Unfinished Nation

Unfinished Nation
Indonesia Before and After Suharto

MAX LANE

VERSO
London • New York

First published by Verso 2008

1 3 5 7 9 10 8 6 4 2

Verso
UK: 6 Meard Street, London W1F 0EG
USA: 180 Varick Street, New York, NY 10014-4606

www.versobooks.com

Verso is the imprint of New Left Books

ISBN-13: 978-1-84467-237-0 (pbk)
ISBN-13: 978-1-84467-236-3 (hbk)

British Library Cataloguing in Publication Data
A catalogue record for this book is available from the British Library

Library of Congress Cataloging-in-Publication Data
A catalog record for this book is available from the Library of Congress

Typeset in Garamond by Hewer Text UK Ltd, Edinburgh

Printed and bound in Great Britain by
Marston Book Services Ltd, Oxfordshire

Contents

Acknowledgments

This book would not have been possible without the opportunities I had to travel to Indonesia (and to the Netherlands) several times during 2000 and 2004, or the chance I had to put aside time to translate more works by Pramoedya Ananta Toer and to write. This, in turn, was made possible by two lots of financial support I received from the New York Foundation of the Arts.

A part-time research fellowship at the Asia Research Centre at Murdoch University in 2004 was also crucial. Much of the more recent research has been carried out while I have been a Ph.D. student at the University of Wollongong. Some of this book material will, I think, find its way into a Ph.D. thesis.

Smaller financial support earlier during this period from the Institute of Popular Democracy in the Philippines and from the Centre for Asia Pacific Social Transformation Studies at the University of Wollongong was helpful.

The thinking-through process involved in developing the ideas of this book could not have occurred with material support only. Most precious were the hundreds of discussions I have been able to engage in with many people. I would like to especially thank for their time and patience Joesoef Isak, Danial Indrakusuma, Dita Sari, Agus Jabo Prijono, Hilmar Farid, Kelik Ismunanto, Zely Ariane, Nico Warouw, Weby Warouw and Hariman Siregar.

In Australia I have had fruitful discussions on Indonesia with Professor Adrian Vickers. Professor Garry Rodan's support and his commentary on the draft manuscript were very beneficial.

This is a work of political analysis and any ability to conduct such analysis has also benefited from my discussions and joint activity with other political activists, and especially the writing I have done for *Green Left Weekly* newspaper in Australia and the work I did with all the activists of Action in Solidarity with Indonesia and East Timor (ASIET). My friend and fellow activist, John Percy, also read through the manuscript.

While at the Asia Research Centre at Murdoch University Toby Carroll was a great friend and gave me extra spirit. Since 2002, my wife and partner, Faiza Mardzoeki, has not only always been supportive but has also been a great discussion partner and someone who has introduced me to new aspects of Indonesian cultural life.

Introduction

In May 1998 a dictatorship was forced out of power. President Suharto was forced to resign in the face of escalating mass protest—mass protest which had begun in the late 1980s, and climaxed in May 1997 and again in May 1998. Large sections of the population, led by university students, were refusing to acquiesce in dictatorship any longer. Suharto's cabinet ministers and politicians, and his generals, were faced with a choice: either deepening ungovernability and radicalization among the population or abandoning Suharto. They chose the latter. The mass protest won its main demand: the resignation of Suharto.

The dictatorship had lasted thirty-three years, thirteen years longer than the period of open politics that had begun with the proclamation of independence in 1945 and ended with Suharto's seizure of power in 1965. Thirty-three out of the fifty-five years of independence (up until 1998) had been lived under a dictatorship, established after a horrific wave of mass murder and the suppression of the most politically active and largest organized political bloc among the population. More than a million people were executed; tens of thousands detained for a year or more; and close to 20,000 detained for ten to fourteen years. The political and indeed the national culture in general, was transformed along with the political system itself.

When such a period ends, and when it ends to the echoes of the demand or slogan *reformasi total* ("total reformation"), the immediate and most pressing question that presents itself both to the observer and to all those caught up in the changes is: What comes next?

This book was originally conceived as an attempt to answer that question: What next? There had already been two Indonesias—that of 1945–65 and then Suharto's Indonesia, 1965–98. With Suharto gone, would there be a new Indonesia and what would it be like?

Any attempt to answer that question could only start with identifying what was already happening. What changes were already under way within Indonesian society and politics? What forces were at work? What were the political ideas evolving among those forces? What were the factors pushing any such forces forward? What factors may be holding them back? The beginning of any answer to the question of what the next Indonesia would be like would be found in the history of how (and also to what extent) the previous Indonesia was abandoned. So this endeavor became a study in contemporary history.

The analysis presented in this book draws the conclusion that Suharto did not just fall from power—he was pushed and the movement that pushed him from power developed as the result of an arduous, conscious effort to build a political movement, based on mobilizing masses of people in action, that could indeed unseat the dictator. In this sense, the analysis differs from the majority of especially Western analysis, which identifies either foreign or elite forces as the main causes for the fall of Suharto.

Chapters 5–8 analyze this process from the time that a small group of activists conceived of the necessity to revive mass action politics as the only way to end the Suharto dictatorship. From the late 1980s, they pioneered the revival of street protest mobilizations, factory strikes and land occupations. All these forms of activity had been violently suppressed and banned in 1965. These actions—or *aksi* as they were called—gradually chipped away at the base of the central pillar of Suharto's political system: the "floating mass"—a demobilized and depoliticized population. These chapters set out the argument that mass action politics, consciously stimulated by an organized political group, was the determining force in bringing an end to the Suharto dictatorship.

However, neither the centrality of *aksi* in this process, the speed at which mass action revived, the patterns of revolt that emerged nor the issues raised in its aftermath can be understood without locating this process in the longer-term history of the country. Chapters 1–4 look at the dynamics of Indonesian history flowing from the anti-colonial struggle up until the seizure of power of General Suharto in 1965 and the counter-revolution he carried out. These chapters set out how mass mobilization politics played a central role in the anti-colonial struggle that began at the beginning of the twentieth century and continued up until 1945 and in a struggle to "complete the revolution" that unfolded between 1945 and 1965. This was a sixty-year-long struggle that began to form and consolidate the Indonesian nation itself: the Indonesian national revolution. It was because of the centrality of this method of struggle, mass mobilization, in the Indonesian national revolution (the nation-building process itself) that crushing it, all ideas associated with it and any memory of that experience, was also central in the counter-revolution that General Suharto implemented after 1965. To the extent that General Suharto's New Order was defined by this counter-revolution and its suppression of mass mobilization politics, the struggle to revive such politics hit out at the heart of Suharto's system.

Chapter 9 summarizes the socio-economic conditions flowing from the imposition of neoliberal economic prescriptions that have underpinned this process throughout the 1990s and into the post-Suharto period. Chapter 10 and the Conclusion attempt an explanation of the fragmented consciousness inside the development of the social protest that has continued after the fall of Suharto. The analysis draws the conclusion that while the mass movement against the dictatorship rewon for Indonesian political culture a key gain of the national revolution—mobilization, *aksi*—the process of rewinning the ideological and cultural gains of the national revolution is only now starting to accelerate.

My aim is to explain as well as I can what I consider to be the real processes that have unfolded during the 1990s which led to the end of the dictatorship and which are setting the framework for political change in the coming period. However, I should declare openly also that I have been a partisan of this process. Since the mid-1970s I have been involved in initiatives which have been aligned with that spectrum of Indonesian political and cultural forces opposed to the dictatorship and advocating an Indonesia different than that formed under the dictatorship.

In 1975, I participated in the dissident theater group led by W.S. Rendra, Bengkel Theater, during the period that Rendra wrote and Bengkel Theater performed his hit anti-dictatorship plays, *Lysistrata* and *Kisah Perjuangan Suku Naga* (*The Struggle of the Naga Tribe*).[1] I later translated *Kisah Perjuangan Suku Naga* into English, and this version was published in the USA and Australia and performed in several countries. I wrote in the Australian press trying to give coverage to this side of Indonesian political and cultural life. Most of the media covered only the political life of Suharto and his generals.

In 1981, after resigning from the Australian Department of Foreign Affairs development aid section, I helped found a new journal *Inside Indonesia*, published in Australia, which also aimed to provide information and analysis about the activities and ideas of those sections of Indonesian society opposed to the dictatorship. I was the editor of this quarterly magazine for several years.

During the 1980s, I also translated the four historical novels of Pramoedya Ananta Toer, *This Earth of Mankind*,[2] *Child of All Nations*, *Footsteps* and *House of Glass*, which he had written while imprisoned on Buru Island concentration camp. I was involved in campaigns outside Indonesia in defense of Pramoedya's rights and in support of the publishing house, Hasta Mitra, that published his books. Hasta Mitra itself was built by former political prisoners asserting their rights in defiance of the dictatorship's edict that such people were not allowed to publish books.

In 1990, after an absence of several years from Indonesia, I came into contact with the new generation of young Indonesian political activists. It was a year after the big campaign in Central Java where students had joined peasant farmers in protests against the World Bank-financed Kedung Ombo dam project. Several other big farmer demonstrations and land occupations had occurred, especially in West Java. My first meeting with them was when I was invited to speak to a gathering at the offices of SKEHPI, an environmental group whose office had become the organizing center for many of the new protests.

It was very clear from this meeting that a qualitatively new phase of political struggle had begun. I was driven to the office by the late Hasyim Rachman, accompanied by Joesoef Isak. Hasyim Rachman and Joesoef Isak were both journalists who had been imprisoned by Suharto as part of the general suppression of the left after 1965. Hasyim had been imprisoned on Buru Island, in the same hut as Pramoedya. Joesoef had spent ten years in a Jakarta gaol. They were the two people who had joined with Pramoedya to form a publishing company to publish Pramoedya's works. By 1990, they had published the four Buru Quartet books, all of which were subsequently banned. Since then Joesoef has had to spend another three months in gaol, after being accused of masterminding an invitation for Pramoedya to speak at a forum at the University of Indonesia. Joesoef's son, who was a student at the university and part of the committee that invited Pramoedya onto campus, was expelled.

Hasyim and Joesoef were welcomed by the forty or so young people in the office, including the young boy—maybe five years old—running around the front yard with a red balloon bearing a yellow hammer and sickle symbol. Among those present, although I didn't know until more than ten years later, was the daughter of the old Indonesian Communist Party's leading intellectual, Nyoto. It was clear that Suharto's policy of instilling fear and hatred of the old left was weakening. The left had been taboo for the previous generation of student protestors.

During the following nine years, I cooperated with a number of these students and activists on different projects: writing articles and publishing magazines. It was from among these activists that emerged the new political party, the People's Democratic Party (PRD). After 1994, when the party— even though still very small—began to become more prominent and suffer harassment, I was active in Australia and internationally in trying to win support for the defense of their rights. In 1996, fourteen leaders of the PRD were arrested. I was active in the international campaign demanding their release and in support of the escalating movement against the dictatorship.[3]

These activities are important to put on the record for the readers of this book, but not only to record my partisanship in the process it describes. My approach to analyzing Indonesian history and society has also been greatly influenced by these experiences, but not simply through the formation of partisan sympathies. In the course of research, reading and discussion—as well as through "participatory observation"—of this period, I have been influenced by two sources of thinking on Indonesia.

The regular reporting, but more especially the analysis of the People's Democratic Party, have proved to be very useful. The PRD have been prolific in producing analysis of developments during this period. Some of these have been published in their magazines and bulletins, some in short books, many in reports to congresses, national council meetings and so on. Some have been the result of the collective analysis of the organization. Some have been the writings of specific leaders, such as Dita Indah Sari and Danial Indrakusuma. Reading these insightful writings, usually also packed with information, but also interrogating them (and their authors) have helped me understand things better. The writings have also been theoretically strong and marked by a vigorous search to understand reality. In the most substantial study of the role of intellectuals during the New Order, *Intellectuals and Power under the New Order State*, the author places the

PRD intellectuals in the category of "prophetic" intellectuals. Dhakidae, himself a Ph.D. graduate from Cornell University and head of the research department of the country's leading newspaper, *Kompas*, puts them in this category, seeing their writing and analysis as being integrated into a praxis dedicated to the end of the New Order state and therefore bound to the necessity of being anchored in reality. He sees them as neo-Marxist intellectuals for whom: "Theory became praxis in confrontation with a state which has stood for decades."[4]

My analysis identifies their role as initiators of the process of rewinning legitimacy and acceptance among people for *aksi* and therefore of playing a major (very specific) role, despite their small numbers, in the overall process leading to the fall of Suharto. Much of my analysis of events would be similar to that which they have formulated. At the same time, the intellectual process of engagement with their writing and ideas has been interrogative and dialogical—as it is among the PRD membership itself. In the process of interrogation, and in the course of trying to work out how to write this book, another source of analysis and knowledge has had a profound influence upon me.

Through the course of the 1990s, I regularly read—and have since reread—many of the "national situation" reports written by the PRD as well as the articles on the national political situation in their magazine *Pembebasan* ("Liberation"). During the same period, I also read more of the writings of Pramoedya Ananta Toer that deal with Indonesian history, both his fictional and his non-fiction writing. Pramoedya is Indonesia's great novelist and, I also think, the country's greatest historian, although not fitting the conventional model. He also felt sufficiently aligned with and had sufficient respect for the PRD to become a member in a public ceremony on 22 March 1999. He opened his speech at that meeting with the words:

> At this moment, in the midst of this spirited and enthusiastic Young Generation, I truly feel happy. This is the most important event in my life, what I have dreamed of since I was young: to witness for myself the birth of a Young Generation not burdened by bombasticism, and which is rational, corrective, critical, and all of this bound by firmness of commitment.[5]

Despite this alignment, it is clear also that there is a disjuncture between Pramoedya's writings and those of the PRD. This disjuncture reflects the disjuncture that is the major topic of the last chapters of this book. This is the disjuncture, or as yet only weak connection, between the process of recovering the method of struggle of the national revolution (*aksi*, mass action) and that of recovering the ideological and cultural gains of the national revolution and the memory of its experience.

The PRD's analysis is rooted in the day-by-day, month-by-month assessment of political developments. Pramoedya's analysis flows from an attempt to discover the Indonesian nation itself, looking back over one thousand years of history. His historical novel *Arok Dedes* is set in thirteenth-century Java. The great historical novel *Arus Balik* (*The Current Reverses*) is set in the sixteenth century. The *This Earth of Mankind* novels are set at the beginning of the twentieth century. There are a myriad of themes and issues taken up by Pramoedya in his novels and also in his other non-fiction works, such as *Realisme Sosialis dan Sastra Indonesia*[6] ("Socialist Realism and Indonesian Literature"), *Sang Pemula*[7] ("The Trailblazer"), and the scores of essays he wrote in *Bintang Timur* newspaper and other magazines before 1965. Some have been briefly repeated in various speeches more recently. But perhaps the most important of these, and relevant in helping form the framework of analysis in this book, is the understanding that the process of "nation formation" of the first sixty years of the twentieth century was indeed a "revolution".

The most profound statement in relation to this is implicit in the *This Earth of Mankind* novels. These novels were inspired by the life of the first indigenous Indonesian to run a daily newspaper. He used it to promote the struggle against colonialism and the formation of the first organization that used political mobilization on mass scale, namely the Sarekat Islam. In this sense, the novel tells the story of the social and political processes that prepared the ground for the national struggle for Indonesia. Yet throughout the novels, the word "Indonesia" does not appear—because the concept did not yet exist. One thousand pages of powerful fiction, telling Indonesians where their country came from but fully aware that at that time neither the entity itself nor the concept existed.

Indonesia had to be created as something totally new, that is, as a qualitative change and product of the creative power of revolution. This idea that Indonesia is a new creation is fundamental to all of Pramoedya's thinking. Further, Pramoedya saw nation building (the national revolution) as a process and not an instantaneous event. It would require a conscious revolution to create the nation and consolidate its creation, a process that would have to be completed through political struggle. For Pramoedya, even at the moment of its conception, the conception itself was unfinished:

> They, university students who received scholarships from the colonial government in the Netherlands as well as the exiles of the Indische Party, discovered a homeland and nation and they called it Indonesia. This was a glorious and great discovery. It is a pity, but the flaws of this discovery were as great as its glory. There was no socio-political concept and it was imbued with antipathy to history. For example, the name Indonesia means Indian islands. The name itself was invented by an Englishman and then popularised by the German ethnologist, Adolf Bastian (1826–1905). The name "India" for Indonesia originates from the Western nation's hunt for spices in the Moluccas starting in the early 15th century, a hunt that led to the whole of the non-Western world being dominated by the West. These spices came from what is known today as Indonesia, but always traded as "made in India." While under Portuguese domination, it was known as Portuguese India. Under Dutch colonialism it was called Dutch India. And to disguise this association with India from the native people, this name was written Hindia.[8]

Completing the revolution was essential, in Pramoedya's eyes, for solving any of the social, economic and cultural problems of the country. The "physical revolution," that is, the guerrilla war against the Dutch in 1945–9, did not complete this process. It required another period of mass mobilization, basing itself on the popular classes, to establish national independence of political action, economic sovereignty and character in culture. For Pramoedya, this was the goal of the political campaigns of the period 1959–65, led by Soekarno, and basing itself on broadening mass mobilization and participation in political life. In 1998, at another PRD event, he stated:

> As regards the building of a nation-state, Bung Karno added three lines of march: which he called the Tri Sakti. The first was to be sovereign in politics. The second was to stand on one's own feet in economics. And the third was to have character in culture. And this remains absolutely correct.[9]

This movement, despite President Soekarno being at its head, never won state power and thus was never able to implement the policies it proposed in order to complete the revolutionary process as it saw it. The mobilized mass forces that supported Soekarno, organized in the left wing of the Indonesian National Party, the Indonesian Communist Party, the Indonesia Party, and scores of mass organizations affiliated to these parties as well as left-wing military officers remained marginal in the cabinet and state apparatus. General Suharto led a pre-emptive counter-revolution in October 1965 which ensured that they never moved from the margins of power and which also established the New Order.

Before the national revolution was completed, that is, before a nation was fully created and consolidated, a counter-revolution was carried out which had the effect of rolling back many of the gains made by the national revolution up until then. The political campaigns which the PRD (and many other groups) was carrying out in the 1990s and the political developments it was analyzing were taking place in the context of an unfinished national revolution that had also suffered thirty-three years of counter-revolutionary suppression. The PRD's analysis assessed each development as a new conjuncture. Pramoedya's comments and speeches in the 1990s and the analysis and logic of his earlier writings drew out the long-term dynamics of Indonesian history and thus set the broader, but still immediate, context for these conjunctural developments. But the two perspectives have not yet integrated.

This book draws inspiration from the thinking of Pramoedya Ananta Toer about the long-term dynamics of Indonesian history and from the conjunctural analysis of the PRD. It attempts to meld, or at least begin to meld, these together. But addressing this disjuncture between the conjunctural and the long term also introduces an "imbalance" of sorts into the book. The primary focus of the material is on the developments of the 1990s, the role of *aksi* in the overthrow of Suharto and in the political processes unfolding after Suharto. At the same time, I aim to address the significance of these developments for an ongoing, long-term process, namely, the Indonesian national revolution and the counter-revolution which halted it for thirty or more years. This has meant that I have also had to relate the whole period from the beginning of the twentieth century until the 1980s all in just a few chapters. This has meant that, inevitably, these first chapters of the book present a bird's-eye view of what I think happened and have summarized, with some aspects of the development of society just mentioned in passing. This may contrast with the greater detail—although still summarized given the richness of developments—of the later chapters.

There is much work to be done in rewriting the history of Indonesia. While I hope to make more contributions to this process in the future, I am sure it will be the new generations of Indonesian historians and activists who will complete this task. It has already started with a huge explosion in writing about history since the fall of Suharto. We are at the beginning of a process where the center of "Indonesian Studies" will return to Indonesia itself, wresting it away from 100 years of Dutch and then American and Australian academic colonialism.

These have been the main theoretical or analytical influences on the analysis I am presenting rather than ideas coming from either Indonesian or foreign scholarship. Theoretical debates have not been a feature of the non-Indonesian scholarship on Indonesia since the 1970s and the early 1980s when scholars such as Herbert Feith, Ben Anderson and Richard Robison were widely read among student activists and other dissidents in Indonesia. While some scholars, particularly Robison, have retained strong theoretical interests, the overwhelming character of Indonesian scholarship has been its empiricist, case-study character. I have sometimes drawn on these case studies.

During the New Order, university scholarship in Indonesia suffered both the censorship of the dictatorship as well as the effects of the counter-revolutionary suppression of the memory of the national revolution. Dhakidae's book on *Intellectuals and the New Order* and the volume of essays on the *Social Sciences and Power in Indonesia*, edited by Dhakidae and the Singapore-based Indonesian scholar, Vedi Hadiz, analyze and document the limitations of this scholarship.[10] However, despite this suppression, Indonesian intellectuals who defied the oppression, often outside the universities, have contributed much to the development of contemporary political analysis. Since the fall of the dictatorship, there has been an explosion in the publication of books about history, politics, culture and society. These have also been an important source of ideas for this book and provide the majority of citations.

The analysis in this book is, I hope, strengthened by drawing insights from the ideas of both Pramoedya and the PRD and by, however partially, trying to deal with the disjuncture between the two perspectives.

1

Indonesia

There are over three hundred different ethnic groups in Indonesia, each with its own cultural identity, and more than two hundred and fifty distinct languages are spoken in the archipelago. Religious beliefs too are varied: nearly all the important world religions are represented, in addition to a wide range of indigenous ones. Economic adaptations include such differing modes as seminomadic shifting cultivation, sago gardening, small holder rubber tapping, irrigated rice farming, highly capitalised plantations for export crops, small itinerant peddling, large scale commerce, cottage industries, and modern manufacturing. Forms of community also vary, from small isolated villages to huge modern cities; the many different types of kinship systems include matrilineal, patrilineal and bilateral patterns; while the traditional political systems range from tribes to kingdoms.[1]

This passage, by American anthropologist Hildred Geertz, first published in 1963, is a typical introduction to describing the social and cultural diversity of Indonesia.

The description captures well the kind of diversities that existed within the archipelago in its first decade or so after independence. There are many such descriptions in both Indonesian- and non-Indonesian-language literature. When trying to describe this diversity, there is frequently a mention of the national motto that was adopted when the country won its independence: "Unity in Diversity." Most of these descriptions, however, have a blind spot, an aspect they ignore or downplay. Cultural development in the various parts of the Malay archipelago had been held back by colonial intervention, suppression and manipulation that had lasted over at least 300 years before Indonesia's independence.

Most of the traditional political systems referred to by Geertz, for example, had long been subdued and significantly reformed or controlled through Dutch, British, Spanish or Portuguese intervention. Kingdoms had been reduced to tributaries or simply conquered. Tribal systems had new structures imposed on them as Dutch scholar administrators wrote their customary law for them, often restructuring their political organization in the process. Even where kingdoms or communities had been left free of direct colonial administration, they existed within an archipelago whose economic, cultural, social and political life, and most intercourse between the communities of the archipelago, was dominated by colonial interests and policies.

When Europeans first began to interfere in the life of the peoples of the archipelago there was great unevenness in the social and economic development of its different parts. Some regions had kingdoms or sultanates which had long histories of influence throughout the archipelago and even beyond. Some kingdoms had operated only locally, and some for very short time spans. Some societies had developed writing scripts and bodies of court literature; other areas were still tribal societies, some with no developed writing at all. Some had a long history of contact with peoples outside the archipelago, others had little or no contact. A key part of the process of both the economic and cultural development of societies in the archipelago was linked to the dynamics of interaction among the peoples across all the islands.

That interaction, *as an internally generated process*, slowed down and then stopped under the impact of European intervention, domination and finally colonization—until the beginning of the twentieth century. The dynamic element of the archipelago's cultural life, its collective interaction with the outside world through trade, had been conquered by colonial power, most particularly that represented in the Dutch East Indies Company. Before the end of the seventeenth century, all the major trading cities of the archipelago had been conquered—on the Malay peninsula, on the north coasts of Java and in the eastern archipelago. The historian Anthony Reid has commented that Europe also fell at one point to the commercial power of the Dutch but, he added, "Their [Southeast Asian maritime traders] defeat was more permanent, however, precisely because the maritime trade played such a role below the winds [that is, across the archipelago]."[2]

In several places in the archipelago, the original political communities remained in place, but the dynamism was finished and the political forms, and the cultural traditions associated with them, atrophied. Interaction between the peoples of the islands was channeled through the colonial infrastructure and policies. What interaction continued outside the colonial framework between the sixteenth and nineteenth centuries remained that of contact between small traders and petty rulers.

The diversity of the archipelago at the beginning of the twentieth century was a diversity of defeated cultures that had been turned into "traditions." They were virtual museum cultures, maintained for observation or for distorted usage by colonial rule. It was the national awakening, beginning at the start of the twentieth century, that led to a new Indonesian consciousness where some old cultural elements were revived but subordinated to a completely new Indonesian culture—which was itself in the process of being formed. This latter cultural process was laying the basis for the future unity among diversity of the archipelago.

Since his novels were published in 1981, it has been difficult for any historian or commentator, within or outside Indonesia, not to refer to the four great novels of Pramoedya Ananta Toer, known collectively as the Buru Quartet. When the first volume, *This Earth of Mankind*, was published in 1981, the Indonesian Vice-President, Adam Malik, defying his military boss, then President General Suharto, called for the books to be compulsory reading for every Indonesian school child. His wish was not fulfilled then, and is still not fulfilled today. These classic novels by Indonesia's greatest novelist are still banned from the Indonesian state schools' curriculum.

These novels by Pramoedya, *This Earth of Mankind, Child of All Nations, Footsteps* and *House of Glass*, have often been described as novels of the Indonesian national awakening. Yet not once in more than 1,000 pages of rich fictionalized social history does the word "Indonesia" appear. It is not spoken by a character, it does not appear in any writings or newspapers, or on signs or in a poem. It is not there because the idea did not exist and the idea did not exist because the entity, an Indonesian nation, did not exist.

At the beginning of the twentieth century, the Malay Archipelago was in the grip of Dutch, British, Spanish and Portuguese colonialism. Not every

piece of territory was under direct colonial administration but the economic, cultural and political life of the archipelago had been contained
within the limits of colonial policy and interests since the early sixteenth
century. European colonialism had become the determining influence in
the economic, social and cultural life of the archipelago. The archipelago
had a colonial division enforced upon it: the Malay peninsula was cut out of
the archipelago into a separate unit; the southern Philippines was separated
from the Celebes islands; and the eastern half of the island of Timor was
divided from the western half.

The economic, political and cultural development of an archipelago-
wide geo-cultural entity was blocked. The Portuguese and Dutch navies
and armies destroyed the naval capacities of the Malay, Sumatran, Javanese
and other kingdoms. Individual kingdoms, sultanates and other territories
were conquered, or subordinated through treaties, on a one-by-one basis,
making permanent the state of separation of each area from the other.
Inter-regional linkages, generated within the archipelago as a result of the
needs of the archipelago's own social classes, withered to be replaced by
linkages arising from the operations of the colonial merchants and navies.
Indonesian nationalists often talked about 300 years of colonial oppression
and this has often been disputed by the pedants who argue that it was only
in the early twentieth century that the Dutch colonial administration of the
Netherlands Indies conquered and administered the whole archipelago.
However, the archipelago became the site of societies which had been either
conquered or, if not conquered, deprived of the kind of dynamic trade and
cultural contact between its regions that had always been the motor of real
social progress.

Hinduism, Buddhism and then Islam had all moved through the
archipelago—to different extents and depths—through this local, dynamic
process. In every case, they brought new ideas, new literatures and new
technologies, adapted and utilized in a process controlled and developed by
social forces located in the archipelago itself. From the sixteenth century
onwards extraction of wealth by European powers and restriction on the
transfer of knowledge became the norm. The culture of the archipelago
became its "traditions," to be preserved deliberately by colonial policy or
prevented from changing into something new by enforced isolation.

This situation of cultural stagnation and regional separation had existed
for almost 400 years when the Indonesian national awakening began at the

beginning of the twentieth century. This awakening led to a movement struggling for freedom from colonialism, for independence, for the foundation of a new and independent nation and state. This movement was a revolution, a national revolution.

The words "nation" and "revolution" have played such central roles in modern history that they have become words which have attracted to them many usages and meanings. "Peoples," ethnic groupings, tribes, clans, kingdoms and states of one kind or another have existed for thousands of years. But nations are a new phenomenon, created out of the struggle to overthrow European feudalism and its system of fragmented principalities and fiefdoms, each with its own language, laws, borders, identities and pride. This struggle was driven by the bourgeoisie, the new moneyed and propertied class whose commercial activities were hemmed in and blocked by, among other things, the decentralized fragmentation of the feudal system. The Dutch, English and French revolutions not only overthrew the feudal ruling classes of those societies but also began the process of establishing something totally new on the face of the earth, the nation.

These new entities evolved in fits and starts before, during and after the great revolutionary upheavals. Over a century or more, they developed into a stable community of people, formed on the basis of a common language, territory, economic life and psychological make-up, manifested in a common culture. States developed out of their wealthy and powerful bourgeoisie's will to rule over these nations. The rise of the nation state as the location of the rise of capital and the spread of the power of European (and later American) capital throughout the world organized the world economic system on the basis of nation states and national economies.

By the eighteenth century, the European national states mobilized their armies and navies and civil servants to model their colonial possessions on the national state and economy. These colonies are carved out and registered on maps as if they were nations. But they were not nations. They were given some, but not all, of the elements of a national economy: a currency, taxation and customs laws, and their administrations followed policies designed to encourage or protect this or that sector of business and economic activity, depending on the current needs of the stronger sections of capital back in the home country.

The Netherlands Indies was like this. It was there on a map of the world. You could see the borders and the capital, Batavia, and locate the international ports where customs and excise would be collected. But this entity was not the creation of great forces that had developed within the societies of the archipelago and that had burst asunder the old system, establishing something completely new. The European nations had been established by revolution: a process that had created something completely new by overturning the old system and ways, and by using new methods, mobilizing the mass of ordinary people, peasants and town poor, in direct political action behind revolutionary slogans. The entity of the Netherlands Indies was imposed on the archipelago (minus the Malay peninsula, East Timor and the southern Philippines) for the purposes of facilitating colonial extraction of wealth.

Integration of economic life, the spreading of a common language and the forging of a common cultural outlook were never part of this process. In almost all of these areas, colonial priorities meant the opposite. The economic life of the archipelago was characterized by what its own colonial economists described as a "dual economy." One sector was ruled by and served the immediate interests of colonial capital; and then there was the rest, starved of capital, restricted to the local, with inter-regional links stuck at a petty trading level. There were no indigenous-owned large archipelago-wide trading houses. Extraction from plantations, forced cultivation and mining dominated the colonial sector. It funded the expatriate colonial population and its hangers-ons who did develop their own shared colonial psychological outlook and culture. Outside of these enclaves, none of these features even began to develop on an archipelago-wide basis until the beginning of the twentieth century.

From Outside the Enclaves

The primary character in Pramoedya Ananta Toer's novels, called by his nickname Minke, was inspired by the writer, journalist and political leader, *Raden Mas* Tirto Adhisuryo. Pramoedya never spells out his name in full in the fictionalized account of his life and achievements in the novels,[3] but his life and a selection of his writings were published in *Sang Pemula*, written and edited by Pramoedya in the mid-1980s.

Tirto Adhisuryo published the first newspaper owned and run by a *pribumi*, a native of the archipelago. There were Dutch-owned papers and some advertising sheets owned by Chinese merchants that also published both journalism and fiction. This first native newspaper was not published as the voice of either "Indonesians," who did not exist even in people's minds, or *pribumi*. It was published under the motto: "the voice of the governed." It started first as an appeal to those from among the governed who were working for the Dutch government. These were the native civil servants employed by the Dutch and usually recruited from the lower levels of the long-defeated, remnant aristocracy and descendants of hereditary rulers of one kind or another. In Java, they were known as the *priyayi*, a term which has stuck until today. But this appeal failed. Their conservatism and timidity, flowing both from the anemic nature of their remnant feudal cultural background and from their material dependence on the colonial wage, meant that they always retreated from speaking out for "the governed" against those governing. They were integrated into the enclaves.

Tirto Adhisuryo eventually turned to those outside the enclaves, who were not dependent in any direct way on the Dutch, or even subordinated to the operations of the enclave. He dropped his attempts to organize a "Union of Priyayi" and joined in the effort to organize a "union of Islamic traders." The trader was the motor of independent political and cultural life outside the enclaves. This was not because of any great accumulation of capital and therefore resources. It was simply because these traders had some resources at least and were independent of the colonial enclaves. They were an independent social force, independent of Dutch capital, Dutch power and the social norms of the enclaves. Their separation from the enclaves was stated clearly also by their adoption of the banner of Islam.

The Union of Islamic Traders (Sarekat Dagang Islam, SDI), founded in 1909, spread like wildfire outside the enclaves, recruiting every kind of small and "large" trader, peddler as well as peasant farmer, even urban worker as well as Islamic teacher. Its momentum grew so strongly that its presence could be felt inside the enclaves, even recruiting those *pribumi* working as labor there. In 1912 it changed its name to just the "Islamic Union" (SI) and, by 1919, claimed a membership of 2 million, making it one of the largest, possibly the largest, mass organization in the world. In 1921, the SI split, and a massive left wing, opposing both colonial rule and capitalism, formed the People's Union (Sarekat Rakyat, SR). The SR was the first overt mass organization reflecting the growth of the popular radicalism in Indonesia. The split between the SI and the SR reflected the class divisions outside the enclaves.

These developments reflected a growth in a sense of identity, even community, among the peoples outside the enclaves. The enclaves were scattered throughout the archipelago wherever there were colonial economic or military interests, from Aceh at the far western tip to Papua in the east. Dutch was their ruling language. Another language emerged as the embryonic language outside the enclaves, Malay. This was the language of the Malays living on both sides of the straits of Malacca, and the site of two of the major maritime kingdoms that had brought Indic culture and then Islam to other parts of the archipelago. Srivijaya dominated the Malacca Straits from the seventh to the early eleventh centuries. Trade from both eastern Indonesia and China as well as from India, the Middle East and Europe moved through its main port on the southeast coast of Sumatra. Malacca (or Melaka), with its main port on the Malay peninsula, dominated the strait in the fifteenth century. Its trading activity also reached right across the archipelago to the east, strengthening the use of Malay in all the ports.

In 1928, at a youth congress in Batavia, young political activists from across the archipelago affirmed their commitment to creating a new nation when they announced a Pledge of the Youth (Sumpah Pemuda) to achieve liberation from colonialism: "One nation with one language, Indonesian; and one homeland, Indonesia." The language, Indonesian, was to be based on Malay, the lingua franca of the archipelago. There was no serious attempt to adopt any of the regional languages, even that of the Javanese who were the single biggest ethnic grouping, as the national language, or even as some kind of official language for use at an archipelago-wide level.

In 1928 there was still only a small body of Malay literature, defined even in the broadest sense. While the Dutch had used Malay at the lower levels of the civil service, it was an awkwardly standardized language of rules and regulations. As the language of inter-island trade it was a language of contracts and haggling in market places. Malay-speaking Chinese, writing in the early newspapers as well as novels and short stories, began to develop the language as one fit to discuss all the issues of modern life, laying the foundations for it to become a language of national affairs and national liberation. Its growth was then given a big push by the mass anti-colonial movement. After 1928 the political leadership wrote and made their main speeches in Malay, which was more and more often called Indonesian. "Indonesia" had been adopted by "Indonesian" students in the Netherlands in 1917 as their term for the Netherlands Indies, asserting the legitimacy of their claim to the right to strive for nationhood. By 1928, the term was more widely used in the anti-colonial movement. Many sections of society coming into political motion adopted "Indonesia" as the name of the country they were struggling to liberate. In December 1928, the first archipelago-wide assembly of women activists organized the Indonesian Women's Congress, for example.[4]

The man who was to become the most popular political leader throughout the archipelago was already writing articles in Indonesian, published in journals such as the *Suluh Indonesia Muda* ("Torch of Young Indonesians") by 1926. The Indonesian Communist Party had dropped reference to Indies and started using Indonesia soon after its founding in 1920.

From inside the enclaves, the Dutch insisted that "Indonesia" implied a level of cultural unity among the ethnic groups and traditional societies of the archipelago that did not exist. Of course, they were correct. There was no unity, integration or even any real interchange between all the cultures of the archipelago. The interchange of ideas across the archipelago had been restrained drastically with the arrival of the Europeans in the sixteenth century. "Indonesia" did not represent a fusion of existing "traditions," those half-embalmed, selected elements from the cultural life of the societies at the time of their first serious engagements with colonial power.

An Indonesian cultural outlook was being forged but, just as with the revolutions that produced the first European nations, elements from the past were not the dominant ingredients. Within the context of the societies of the archipelago at that time, the new and the future dominated. Even the idea of nation and the word "Indonesia" were new, completely new. For 90 percent of inhabitants, the language being proposed as that of the united community was new. In the past, political identity had been defined on the basis of being the subject of a particular ruler, not membership of a national community. Such a concept of nation also amounted to a rejection of any return to feudal rule. New forms of political state and life were proposed, borrowing from the ideas of the two great types of revolution that had occurred before the 1920s: the bourgeois revolutions of Europe and the

USA before the twentieth century, and the proletarian revolution that had taken place in Russia in 1917. In addition to this were the ideas thrown up by the other Asian anti-colonial revolutions, in China and the Philippines.

The new identity that was being forged owed more to the heritage of the modern revolutions than it did to any borrowings from the traditional cultures. The community that was most concrete in the eyes of those at the forefront of the national awakening, even before the idea of the new nation had crystallized, was that recorded under the banner of Tirto Adhisuryo's first indigenous-owned newspaper: the voice of the governed. Indeed, Pramoedya presents Adhisuryo's own intellectual and political development as heading in the direction of pan-archipelagoism. In *Footsteps*, where Pramoedya follows historical events more closely, Adhisuryo is arrested by the Dutch authorities just as he is about to travel beyond the Dutch Indies to (British) Singapore, Malaya and the (American) Philippines. The new identity that was just starting to be formed was that: *new*, and only very tenuously connected to the past, to "tradition." In many respects it was based on a conscious rejection of tradition.

The new dominated in everything—not just in ideas but also in methods. Armed rebellions against the Dutch, usually under the leadership of a prince or religious leader, had been regular occurrences during the previous 300 years. Now a revolutionary change was taking place. The organization of workers and peasants was developing, organized around the defense of their own immediate interests. Unions arose among the small working class in the towns, becoming the engine behind much of the growth of the anti-colonial movement throughout the 1920s, 1930s and 1940s. Farmers also organized. And their weapons were generally not sword or spear or rifle. Their weapons were the newspaper and magazine, the leaflet, the placard and poster, the street march, the public meeting, the mass assembly, the strike and the boycott. Ideas, expressed in the written word, and organization were the new weapons, and every kind of new idea, taken from all the revolutions, was present in the speeches of the new leaders.

In contemporary Western society, these methods no longer have a sense of newness and power, having atrophied through underuse since the economic boom of the 1950s (with the exception of the period of the 1960s). But in the Netherlands Indies, they were truly revolutionary. Passivity characterized the subject of the feudal ruler and colonial master; to be led by force of status alone gave way to strength of organization and the sharpness of language and ideas. Everything was being turned upside down, and this was renewing the society outside the enclaves with energy.

This process unfolded, of course, unevenly. There were armed rebellions initiated by the Communist Party of Indonesia (PKI) in 1926 and 1927. Plantation workers in Sumatra, peasants in West Java, harbor workers in Sumatra and Batavia rose up and were crushed. Many rushed to their death, hundreds of others were imprisoned or exiled, some to the colonial death camps in West Papua. The political leaders, some from the trade unions, others from the tiny layer of educated natives, were exiled across the archipelago. Soekarno and others went in and out of gaol and exile during the 1920s and 1930s.

Mass organization and mobilization also ebbed and flowed, responding to changes in the political and economic conditions, and colonial policy. Parties rose and fell or stagnated or went underground. But the revolution continued. The new methods became embedded. The new ideas formed the real basis of a new Indonesian culture, pushing aside the influence of the remnants of the "traditions." It was *aksi* (action), *mogok* (strike), socialism and democracy, *sarikat* (union) and *vergadering* (mass assembly) that were central to the vocabulary of the anti-colonial movement, not the folk tales or courtly discourses of the so-called ethnic traditions. Most of all it was *revolusi* (revolution) and *merdeka* (freedom).

It is important not to underestimate the impact of these then revolutionary methods, as it is also not to romanticize the way they asserted their impact. In 1919 SI claimed 2 million members. No doubt the level of activity and participation among this membership was very uneven. However, the fact that the first big anti-colonial mass organization reached such huge levels of membership, and then gave birth to a large leftist formation (the PKI), is a signal that the phenomenon was real and widespread. Even after the suppression of the PKI, in 1926–7, there was constant renewal of the movement, manifesting both in political parties, workers' strikes, educational campaigns and literary activity.

The idea of "voice of the governed," first expressed by Adhisuryo in 1907, was transformed over the next two decades into a different, more dynamic conception, that of *pergerakan* (movement). This was the word on the whole nationalist movement's lips to describe what was taking place in society. The word *pergerakan* conveys a more active sense of everything in motion than the word *gerakan*, which can also be translated as movement. It was deep motion that was a fundamental characteristic of the unfolding process. In his book, *An Age in Motion*, which depicts all this so vividly, Takashi Shiraishi writes:

> The Indonesian national consciousness, with Malay/Indonesian as their political language, newspapers, rallies, strikes, and ideologically divided parties—all were inherited as the new generation as the pergerakan tradition. In the last month of 1926 Soekarno, a leading figure of the Bandung Algemeene Studieclub (Bandung General Study Club), wrote a serialised article under the title "Nationalism, Islam and Marxism" and called for the unity of nationalist (that is, non-Islamic and non-Communist), Islamic and Communist parties in the struggle to achieve a Free Indonesia. Soekarno's call marked the opening of a new era, not only because he was to become a leading figure of the new generation but also more important, because he voiced a new consciousness.[5]

Dutch power was smashed by the Japanese invasion in 1942, but the anti-colonial movement, the *pergerakan*, the national revolution, had created the ideas about political structure, the methods of struggle and the leaderships to fill the vacuum that emerged immediately after the defeat of Japan. All the structures and methods of the revolution came to the fore, filling the whole of the political vacuum: parties, united fronts, unions, armed organizations of rebellion, newspapers, leaflets, conferences, congresses, mass assemblies, *aksi, revolusi* and *merdeka*. In fact, this time, with Dutch repressive power confined only to certain locations, the revolutionary impulse and energy frightened many of the new Indonesians away from this new Indonesian culture. Some started to hanker for the culture of the enclaves. These elements, perhaps best represented by the nationalist Mohammed Hatta, promised the Dutch all their colonial wealth would be returned, the plantations they had thieved, the mines that had been worked with slave and coolie labor, their trading licenses and shipping lanes. They promised to disarm those who were too revolutionary, leading to armed clashes within the liberation movement, and a large massacre in the Javanese town of Madiun in 1948, when thousands of left-wing activists and fighters were shot and thousands more imprisoned. Central leaders of the left were assassinated.

Creating a New Indonesian Culture

The proclamation of the Independence of Indonesia on 17 August 1945 created the Indonesian state, which then fought a four-year guerrilla war to defeat the colonial Dutch attempt to restore the Netherlands Indies. The Dutch conceded defeat by signing recognition of the transfer of sovereignty to a United States of Indonesia in 1949. The Hatta government had also surrendered to the Dutch who had demanded that Indonesia form itself as a federal state. The Dutch hoped that this would allow them some continuing influence in areas where they retained strong ties with some sections of local elites. However, the United States of Indonesia was soon disbanded and replaced again by the Republic of Indonesia.

The territorial boundaries of the new nation were the boundaries of the Netherlands Indies. But for the first time, other features of nations that had emerged in other parts of the world had a chance to develop, to be developed. This Indonesian language had been the language of the anti-colonial movement and was the language of the national revolution. These words of the new Indonesian language, of whatever original linguistic origin, had literally become household words across the archipelago: *revolusi, aksi, merdeka atau mati* (freedom or death), *pemerintah* (government), *partai, perjuangan* (struggle), *pejuang dan berjuang, semangat* (spirit) and others. These words also embodied the core of the cultural development that had been generated by the nationalist movement, manifested also in literature and the arts.

Even during the years of the guerrilla struggle, the first steps were taken to accelerate the spread of a common language and the development of a common culture. The key vehicles were schools and political parties. After 1949, the new government was able to spread schools very quickly throughout the country. The progress made in establishing school buildings and giving initial training to teachers during the 1950s was remarkable. In 1950 literacy was estimated at 10 percent and there were an estimated 230 Indonesians with tertiary education from the small tertiary education institutions established by the Dutch. Within ten years literacy had increased to over 80 percent and schools were present in almost every village. Apart from the state education systems, religious schools also introduced a new curriculum and spread literacy in Indonesia.

But the forging of a new common culture was something that progressed more through politics than formal education. It was the political parties and the struggle between them that was the cauldron in which the elements of a new culture were being mixed and formed. Within a few years of the end of the guerrilla war against the Dutch in 1949, political party life came to dominate almost all social and cultural life. The phenomenon of the *aliran* developed where almost all citizens belonged to one or another political organization or affiliated group.

Political parties, and the mass organizations affiliated to the parties, filled a social and cultural vacuum. Four hundred years of colonial intervention had held back energies that were now unleashed, energies to organize social life. During the 400-year colonial period, Indonesia's social classes— peasantry, nascent bourgeoisie, with its massive petty bourgeois sector, and proletariat, with a massive semi-proletarian sector—had not had the chance to organize freely, either in the social or the political sphere. There had been atrophy of most social and cultural organization. New organiza- tions had begun during the anti-colonial movement and the ideas of organization and activity had become widespread. However, colonial suppression had meant that any organization was always short-lived, having to engage in never-ending maneuver just for survival.

This situation was overturned through the national revolution and all social classes could organize again, freely. And the political parties filled almost the whole vacuum. They were also continuations of the ideologi- cally affiliated parties created during the time of the *pergerakan*. Parties had affiliated organizations for almost every sphere of activity. Credit coopera- tives, chess clubs, prayer groups, housewife auxiliaries, cultural associations, worker and peasant unions, women's groups, high school, university student and youth groups were all associated with one or another party. These conglomerations of parties and affiliated organizations became known as *aliran* or streams. They operated on a day-to-day level, every day, and not just in the lead-up to elections. They often represented the primary identity for any individual.

These *aliran* combined appeals to remnant religious and cultural ideas with both modern ideologies and modern political methods. There were religious-based parties as well as secular parties, but even the religious parties used their religious vocabulary to try to describe some form of modern state: usually liberal democratic or socialist. Dues-paying, active membership was the basis for all these parties and organizations. Rallies, marches, demonstrations, conferences, congresses, cadre training courses, leaflets, placards and banners became a central, even the central, feature of the cultural life of most of the population. Politically affiliated newspapers and magazines proliferated, making the most important contribution to the production of regular general reading material.

When the first general parliamentary elections were held in September 1955 the voter turnout was almost 100 percent. Herbert Feith described election day:

> Election day itself . . . was a momentous occasion—a ceremonial act of participation in the nation which was carried out with great dignity and seriousness. The balloting was orderly and free. . . . The choices made by the village voters were meaningful—not as assessments of the performances of particular governments, but as quasi ideological identification of the villagers.[6]

The "quasi ideological identification" of the villagers reflects the organization and mobilization of the whole population into *aliran*. Four major *aliran* were reflected in the 1955 elections. These were those organized through the Indonesian National Party (PNI) who won 22.3 percent of the vote, MASYUMI with 20.9 percent, Nahdlatul Ulama with 18.4 percent and the Communist Party with 16.4 percent.

People's daily lives were as much organized through these *aliran* as was their voting. The party and affiliated mass *aliran* were forged out of a nexus between two phenomena. One was the social organization vacuum that had been created by colonial suppression. The second was the necessity for the nation-building process to have a real socio-economic and political content: independence meant nothing to people separate from the struggle to improve their material lot and increase their empowerment, as compared to their life as "subjects." *Demokrasi* and prosperity were seen as almost one and the same thing, and in many respects, for most people, they had to be fused. For the mass of the population—proletariat and peasantry—improvement in living conditions was tied up with struggling for better conditions, and that needed mass organization and political campaigns and

advocacy. For the bourgeoisie and petty bourgeoisie it meant access to the
decision-making process within the government.

The struggle for improved living conditions saw a massive growth in the
trade unions and peasant organizations, especially those affiliated to the
PKI and the PNI. Trade unions claimed 6 million members by March
1958. Between 1952 and 1956 the number of workers registered as having
been involved in disputes rose from just over 1 million to more than 5
million. Hundreds of thousands of workers were involved in strikes. And
more than 1 million workers went on strike in 1957 in the campaign
against the Dutch colonial presence in West Papua and its integration into
Indonesia.[7]

During 1956–7, almost every Dutch-owned company in Indonesia,
almost the whole of the modern sector of the economy, was occupied by
workers in unilateral actions. The Dutch managers were thrown out of the
plantations, mines, factories and import-export houses. These occupations
had come at the peak of five years of mass mobilizations against the Dutch
presence in Indonesia, spearheaded by the nationalist left, mainly Soekarno
and the PKI. This campaign fused two strains in the national revolutionary
process under one banner. Socio-economic improvement (broadly referred
to as *adil makmur*—justice and prosperity) and gaining full sovereignty
over the economy were fused as a single process under the banner of
"finishing the revolution." The return of the Dutch companies to Holland
after 1949, the Hatta government's recognition of a massive foreign debt to
the Dutch colonizers and its concession of agreeing to continuing Dutch
rule in West Papua were seen as symbols of the unfinished revolution.

The campaign to oust the Dutch presence added extra energy to the
mobilization of millions of people over a five-year period through the
aliran, especially that of the PKI and PNI.

It was out of all this campaigning activity, an extension of what had been
happening since 1909, that a new common cultural outlook was in the
process of being created across the archipelago. The newspapers were also
almost all associated with an *aliran*. Literary and cultural activity also
became overwhelmingly organized through the *aliran*, and all of the four
parties had large cultural organizations attached to them. A national
literature began to emerge and make its presence felt beyond literary
circles as new texts entered the school curriculum or were turned into
drama, film or radio plays. Political mobilization right down to the

grassroots, polemical debate, and the ideas of the major world revolutions and, increasingly, of the wider anti-colonial revolution were the building blocks of this new cultural outlook in the making. The anti-oppression elements in Islamic thinking, spurred on as part of the Arab national revolution in the Middle East, also became more widespread. Besides Marxist socialism stood Islamic socialism, village socialism and Indonesian socialism.

As this process deepened and spread, differentiation, indeed polarization, also sharpened. The problem (for some) was that the national revolution was increasingly being led by the left, by political forces whose strength arose from their organization and mobilization of the proletariat and peasantry. The ideas associated with the rise of these movements, and the spread of the political culture associated with them, were threatening to those still influenced by the culture of the enclaves and with privileges stemming from their hold over property, either land or capital. The ideas of the rising political culture were clearly reflected in the vocabulary that was becoming dominant: again the vocabulary of the national revolution. The keywords were: *revolusi, aksi* (action), *semangat* (spirit), *organisasi, massa, rakyat* (the people), *kedaulatan* (sovereignty), and increasing socialism and imperialism. The increasing influence of socialist ideas, reflected in the growth of the PKI and of a militant left wing inside the PNI, was giving a more specific content to the old formulation of *adil makmur* (just and prosperous). These ideas were not only the daily substance of newspapers, leaflets and meetings, but even by the late 1950s also began to find their way into every form of art and literature.

The political leadership of the opposition to this rising political culture, this nascent new national culture, was drawn from those who had been forged in closer proximity to the old colonial enclaves. These were either intellectual politicians educated in the Dutch system, even in the Nether-lands, or Indonesians who had been military officers or non-commissioned officers in the old Royal Netherlands Colonial Army. The intellectuals were concentrated in the Indonesian Socialist Party (PSI), whose alienation from the mass of the population had been demonstrated by its 3 percent showing in the 1955 elections. They were the politicians whose models were free enterprise economy, liberal parliamentary democracy and the welfare state but who wanted to achieve these without going through the same mobilizational upheaval that Europe had passed through with its revolu-

tions. One of the great, early Western analysts of Indonesian politics, Herb
Feith, described this divide as between the "solidarity makers" and the
"administrators." For Feith, the "solidarity makers," that is, Soekarno and
the left, were denying rationality. Feith failed to grasp what was actually at
stake, the completion of a revolution which would not only overturn the
old colonial system but also create a new nation and culture. Such a process
required, above all, participation, that is to say, organization and mobilization, which could only occur around the issues of actual concern to the
mass of people, the proletariat and peasantry.

There were many Dutch-trained military officers in the new officer
corps. These included the Armed Forces Chief of Staff, General Nasution,
as well as Colonel Suharto, a former sergeant in the colonial army, later to
seize state power in a move to pre-empt a victory for the forces of the
mobilized left and Soekarno. Many of these army officers, and some whom
they in turn trained, quickly integrated themselves into moneymaking
activities, especially smuggling and gambling. In 1956 when workers took
over the Dutch factories, which were then nationalized, military officers
were appointed to manage them. These armed capitalists were very early
located as the real embryo of the new capitalist class. The extremes to
which some of them would go in order to defend their interests was
exemplified in 1952 when General Nasution surrounded the presidential
palace and ordered Soekarno to disband parliament after a dispute over
civilian control of military appointments. Soekarno talked them down. In
1956, other officers in Sumatra and Sulawesi initiated armed rebellion and
stated they would set up an alternative Indonesian government. Threats
from the central government, under pressure from the left, to stamp out
their smuggling activities had provoked the rebellions. It was during these
rebellions that Indonesia saw its first political prisoner camps since 1948
where PKI *aliran* members were detained.

Radicalization

The anti-colonial movement was explicitly committed to the establishment
of a new Indonesian nation and state. The political organization and
mobilization of masses of people between 1909 and 1945 became increasingly explicitly oriented to this. After independence, the struggle between
political parties, and the class interests their leaderships represented, was

essentially a struggle over what kind of country and society Indonesia would be. Despite the deep antagonisms that were brought to the fore, this struggle also intensified the sense of Indonesian identity growing within society. What kind of society would Indonesia be? This was how political debate posited the central issue before the whole people. Even movements that presented themselves as partially responding to regional grievances, such as the PERMESTA movement, presented their solutions to these grievances within the framework of Indonesia. Likewise, Islamic fundamentalist currents, such as those based among minority tendencies in Aceh, Sunda (West Java) and South Sulawesi, proposed an Islamic Indonesia.

Whether Islamic, federalist, social democratic or socialist, all of the political streams were struggling for Indonesia to be created in their image. This crossed ethnic and traditional cultural boundaries and was a part of the foundation of the process of nation formation.

At the same time, a different division was being sharpened. A difference quickly emerged which was reflected in the question of whether the national revolution had been completed in 1945–9, with the formal establishment of the independent Indonesian state. Soekarno and the organized left, found mainly in the PKI and the left wing of the PNI, took the view that the revolution had not been completed. Their view was that the economy was still in the grip of Dutch and general Western imperial interests and that a strong national (that is, commonly shared) culture and character had not been fully developed. This view was opposed by the army, the right wing of the PNI and the larger Islamic parties which sought cooperation with the West and its corporations and which wanted an end to the political mobilization of workers and peasants, especially as the latter were demanding nationalization of more foreign enterprises, a role in the management of state-owned corporations and distribution of land away from landowners to tenant farmers and the landless.

There was also growing support for a more active alignment with the non-aligned and socialist bloc in world politics. The Soekarno–PKI alliance supported the Vietnamese revolution, developed a diplomatic alliance with the People's Republic of China, and began a campaign against the formation of Malaysia when Britain and the Malayan elite did not allow a referendum in Sabah and Sarawak on their incorporation into the new nation. A large campaign of mobilization against Britain and Malaysia was supported by millions of people.

The foundation process of nation formation, especially at the cultural level, namely mobilizational political struggle, was a deeply contradictory process. It strengthened commitment to the concept of an Indonesian nation but reflected deep divisions over what kind of country the as yet still to be established Indonesian nation should be. There was an ideological civil war over the fate of the nation, a civil war that was a basic element in the completion of the national revolution.

Just as in other great civil wars involved in the creation of nations, the two sides in this war were anchored to basic class interests. Political mobilization was more and more propelled by the energies of the proletariat and peasantry mobilizing behind demands that they saw as reflecting their interests and behind a political leadership embodied in the alliance between President Soekarno and the Indonesian Communist Party (PKI). This was reflected in the astounding growth in the membership of the PKI and the other main Soekarnoist organization, the Indonesian National Party (PNI), in the years before 1965. By 1965, the PKI and its mass organizations were claiming a total membership of 25 million. The PNI also had several million members. This 25 million plus represents a massive proportion of the adult population: it was more than half of the 37 million voting population of just ten years before and was probably more than half of the 55 million voting population recorded in 1971.

Ideologically, and reflecting upon the process of national identity, Soekarnoism itself had started to win a position alongside the concept of Indonesia as the most popular basis for the completion of the revolution. During the 1950s, left and right, Islamic and secular, unitary and federalist all formulated their ideas as an answer to what kind of Indonesia was wanted. Indonesia was the common shared central concept. During the 1960s, differing ideas about the future started to be represented as either false or genuine Soekarnoism. Even those most opposed to the direction and character of mobilizational politics established themselves as, for example, a *body in support of Soekarnoism.*

All political forces adopted the vocabulary of "finishing the revolution," of socialism, of being "progressive revolutionary." This was not the result of totalitarian censorship or central state control. In the 1960s, the state apparatus itself was a central site of the sharpest possible conflict. The closest structure to a so-called "hard state apparatus" was the armed forces, whose leadership was in fact more and more opposed to mobilizational politics and to the left. The army leadership had even established its own organization, the Joint Secretariat for Functional Groups (Sekber GOLK-AR) to propagate a form of socio-political organization that eschewed both mobilization and ideological conflict.

The force propelling all groups to adopt the leftist language of the national revolution was the growing popularity of these ideas and the level of mobilization of the mass of the people. The membership numbers of the PKI and PNI underline this reality. Moreover, there was a deep level of participation in this political life, which gave it extra strength, fusing together the development of a national cultural outlook with a specific political outlook. One manifestation of this participation was the explosion in availability of reading material, especially newspapers. Another manifestation of the fusion of the two processes was the massive recruitment of teachers, from primary through to high school, into the radicalizing *aliran*, transmitting this radicalization to the school population as part of the national culture.

As tension increased, especially in late 1964, the army regularly arrested members of the PKI, especially farmers involved in leading occupations of land due for land reform. In some areas, the army also banned left-wing publications. After five assassination attempts on Soekarno in the late 1950s and early 1960s, and rumours of possible military coups and similar plots against him, he agreed to the detention of opponents who were accused of cooperation with US intelligence agencies. Although these repressive actions further heightened tensions, there was no systematic repression by Soekarno. Soekarno, in fact, did not have control over the repressive apparatus, namely the army, police and courts, which were controlled by his enemies.

The real terror for the conservative and right-wing bloc was not one of physical intimidation, or even arrest or arbitrary purge. The anti-Soekarno anti-PKI camp was able to organize major conferences and other political activities throughout the period 1960–5. The real terror was that of being marginalized by opposing ideas actively supported among the population. This did threaten, at some future point, possible loss of the dominant position in various associations and unions as well as in state institutions, including educational institutions. Three leading figures from the intellectual right lost their positions in universities and the state radio organization in this period. A manifesto opposing the mobilization of art and

culture for political purposes, the Manifes Kebudayaan (MANIKEBU—
Cultural Manifesto), was issued by anti-left writers. This was banned on
the initiative of the Minister for Education and Culture, Prijono, a member
of the centrist Murba Party.

Between 1962 and 1965, the Soekarno–PKI alliance gained more and
more support, isolating its opposition who increasingly turned to the army
for protection. By 1965, the prospects of the Soekarno–PKI alliance
coming to power were very great. The pro-capitalist political parties
had lost all momentum. Two—the MASYUMI and PSI—had been
outlawed for participation in the unpopular and easily defeated 1956–7
armed rebellion. The PNI was undergoing a virtual split as left-wing forces
gained greater support among its peasant and lower middle-class base
leaving an isolated and weak right wing. The rural village-based Islamic
organization, with its strong ties to landowners, the Nahdlatul Ulama,
adapted to the national trend, accommodating to Soekarno's vocabulary
(while inculcating its militia with an anti-left perspective).

At the level of governmental power, both nationally and in the
provinces, however, the growing left alliance, comprising Soekarno, the
PKI and the left-wing of the PNI, represented a minority. While Soekarno
was President, he did not have the power to form a cabinet based on the
alliance of pro-Soekarno and pro-left forces. The cabinet comprised a
coalition of centrist and right-wing politicians from the PNI, the Murba
Party and Nahdlatul Ulama and from the armed forces. PKI leaders Aidit
and M. Lukman were ex officio members of the cabinet due to their
position as deputy speakers of the Provisional People's Consultative
Assembly but they were not given ministries to head. Any attempt to
shift the balance of power in the cabinet in a leftward direction held the
potential to provoke a reaction from the armed forces, whose officer corps
was dominated by anti-left elements. The other important arena was the
parliament. Soekarno had dissolved the parliament elected in the 1955
general elections and appointed a new one. However, in this process, he
had gone out of his way to be "representative," even reducing the
representation of the PKI. The pro-Soekarno left forces in the parliament
were in a minority. They were forced to accept watered-down versions of
some of the legislation that had been championed, such as new agrarian
laws calling for the redistribution of land from large landowners to landless
peasants.

A political victory for the Soekarno–PKI alliance could come with nothing less than a deepening of the revolution, a complete displacement of current state power. The PKI leadership itself had developed the concept of "the state with two aspects" whereby it posited that there were "pro-people" and "anti-people" elements in the state apparatus and that the "anti-people" elements had to be removed. Soekarno also gave support to this perspective through his support for the "retooling" of corrupt and conservative bureaucrats out of the state apparatus. In the "retooling" process, the PKI identified as primary targets the *kabir*—capitalist bureau-crats—primarily army officers who had gained control of nationalized enterprises and associated government departments and institutions.

"Retooling" was not the only policy aimed at the enemy within the state apparatus. Soekarno, the left PNI and the PKI also supported the program of "NASAKOMization" of both the civil service and the armed forces. NASAKOMization meant placing leading personnel from each of the nationalist (*nasionalis*), religious (*agama*) and communist (*komunis*) poli-tical streams into key positions in the civil service and the armed forces.

Support for a socialist direction—for nationalization of foreign business, for land reform, for worker participation in management, and for coopera-tion with the socialist states and the non-aligned bloc—was overwhelming at the mass level, but isolated within the state apparatus. The struggle over the nature of the new national entity became more and more a struggle between a mobilized movement of the popular classes led by the Soekarno–PKI alliance and an increasingly politically isolated alliance of parties representing the interests of landowning and business groups, and under the leadership of elements that were strong within the state apparatus, particularly the army.

Several things had become intertwined. The activity—mass mobilization political struggle, the post-independence *pergerakan*—that had been spreading the vocabulary, ideas and methods of the new national culture was also the activity through which political (and social class) interests were struggling for sway over the process of completing the process of forming of the new Indonesian nation and state. It is crucial to keep reminding oneself here that Indonesia as a nation, a national social formation, had not yet been completely established in either 1945 or 1949. It was a nation in the process of formation. The huge political mobilizations were not taking place in the aftermath of the completion of a national revolution, when the nation in all its aspects had been formed. These mobilizations were taking place as an integral part of the struggle for the nation.

Protection of the existing social order, including the new privileges of the military business managers' caste, became intertwined with opposition to mobilizational politics in general. This was reflected in the struggle around another slogan of the period: "Politik adalah panglima" (Politics is in command). The Soekarno-PKI alliance was proposing a reorganization of politics and society requiring the removal from the state apparatus of conservative personnel and a redistribution of power that would be constituted through a series of changes in the political format. This would involve NASAKOMization, worker participation in state-owned enterprises, distribution of land away from large landowners and the arming of the trade unions and peasant organizations. The political mobilizations in rallies, demonstrations, strikes, land occupations, formation of new branches of all organizations, cultural campaigns in the villages, educational courses, congresses and conferences were all aimed to achieve these goals. This was the concrete content of the various political declarations issued by Soekarno. Prioritizing these campaigns was described as putting politics in command.

Various political groups, in alliance with the army, started to actively oppose this idea. All politics, in particular mobilizational politics, was viewed as destructive. The "functional groups" concept (*golongan karya*— GOLKAR) propagated by the army was meant as an alternative to mobilization. An individual's place in society was seen solely through their occupational role and their role in life and society, including their political role, which was simply to carry out their (occupational) function: workers labored, farmers farmed, fishermen fished, housewives served their husbands and children and so on. They were to belong to organizations under the effective control of the state and the army. The Joint Secretariat of GOLKAR in the 1960s, and later in the 1970s and 1980s, was comprised overwhelmingly of military officers.

The phenomenon of opposition to "politics" also began to surface within some intellectual circles and at the margins of student activity. By 1962 most intellectuals and artists had also joined one of the *aliran*. The People's Cultural Institute (LEKRA) and the National Cultural Institute (LKN), connected to the PKI and PNI respectively, were the biggest and most active cultural organizations. The Indonesian Scholars Association

(HSI), also connected with the PKI, was growing rapidly. Among intellectuals and artists, these organizations were countered by new "anti-political" groupings, in particular, the Cultural Manifesto (MANIKEBU) group. The MANIKEBU group adopted the GOLKAR idea that different occupational groupings should stick to their role: so artists, for example, should stick to art and stay out of politics—but in alliance with the army. Among students in Jakarta, a small, new group arose, called Serikat Mahasiswa Lokal (SOMAL), whose basic outlook was to keep out of mobilizational politics. The MANIKEBU group alongside the SOMAL students and a few of their academic mentors were to be the central political partners and to provide the democratic cover for General Suharto's army leadership group when it seized power in October 1965.

Thus the scene was set for a confrontation between the Soekarno-PKI-led coalition, whose strength was based on the heightened mobilization of the worker and peasant mass of the population, and the army leadership, the right-wing parties dominant in the government alongside a small coterie of corrupt business managers and landowners, who were increasingly frightened of and opposed to any kind of mobilizational politics, a form of politics that they could not successfully pursue themselves. This later camp's strength was based in its overwhelming domination of the state apparatus, including the army. In the armed forces, while pro-Soekarno officers had increased in numbers they were still a clear minority, especially in the land army. The often held popular image of Soekarno as some kind of all-powerful leader is completely false. His ideas were powerful among the people and even his enemies had to accommodate to their popularity, but primarily at the level of choice of vocabulary. The conflict did generate repressive acts on both sides. MANIKEBU was banned and three of its signatories lost their jobs in universities and state radio. Several prominent figures associated with the anti-Soekarno camp were also detained. The army continued its banning of PKI publications in the regions and, more ferociously, continued its attacks on peasant land actions in the countryside.

A cultural revolution had been underway since at least 1909 and it had deepened and spread after independence as schools, parties and the new *pergerakan* spread their reach and deepened their contact with the people. This accelerated after 1962 when the Soekarno–PKI alliance surged in support before it was suppressed in 1965. A new discourse on the future of Indonesia was providing the basis for the emergence of a shared national cultural outlook. The outcome of the confrontation that developed between 1962 and 1965—mass suppression of the Soekarnoist/PKI *pergerakan*—would have enormous ramifications for the process of cultural unification throughout the archipelago.

"Guided Economy"

The revolutionary process in the arena of political culture and national consciousness was paralleled by a struggle in the economic sphere. Independent Indonesia had inherited a dual economy, with a modernizing enclave sector operating as a virtual economic extension of the Dutch economy. Extraction of wealth had been the overriding principle of the previous four centuries, including during the modernizing one hundred years before independence. This enclave sector was based primarily on mining, plantations and various forms of forced cultivation among small farmers. Extraction primarily took the form of repatriation of profits back to the Netherlands. Little of the surplus stemming from Dutch and other foreign investment in the Netherlands Indies stayed within the country. Wages were miserably low, accounting for hardly even a few percentage points of costs. Construction of infrastructure often used slave labor, or the equivalent, and was often also paid for by taxes extracted from the local population out of the surplus they produced themselves in the traditional sectors. A minimal proportion of the country's wealth was reinvested in improving human resources. There were only 230 Indonesian tertiary graduates in Indonesia when the country won its independence—at that time it already had a population of around 80 million people. The only school system that had existed was for training clerks for the civil service of the colonizers.

During the 1950–65 period, there was a steady escalation in efforts to break out of the dual economy. These efforts were driven by two different class forces. There was one effort driven by the country's small capitalists or aspiring capitalists (sometimes bureaucrats, politicians or rural landowners) to develop themselves as a new class of Indonesian national entrepreneurs. Such efforts began as early as 1950 under a program known as Indonesianization. This program was based on policies of protection, providing privileges for and subsidization of aspiring Indonesian private capitalists.

Another effort came out of the organized left, and was aimed at achieving both nationalization and worker control within a general socialist frame-work. In 1956, trade unions occupied almost all of the Dutch companies, which were then nationalized. More than 400 plantations and scores of commercial, industrial and banking enterprises were nationalized, account-ing for 90 percent of the country's plantation output and 60 percent of foreign trade. The army was in a powerful position at that moment as martial law had been declared in response to rebellions by ultra-rightist army officers based in Sumatra and Sulawesi who were moving to proclaim an alternative Indonesian government. Army officers became the managers of these nationalized companies.

The nationalizations, combined with the 1956 repudiation of 85 percent of Indonesia's debt to the Netherlands which it had also inherited from the Netherlands Indies, broke the international connection associated with the dual economy. Between 1956 and 1965, extraction of wealth from Indonesia was no longer the major problem of the economy. The focus of economic problems shifted to maintaining and increasing production across the archipelago.

The nationalizations of 1956 and the placement of army officers as the managers of the new state-owned companies meant that the basic contra-dictions of Indonesian politics became sharply focused within the natio-nalized sector. The trade unions, under the leadership of the left, campaigned for worker participation in enterprise management councils and for the "retooling" of corrupt and inefficient managers. Pickets, strikes and demonstrations, combined with lobbying of the President, were the main campaign methods. After almost ten years of campaigning, by 1965, one-third of enterprise management councils had trade union representa-tion but they were often thwarted by having no real say in management.

The nationalizations were also to provide the basis for what Soekarno and the PKI called "Guided Economy," proposed in 1959. This was to be an effort to develop the economy through a program of direct state intervention and regulation of the business sector. It was also to involve a refusal to accept any "strings attached" aid from the West and greater economic cooperation with the socialist and non-aligned blocs. "Guided Economy," however, never had a chance to be seriously tested. The Soekarno–PKI camp was still a minority in the government, and the major state corporations were in the hands of the army. Resistance within the government to this path continued. As late as 1962, the Indonesian government still accepted a delegation from the World Bank to discuss possible cooperation.

At the political level, the Soekarno–PKI camp won a battle when the government rejected the World Bank package offered in 1962, which would have required the government to restrict public spending, thus threatening, for example, its programs of subsidizing school education. At the same time, the government was able to negotiate new, soft loans from the Soviet Union and to begin some projects with Soviet assistance. In March 1963 Soekarno issued the Economic Declaration (DEKON), giving further political backing to the socialist ideas embodied in a "Guided Economy." However, a "Guided Economy" was still impossible. One problem was that the country's major export earner, rubber, faced a price collapse in 1960 as a result of competition from synthetic rubber. However, the real issues were political. The government had no real control over the modern sector of the economy, which remained in the hands of an unaccountable army, which was also politically hostile to the whole leftward trajectory of Soekarno. All energies were in fact being absorbed by the political battle between left and right, reflected in both the domestic and international arenas, that was becoming more desperate with every passing day. The economy became increasingly chaotic between 1962–5, and by 1964 production began to collapse. Only a fully fledged Soekarno–left PNI–PKI government could have tested the feasibility of developing the economy under "Guided Economy" socialism and in cooperation with the socialist bloc countries, rather than with the West.

Political Mobilization and Indonesia

Political mobilization—mass *pergerakan*—was the process which was creating Indonesia, including a new national cultural outlook. At the same time there were the beginnings of an attempt to restructure the Indonesian economy to end the dual economy and bring it under greater control of the Indonesian state. In October 1965 both mass mobilization politics, which had become the dominant form of politics, and a "Guided Economy," which had hardly begun, were brought to an abrupt halt when General Suharto and other elements from the Indonesian army officer corps seized power in the wake of the failed attempt to remove some of the anti-left army leadership by Soekarnoist officers sympathetic to the left. This event set the scene for the emergence of a completely different Indonesia during the coming decades. In his book, the *Indonesian National Revolution, 1945–50*, Anthony Reid ends his description of the 1945–50 period with some comments on how history unfolded after 1950:

> The romantic pemuda [youth] vision was increasingly revived by Sukarno's rhetoric of unity, struggle, and sacrifice. The spirit of the revolution continued to live in a dozen divergent but passionate forms, at least until the terrible crisis of 1965–6 drove them all out of sight.[8]

Putting aside Reid's use of the pejorative "rhetoric," there is no doubt that any "spirit of the revolution," that is, the revolution that was creating Indonesia, was eliminated from politics and society after 1965 by the policies implemented by Suharto. The nature of these policies and how they not only removed the spirit of the revolution but also brought the process of completing the national revolution, of completing the nation formation process, to a point of stagnation will be discussed in the next chapter.

One question will, however, remain unanswered: What kind of Indonesia might have emerged if the Soekarno–PKI alliance had won power, if the spirit of the revolution had been able to keep driving politics and culture and if a "Guided Economy" had been given a real chance? In regard to both aspects of this question, we can only speculate. In the sphere of the economy, we should note that Indonesia under a "Guided Economy" would have had serious cooperation with the Soviet Union for at least two decades and with the People's Republic of China until today. India was able to make serious advances in its economy, especially industrialization and technology transfer, as a result of its cooperation with the Soviet Union. Within ten years, Indonesia's oil production was also to surge. But who knows?

A defeat for the army and conservative Islam would have certainly changed the political and cultural map of Indonesia. Of course, there were also very visible contradictions within the new *pergerakan* movement. One central contradiction was that between the creative ideological ferment being developed within the movement and the almost totalitarian acceptance of Soekarno's vocabulary for discussing politics. The question of succession and the balance between the Soekarnoist and PKI left might have developed as a new point of struggle. There had been such a sweeping dynamic behind the amazing growth of the Soekarnoist left movement during the previous twenty years that discussions of differences within the movement had not been a priority. There probably would have been new struggles between new streams created from within a victorious Soekarno–PKI-led revolution.

It is difficult to make a thorough assessment of the experience of the Indonesian left, which included the biggest communist party in the world outside of the Soviet Union and the People's Republic of China. There are a few Western academic studies and only very few initial assessments by survivors of the PKI itself.[9] However, the totality of suppression, including the physical elimination of so many party members, has meant that a real study of the internal life and thinking of this huge party is yet to be undertaken. Today, younger historians have made a start with various oral history projects, interviewing survivors. However, this work has concentrated on their experience of the violence after 1965 rather than their party experiences in the 1950s and 1960s.

The assessment that is required is not just of the PKI, but also of Soekarno and his thinking, and of other thinkers and activists on the left. Again and again I have interrogated survivors from the left of this period, including Pramoedya Ananta Toer. There is little doubt in my mind that the popularization of socialist ideas was the result, in the first instance, of the writing and oratorical work of Soekarno. He had the skill to present socialist ideas to the huge audience of urban and rural semi-proletarians and pauperized petty bourgeoisie mobilized for the new project of Indonesia. The PKI organized those influenced by his agitation, sometimes giving more theoretical infrastructure, whether weak or strong, to his ideas. There was a symbiotic relationship between the two—but a relationship which, in 1965, was still evolving. Soekarno was a radical populist socialist moving to the left. The PKI was a mass communist party that had evolved and developed in a period when such parties were influenced by the example of Stalinism and Maoism. How might a relationship have further developed between an increasingly anti-imperialist socialist and a Stalinist-influenced mass party if the events of 1 October 1965 had not occurred? Sometimes I have heard talk of divisions between PKI Chairperson D.N. Aidit and the second-ranking PKI leader, Nyoto, who was said to be close to Soekarno. I have heard quite a few of the survivors say Soekarno was trying to convince him to break from the PKI and help form a new party. Was this true? What kind of party?

What we do know is what actually happened. In the face of an impending victory for the movement led by the Soekarno-PKI alliance, reflecting the massive growth in support for its ideas, Suharto and the army led one of the biggest massacres of human beings in modern history, a massacre based almost entirely on targeting political opponents. With more than 25 million members of the PKI, let alone millions of other sympathizers of the impending social revolution, the massacre would need to be huge.

2

Counter-revolution

Radicalization deepened and the organizations of the social revolution—
the PKI, the left wing of the PNI and affiliated mass organizations—grew
rapidly after 1962. The struggle for power—even the preparation for social
revolution itself—was more and more situated within the theoretical
framework of the struggle between "the two aspects of the state," that
is, pro- and anti-people aspects. Campaigns to "retool," that is, have
dismissed conservative officials and *kabir* from the state apparatus and also
from some mass organizations, developed as the central struggle. There
were many mass mobilization campaigns demanding the dismissal of
conservative governors and district heads. Students demonstrated for
the dismissal of conservative university professors. Some mass organizations, such as the Indonesian Journalists Association, dismissed conservative leaders. It is not surprising that the "retooling" campaign manifested
itself inside the armed forces.

On 30 September 1965, pro-Soekarno officers began to conduct a
unilateral "retooling" of the armed forces high command. It is still unclear
what, if any, were the overall plans of Colonel Untung and his fellow
conspirators when they ordered the detention of seven of the top generals
in the armed forces high command and moved to replace them themselves
and with other pro-Soekarno officers. The most recent scholarship reveals
that the initial aim was to remove the right-wing of the high command and
then to provoke a mass mobilization across the country for the purge of the
right wing from the officer corps as a whole.[1]

The mass murders were carried out by the Indonesian army as well as
anti-communist Islamic and nationalist militia. These militia were led by
the most right-wing elements attached to the Islamic party *aliran* as well as

those attached to the Indonesian National Party (PNI). Which militia played a major role and which of the anti-communist parties was dominant depended on local conditions.

Most analysis estimates that between 500,000 and 2 million were slaughtered.[2] Most of these people were leaders, activists or supporters of one component or other of the Indonesian left which had been looking to the PKI-Soekarno alliance for leadership. Many of those killed died horribly, as part of a terror campaign. They were decapitated, disembowelled, dragged behind a truck or otherwise cruelly killed. In addition to those killed, hundreds of thousands more were detained for between a few months and a year, often in unlisted safe houses. At least 12,000 were further detained for another ten to twelve years. Tens of thousands were dismissed from their jobs, especially in the teaching service, civil service and railways.

This terror, however, must be seen as aimed at more than the annihilation of the organized left, the PKI and all other groups following Soekarno's left direction. This terror was aimed at ending the processes of the national revolution. It was meant to end the politics of *pergerakan*: all of the ideas and methods that had been an integral part of the Indonesian national revolution between 1909 and 1965. It is not difficult to understand why Suharto and the rest of the leadership of this counter-revolutionary offensive felt the need to annihilate these ideas and methods. In 1965 they faced an impending social revolution. More than half of the voting population were actively mobilized behind demands that, if fulfilled, would completely undermine the privileged position of aspiring military businessmen and rural landowners. This movement for worker control of state enterprises, land reform, further nationalization of the economy and deeper cooperation among non-aligned countries had developed as an extension of the national revolution itself, as an extension of the struggle to consolidate Indonesia as a stable and sovereign nation. There was no way to separate out the basic ideas of the national revolution—*aksi* (street protest), *mogok* (strike), *vergadering* (mass rally), *rapat massa* (mass meeting), *sarikat* (union), *berontak* (rebel), *semangat* (spirit), *pemuda* (youth), *massa* (the masses), *rakyat* (the people), *revolusi* (revolution), *sama rata sama rasa* (equality), *berdaulat* (sovereign), *kepribadian nasional* (national character)—from the movement threatening social revolution.

The counter-revolution launched by Suharto in October 1965 was a counter-revolution in the sense of being an act of massive suppression not only of the organizations of the left and of the social revolution, but also of the national revolution itself. The first part of this counter-revolution was perceived clearly by its perpetrators. On this their cry was *ganyang PKI!*— crush the PKI! On the second aspect, they were probably blind to the destruction they were wreaking on the Indonesian national revolution, although the following decades were to show that they did indeed have only little conception of and commitment to a genuine development of an Indonesian nation.

The terror, murder and massive arrests were the first step in ending open mobilizational politics. The physical elimination and the psychological destruction of the movement itself, right down to the grassroots, was the first task. Suharto's purges were not aimed only at decapitating the leadership of the movement. Nor were they aimed at simply combining decapitation of the leadership and some modest "shock therapy" to demoralize and unbalance the rest of the movement. It went further than that. The violence was aimed at the class base of the movement itself. Factories with a reputation for militancy had their whole workforce slaughtered. Villages that had supported the left were annihilated. Of course, this policy was implemented unevenly, depending on the intensity of the local social conflict. However, the fundamental policy behind all the killings was to decapitate the leadership, eliminate the activist base and terrorize the millions of sympathizers of the PKI, the left wing of the PNI and all affiliated mass organizations—all of Soekarno's supporters.

This slaughter and terror was accompanied by policies of immediate suppression of the organization and press of the left. While the new Suharto regime felt compelled to continue to refer to socialism and revolution in its rhetoric for some time, Marxism and Leninism and, not long after, the writings of Soekarno were banned. The PKI and Soekarnoist left press was closed down. Papers with obvious organizational affiliations with the PKI were immediately closed; others lasted a few months before being closed. The PKI itself and its mass organizations were banned. In the case of the PNI, both the party and its mass organizations were allowed to continue but they were subject to purge. The secretary general of the PNI, Surachman, was detained, tortured and killed.

De-organization: "Floating Mass"

The deeper purpose of the counter-revolution was then more clearly revealed in the policies that were pursued in the aftermath of this slaughter, terror and suppression of the left. Once the immediate threat of social revolution had been dealt with, the new counter-revolutionary government began a policy of political restructuring aimed at making permanent the end of any form of open mobilizational politics. There was to be no more *pergerakan*, ever. For the new government the revolution was finished.

The classic work setting out the "philosophy" of the counter-revolution is by the architect of the new political format, the late General Ali Murtopo. Murtopo was a special intelligence advisor to General Suharto, headed a Special Operations unit for several years, held the position of Personal Assistant to the President for almost ten years and later became Minister for Information under Suharto. It was his book, *25 Years of Accelerated Modernisation of Development*, that set out the counter-revolution's ideas. At the core of his concept was the idea of the "floating mass." It is worth quoting at length from his book on this idea:

> The political parties were always trying to marshal mass support by forming various affiliated organisations based on the ideologies of their respective parties. The mass of the people, especially those in the villages, always fell prey to the political and ideological interests of those parties. Their involvement in the conflicts of political and ideological interests had as its result the fact that they ignored the necessities of daily life, the need for development and improvement of their own lives, materially as well as spiritually.
>
> Such a situation should not repeat itself. Nevertheless, even now the parties continue to be narrowly ideology-oriented as before. Therefore it is only right to attract the attention of the mainly village people away from political problems and ideological exclusiveness to efforts of national development through the development of their own rural societies. For this reason it is justifiable that political parties are limited to the district level only [that is, are banned from the villages]. Here lies the meaning and the goal of the *depoliticisation* (the process of freeing the people from political manipulation) and

the *deparpolisasi* [the process of freeing the people from political party allegiances] in the villages.

Nevertheless, this does not imply the people in the villages are barred from maintaining political aspirations. Besides their opportunity to pour their aspirations into development of their own societies, in the general elections they can also vote for whichever political party or Functional groups (Golkar) they regard as capable of channelling their aspirations and whichever has platforms in accordance with their own aspirations.

In this way people in the villages will not spend their valuable time and energy in the political struggles of parties and groups, but will be occupied wholly with development efforts. Through this process there emerges the so-called "floating mass," i.e. people who are not permanently tied to membership of any political party.[3]

Murtopo grasped perfectly the link between mass mobilization and the role of political parties and the groupings of mass organizations around them. The policies of slaughter, terror and suppression had been aimed at parties most effective in attracting people into activity. The ban on villagers participating in any party activity at all—except voting at election time—was a central follow-up policy to institutionalizing political passivity. The concept that people would be "occupied wholly with development efforts" reminds one of the idea of a "tool with a voice" that was prevalent during slave society. The village people, who were the overwhelming majority of people in the 1965–75 period, were simply to work, to produce and to have no ongoing role in politics. In fact, however, the "floating mass" idea was inspired more by the perception of mass political passivity in the two-party system of Western parliamentary democracies in the 1950s and early 1960s. In the Indonesia coming out of fifty-five years of national revolutionary struggle, the only way to achieve this passivity where people "are not permanently tied to membership of any political party" was through the deployment of mass counter-revolutionary violence. No other way was possible. Parties and political mobilization were too deeply embedded in the foundation of the nation-creating process itself.

The deep roots of the culture of political mobilization meant that even after the slaughter, terror and suppression of 1965–8, the New Order needed an extensive and active system of repression to maintain "depo-liticization." At the core of this system was the territorial command system of the armed forces. From the very beginning of the establishment of the Republic's armed forces, there had always been a section of the officer corps who had argued that the military should have a central role in politics. By the late 1950s, these officers had developed the concept of *Dwifungsi* (Dual Function) which stated that the armed forces had a civic as well as a military role. During the period of the late 1950s through to 1965 the armed forces' role in political affairs was strengthened as a result of extended periods of martial law which had been declared either as a response to mutiny from within the army or as a part of external military campaigns. The key structure for the armed forces' surveillance and intervention into politics throughout the country was a system of territorial commands that had developed during the period of guerrilla struggle against the Dutch. The guerrilla struggle had taken place in almost all areas of the country and so the army had established regionally based army units with local command headquarters and other outposts. The Indonesian army's structure there-fore was never built around a system of forward bases to defend the country from external attack, but rather was structured to manage military activity within the country. Pro-*Dwifungsi* officers developed theories to justify the retention of this system, which then became a parallel domestic admin-istrative structure to the civilian bureaucracy.

This structure was strengthened under the New Order and, for most of these thirty-two years, was invested with special authority to intervene in political affairs. Special national coordinating bodies, based in armed forces' headquarters, were established to coordinate this system of political management. The first was called Command for the Restoration of Stability and Order (KOPKAMTIB), and later slightly restructured and renamed the Body for Coordination of National Stability (BAKORSTAN-NAS). Military command posts existed at almost every level of society, with military personnel posted to all villages. This structure ensured that the ban on political party activity in the villages was strictly implemented.

Some parties were allowed to continue to open offices at the district town level and larger town level. These were the parties that themselves had supported the surrender of political initiative to the army. However, the New Order decided that the counter-revolution needed these parties—nine in all—to be further adapted to depoliticization. First, they had to undergo *simplifikasi.* The Islamic parties were forced to fuse into one party, to be called the United Development Party (Partai Persatuan Pembangunan—PPP). The non-Islamic parties, including the now thoroughly purged PNI, were forced to merge into the Indonesian Democratic Party (Partai Demokrasi Indonesia—PDI). Both the PPP and PDI were also subject to permanent intervention by the government in the selection of their leaderships. The regime's own party, GOLKAR, made up the third party that was allowed to participate in elections.

Of course, these parties were never to be allowed to become vehicles for a return of mobilizational politics. All party campaigning was banned except for a ten-day period before the four-yearly elections. This campaign period was also tightly controlled with each party only able to organize rallies and marches on three out of the ten days. Under "floating mass," the role of the masses was indeed truly to be limited to voting only. Not surprisingly, under these conditions, when elections did occur, the PDI and PPP could never match GOLKAR. GOLKAR had massive funds but also a de facto presence in the villages. The regime had declared a policy of *monoloyalitas* for all civil servants, right down to the village head and his staff. They all had to be active members of GOLKAR.

The attack on the political parties was not only in terms of their role as electoral organizations. Their role in organizing people in trade unions and peasant associations—the whole structure of *aliran* organization—was also demolished. This demolition of the party-affiliated mass organizations was not, however, just aimed at breaking the hold of parties. In most respects, the terror of 1965–8 had already done that. Other policies were instituted to ensure that any such organizations that were allowed to exist played a role of ensuring that the popular classes, disorganized and demoralized by the terror, remained disorganized. The counter-revolution's policy was one of de-organization of the popular classes as a whole.

Initially, during 1966–71, almost no attention was given to the question of long-term policy towards trade unions and similar organizations. As the economy stabilized and both the peasantry and working class began to develop again as a stable social grouping playing a significant role in the New Order's economic program, trade unions as well as farmers and fishermen's organizations were re-established but with a strict policy of ensuring that these sectors were not able to reorganize. All these organizations remained strictly in the hands of officials selected by the New Order government, in many cases retired or serving army officers.

The establishment of these "unions" and other organizations on the basis of one organization for each sector—workers, farmers, fishermen, youth, etc.—was often justified using reference to so-called traditional corporatist ideas, often referring to the so-called "integralist state." There was, however, no interest in either incorporating or integrating these sectors of society into any of the fundamental political processes of the country, except as passive objects of policy, prevented from any possibility of organizing to exercise any level of power. Rather than a manifestation of a so-called "corporatist" philosophy, these were policies of exclusion and suppression.

After 1972, organizations claiming to organize workers, peasant farmers, fisherpeople, youth, civil servants and civil servants' wives were established. All were affiliated to GOLKAR, and were considered to represent key "functional groups." They were consistently used throughout the New Order period to stifle genuine organization. There were internal rumblings from within these organizations from time to time, trying to transform themselves into genuine representative bodies. Such attempts were always suppressed, In 1985 a law was passed to deepen control over all social organizations, legally subjecting them to government control in almost all their activities and committing them to espousing the official state ideology, *Panca Sila*, the meaning of which only the government was allowed to interpret.[4] As a result almost all worker, farmer, youth and student protest during the New Order developed outside these organizations.

All that was left for the majority of Indonesians was to "occupy themselves wholly with development efforts," that is, to work and produce.

Consolidating the Ideologicide: Erasing Memory

The 1965 terror combined with the "floating mass" policies attacked the organization of the forces of social revolution. The massive physical attack on the left ideological community was a virtual "ideoligicide." Of course, such levels of terror also surrounded the ideas of revolution, and of the left in particular, with a deep aura of fear. Anybody associated with the left or expressing left-wing ideas could be subject to such terror. The accusation of being a member of the PKI became one of the most threatening accusations that could be made. Anybody could be asked to obtain documents from local police and state authorities stating that they were "clean" of infection from the PKI. The presence of more than 12,000 left-wing activists on Buru Island prison camp right up until 1978 was a salutary reminder of what would happen if you espoused or were thought to be contaminated with such ideas.

Here too, in the world of ideas, the government realized that the initial terror and suppression would not be enough. The key institutions which could propagate left-wing ideas had been destroyed. They were no longer an immediate danger. The remaining threat came from the national revolution itself, that is, from its legacy, from any memory of what it was and had been trying to achieve. Memory of the national revolution had to be erased from the popular consciousness. Given that the very existence of Indonesia, even as a concept, was a direct product of the revolutionary process, this was a mammoth task. Here too, we see again the necessity, from the point of view of the counter-revolution, of the extent and depth of the slaughter and terror.

In the media, the arts and culture, and the universities these institutions fell quickly into the control of intellectuals who supported or were in sympathy with the counter-revolution. The country's most prestigious university, the University of Indonesia, became the location of joint seminars with the armed forces to map out the country's future. The two massive left cultural organizations had been banned and their writers and artists were gaoled and then exiled to Buru Island. The newspapers, previously attached to political parties and with specific ideological perspectives, either explicitly espoused the political outlook of the armed forces and the counter-revolution or acquiesced in all central matters, as they sought to establish themselves as successful business enterprises. The intellectuals of the MANIKEBU dominated everywhere, hardly raising a single note of concern regarding the hundreds of their fellow intellectuals in prison.

In these institutions a single history of the period of "Guided Democracy" was propagated. Debate about this period was impossible. All the writings of Soekarno, the PKI leaders and intellectuals and other leftists were banned, disappearing from all bookshops and libraries. For the intellectuals triumphant in the victory of the army, the period before

1965 had been one of terror for them. The popularity of their rivals in the arena of the arts and culture was alarming to them. Both their positions in educational and artistic institutions and their markets were under threat. They had survived by cooperating with the army against Soekarno before 1965 and then again after 1965. It was this terror, articulated as the accusation of tyranny against Soekarno, that permeated their representation of the "Guided Democracy" period throughout the media, the arts and the universities. This MANIKEBU generation of intellectuals became known as the 66 Generation and for the first few years the literary work which best displayed their sentiments was a collection of poems by Taufiq Ismail under the title *Tirani* ("Tyranny"), published in stencilled form in 1966. It was this perspective which permeated all ideological institutions. Ironically, this monopoly of perspective was not the result of the popular adoption of one view over another, but was based on a real physical tyranny.

However, the wiping of the memory of the previous sixty years of *pergerakan* history required a more systematic approach. The New Order began a total rewriting of Indonesian history to be propagated in schools, universities and through the mass media. This task was managed by the History Center of the armed forces, headed by a historian who had been recruited into the armed forces and given the title Brigadier-General: Nugroho Notosusanto.[5] An official history of Indonesia was commissioned. New textbooks were written for all levels of schooling and tried out in different forms during the course of thirty-two years. A prominent 66 Generation intellectual was commissioned to produce a feature film depicting the New Order's version of politics under Soekarno and of what it claimed was the 1965 "abortive communist coup," complete with graphic depictions of bloodthirsty communist torturers.. This film was compulsory viewing in schools throughout Indonesia for almost two decades. There were also other feature films commissioned on Indonesian history, especially depicting the alleged heroic activities of Suharto after he had left Dutch service and joined the republican forces.

Even the period of direct armed revolt, 1945–9, was renamed. This period had always been referred to specifically as the period of *revolusi*. In the course of the rewriting it was altered to "war of independence," eliminating the role of the mass of people in the overturning of colonial rule in so many areas of social life.

The new version of history eliminated the *pergerakan* from the narrative. The period of open party politics was depicted as a period of instability and chaos with no redeeming features. The role of the army in creating a sense of instability, such as the 1952 attempt to force the parliament to be dissolved, rebellions by army officers in 1956 and 1957, and assassination attempts on Soekarno by military personnel were never mentioned. The early 1960s was depicted as a period when the PKI and Soekarno wielded total power and the economy was completely neglected. The events of 1965 were depicted as a systematic and malevolent plot by the PKI to seize power. The propaganda lies about the sexual mutilation of assassinated generals' corpses continued for much of the period of the New Order. This was a depiction of history enforced throughout the education system. It was taught by rote with no debate or alternative versions tolerated. It was taught by a new generation of teachers educated under the New Order. Thousands of teachers had been victims in the 1965 slaughter and many thousands more sacked from their jobs. There was a new, "fresh" teaching force. It was like Rome after the rebellion by Spartacus: only one history allowed.

Now, over forty years later, very few people under the age of forty have read a speech by Soekarno or any other of the early nationalist leaders. Two of these leaders, the radical Soekarno and the pro-Western Mohammad Hatta, had their roles in history symbolically revised when the New Order government started to describe them as the *proklamator* of Indonesian independence. They had been political activists and leaders, organizers, public speakers, and prolific writers in the national revolution but the New Order redefined them as simply the two men who read the Indonesian Proclamation of Independence. Nobody needed to know anything more than that; or to have any sense of the richness of ideas and political experience of their own country. The falsification of history has been so intense that even major political events during the period of the New Order, such as the big student demonstrations that almost overthrew Suharto in 1974, are not known in any depth by most people. For many, it is almost as if Indonesian history began some time in the 1980s. By then the combination of 66 Generation domination of the media, arts and universities and the systematic and unchallenged falsification of history through the education system virtually eliminated any memory in the popular consciousness of the national revolutionary process that occurred before 1965. It is not surprising that, as we shall see later, not only the reorganization of society, especially of the popular classes, but also the revival of historical memory, have become focuses of movements for renewal since the 1990s.

Culture

The de-organization of the popular classes and the eradication of historical memory from the popular consciousness have had enormous implications for the development of culture. Until 1965 cultural life, in all its manifestations, was being developed and expanded through mass political activity. Literature, film and art, as well as folk theater and the traditional arts were all being transformed as a direct consequence of being integrated into political activity. A national literature was being consolidated as classic literary works started to find their way into popular consciousness through film and theater. But most massively, political discussion through the newspapers and radio was engaging the whole population, organized through the party *aliran* networks.

The contrast with the perspective of the New Order could hardly be greater. What Murtopo called "conflicts of political and ideological interests" involved massive participation of people in discussion of inter-national politics, the course of Indonesian history, political concepts and pressing national issues. These were discussed in conferences and courses as well as in newspapers and journals. Then, after 1965, these millions of people who had once been so agitated around political questions were expected to become "wholly occupied in development efforts," indeed there was a whole structure of enforcement to ensure that was all they did.

There was also a new kind of state policy in the realm of cultural development and in the conception of Indonesian culture. Murtopo himself played a role here, again conceiving of an idea of archipelagic culture, but one deprived of any dynamism flowing from interaction within the archipelago and with politics. Indonesian culture was redefined, just as it had been under the Dutch, as the federation of the different traditional cultures of the islands. One of the crudest representations of this is the Beautiful Indonesia in Miniature theme park, built on the initiative of President Suharto's wife. This theme park depicts Indonesian culture through exhibitions of traditional arts and architecture, that is, examples of the arts and culture from the regions as they had been preserved since initial European contact (discussed further on p. 66).

The concept of a national culture developing out of the common experience of the people of the archipelago in the course of their collective journey through the twentieth century disappeared. It had to disappear. The journey of the Indonesian people since 1909 had been quintessentially a political journey but now politics was banned to the people. One fundamental manifestation of this turn away from national culture was the extreme neglect of literature in the school education system. First, of course, a huge selection of the body of Indonesian literature was now banned. Great national and nationalist authors like Pramoedya Ananta Toer and Sitor Sitormarang were banned. Their books were no longer published, let alone read by students in school. The same applied to scores of other important writers. But even non-left writers were neglected. Students in high school were given nothing more than the most fragmentary exposure to the writings that had helped form the Indonesian national culture. Textbooks on literature hardly featured any substantial selections of texts. There were no obligatory literary texts at all. Libraries had virtually nothing. Of course, the speeches of Soekarno, including those from the anti-Dutch period, were also unavailable. Very little of the classic literature made it on to film, while versions of myths and legends from the pre-Indonesian period dominated alongside the New Order myths created about its own history.

Outside the scope of official government policy, cultural life did take place, of course. There were two key realms of cultural life that continued. One was that driven by the entertainment industry, frequently borrowing from Western popular entertainment and often selling fantasies of life in the higher echelon of the enclaves. This kind of mass consumer entertainment is not, of course, unique to Indonesia. The other cultural process that began to develop in the 1970s involved forms of art, literature and music that defied the ban on politics. Despite the constant suppression, the role of the art and literature of defiance in maintaining some kind of cultural representation of a common experience throughout the archipelago has been fundamental to keeping a national cultural process alive.

The Social Agency of Counter-Revolution

The Indonesian state—in particular, its core, the instrument of armed repression—drove the counter-revolutionary policies of the New Order, even devising the history curriculums for schools and staffing GOLKAR and the trade unions, especially in the early years described in this chapter. But the state itself acted in the service of specific sectors of Indonesian society: the social forces behind the counter-revolution. Ultimately, these social forces can be traced back to those coming out of or connected to the enclave section of the economy, created in the first place by the colonial economy and reinforced after independence in a neocolonial economy.

There had been one fundamental transformation in this enclave economy. The old colonial power, Dutch capital, had been totally expelled. Indonesia may be the only non-socialist country which completely eliminated the old colonial presence, economically, politically and culturally. When, in 1956–7, all Dutch companies were occupied by the trade unions and then nationalized and placed under the management of military officers operating under martial law, the seeds of a new capitalist class were sown. Different parts of the armed forces as well as individual officers began to operate businesses as if they were private capitalists. They were to overtake the tiny number of Indonesian business families who were operating large, national-scale businesses. Among the first of the armed forces institutions to move in this direction was the Army Strategic Command (KOSTRAD) which, under Major General Suharto, established and operated its own bank.

During the first fifteen years of the counter-revolution, businesses owned by different sections of the armed forces formed a majority of the major new corporations. Later, this started to be overtaken by huge conglomerates owned by the families of a small number of generals. Foremost among these was the huge business empire of the Suharto family. The development of these family conglomerates went hand in hand with the development of business partnerships with Chinese Indonesian businessmen, who supplied skills and contacts. These Chinese Indonesian business people also owned some of the largest business conglomerates. Politically, the Chinese Indonesian capitalists were limited in their direct clout. The anti-communist campaign of 1965–6 had used anti-Chinese propaganda as part of its tactics and the new regime banned the public display of the Chinese language and traditions. This sector was a more behind-the-scenes agency of the counter-revolution.[6]

The core of the state—the armed instrument of coercion—fused with the class whose interests it was defending. Before 1965, the left identified this phenomenon in their campaigns to "retool" *kabir* (capitalist bureaucrats). In 1965 this new capitalist class was still small—embryonic—but it stood at the head of a national structure, the armed forces, which had a command structure that reached down into every village. This gave it enormous capacity in its leadership of counter-revolutionary repression. However, it still required forming a coalition with other parts of society whose privileges were under threat. Civilians, bureaucrats or small business people aspiring to become large capitalists and landowners were the other sectors that mobilized in support of the counter-revolution. It was these sectors that dominated the right wing of the PNI (the urban based Islamic MASYUMI Party (banned, but still organized) and the rural based Islamic party, the Nahdlatul Ulama. These parties closed ranks behind the military leadership. The most right-wing elements in these parties mobilized militia forces to assist the military in the violent repression and murder of the left. Others in these parties offered either political support or acquiescence in the counter-revolution's policies—most, enthusiastically, some with misgivings. Whether it was secular or Islamic militia that assisted the military depended on which *aliran* structures were strong in the regions concerned.

The most aggressive elements were the landowning sector whose property rights had come under attack through the agrarian reform laws passed by the parliament before 1965. The Indonesian Peasants' Front (BTI), affiliated to the PKI and some branches of the PNI's peasant union, had tried to force through the implementation of these laws with land occupations. A coalition of landowners, police and army often physically ejected the squatters. At the core of this sector, notably in East Java where the killings were especially systematic, were landowners closely connected to religious schools or centers.[7] One of the most open expositions of the political psychology of this most aggressive element was in an interview of an East Java-based Nahdlatul Ulama figure, Yusuf Hasyim, on the Australian television program, *SBS Dateline*, in the 1990s. In this interview, Hasyim explained how when the rise of communist activity started to threaten their landholdings, he and his friends gathered together to read *Mein Kampf* and study the methods of Adolf Hitler in confronting communist forces. They modeled their militia, he told the *Dateline* journalist, on the Hitler Youth. He also explained how they were secretly armed and trained by the army.

In other areas, however, such as in Central Java, Bali and eastern Indonesia, secular nationalist, Hindu and Christian anti-communist groups assisted the army. The bulk of the membership of the main conservative parties, whether secular or religious, were, however, mostly passive in this process. The leading role of the army in the counter-revolution and the resort to violence was actually a reflection of the political and ideological weakness of these parties and the forces they represented. They were being politically defeated by the Soekarnoist left and had to be saved by the army. Only small elements of these forces had the confidence and energy to go on the offensive after 1965, and even then only with the backing of the army.

This was also true of the conservative Islamic parties, in particular the urban-based MASYUMI. Despite the fact that it supported the army and that its student arm, the Islamic Students Association (HMI), had played an active role in the street demonstrations against Soekarno in late 1965, Suharto continued to ban its leaders from involvement in party politics and only allowed a pale version of the old party to eventually be legalized. At the same time, this constituency—the small business and trader sector in the towns whose cultural allegiance was to urban modernist Islam—inherited a new, privileged position in the post-1965 middle class. Tens of thousands of university students connected to the PKI and PNI were unable to finish university. In the ten or more years after 1965, it was HMI students who started to fill the civil service positions open to university graduates as well as new management and professional positions in the corporate sector that oil money and foreign investment was later to foster. This was a national phenomenon. In Java, more secular nationalist families, usually of bureau-cratic or landowning background, also made headway, but were dwarfed by those from the urban Islamic sector. In both cases, however, these new, young aspiring professionals, businessmen and civil servants were from a conservative Islamic background but had had a secular education. They became one of the social pillars of the counter-revolution in its early years.

The enclaves, offering some the privilege of an advanced but conserva-tive academic education, had also provided the basis for an anti-populist intellectual sector: those who had been won over to the ideology of technocracy, believing that progress could only come as a result of a long, gradual process of educating the backward masses. The West was primarily dominant because of the extent of formal education in Western societies, not because of colonial or imperial conquest or because of capitalist exploitation. This was the political perspective that was described in the 1950s by some Western writers as the "administrator" stream, counterposed to the "solidarity-makers," those who emphasized populist agitation, such as Soekarno. While this conservative technocratic perspective was present in all the conservative parties, it was represented in its most concentrated form in the Indonesian Socialist Party (PSI). It was young intellectuals under the influence of this party, some trained in the USA and the Netherlands, who became the main intellectual partners of the counter-revolution. Some later became ministers in Suharto's governments in charge of bringing Indonesia into the Western economic sphere of influence. They became known as the Berkeley Mafia, as they had studied at the University of California, Berkeley. Others became civil servants, ran the universities, edited newspapers, joined GOLKAR and became politicians or entered business. In the first years of the counter-revolution this layer of intelligentsia was called the 66 Generation. It was this coalition of armed capitalists (in later years capitalist families separated from the military), landowners, aspiring new capitalists, and a new generation of conservative Western-oriented civil servants, middle-class professionals and intellegentsia that underpinned the counter-revolution for most of the period up until the fall of Suharto in 1998. It is still this coalition that dominates Indonesia, although with power within it now distributed differently.

This was the coalition of forces galvanized together from within Indonesia that were the agents of the counter-revolution. However, the coalition had another powerful component: international capital. Without the support of this force, the counter-revolution would not have been sustained. First of all, the international financial agencies, in particular the World Bank, provided immediate financial backing for the new regime. The major multinational corporations of the world organized a special meeting with Indonesian cabinet ministers in 1966 in Switzerland where together they mapped out an economic strategy for the new government.[8] Almost every major Western government, plus Japan, joined the Intergovernmental Group on Indonesia (IGGI), which met with the Indonesian government every year to make sure its policies were on track and that it had the financial support it needed.

Politically, the Western governments defended the mass murders of the left during 1965 and 1966, hailing them as a victory against communism. British and US intelligence services assisted the army in identifying targets for repression. British warships transported Indonesian troops from Sumatra to Java to assist in the purge operations. International reporting, including through the various Western-controlled radio broadcasts to Indonesia, such as via Radio Australia, made sure the killings were downplayed and negative propaganda against the left was highlighted. In the years following, these policies were continued, with Britain, the USA and Australia equipping and training the Indonesian armed forces, even when Suharto's army was carrying out overt, violent repression, such as during the invasion and occupation of East Timor in 1975–99 and in Aceh in the 1980s and 1990s. Ideological support from the imperialist countries was also enormous. In Ali Murtopo's strategy, ideology was out of favor and development and stability were very much in favor. Western financial institutions, universities and governments produced masses of material to strengthen the regime's claim to be a developmental success and to defend the prioritization of "economics" over political democracy.

It took almost thirty years—until the late 1980s—for a movement to revive that could launch a first challenge against this powerful coalition, with so many resources and with a monopoly on the means of violence. The first challenge came from a group which had been given a unique privilege: the right to political mobilization. These were the university students.

3

Students

There was one sector of the population that escaped the ban on open mobilizational politics, at least for the early part of the New Order. On the campuses all open mobilizational politics by the left parties and student groups was viciously suppressed, with many students being arrested or killed. However, a small anti-left section who were supporting Suharto's counter-revolution were actually encouraged to carry out protests, demonstrations, marches and public meetings and to have their own newspapers. These students, coming from the SOMAL "anti-politics" groups and MASYUMI-connected Islamic student organizations, were used by Suharto to give a civilian face to the counter-revolution. In order to maximize the sense of legitimacy the support of this relatively small sector of the student population gave Suharto, they were allowed to co-opt for themselves the status of representatives of the whole student sector—they became "the students," "the *mahasiswa*."

While Suharto and his allies relied primarily on slaughter, terror and suppression, they knew that the military could not govern alone. It needed civilian allies to help it rule. Suharto and his supporters in the army did not declare a military junta as they concentrated power in their own hands. They proclaimed that all their actions were also in the defense of the revolution and of democracy. They drew in their civilian allies and sought ways of organizing public displays of civilian support for their actions.

Playing a central role in the displays of support were high school, and particularly, university students. Demonstrations by university students against Soekarno occurred throughout the last months of 1965 and particularly in 1966. Most of these demonstrations were carried out under the banner of the Indonesian Students Action Front (Kesatuan Aksi

Mahasiswa Indonesia—KAMI). KAMI was established on the suggestion of Major General Sjarif Thayeb, the Minister for Higher Education and Science, on 25 October 1965. KAMI comprised student organizations with a conservative religious background as well as a range of organizations that had developed before 1965 on a basis of explicitly eschewing political activity. KAMI students had a monopoly of the streets. Their rivals on the left, the Indonesian Students Movement Concentration (Consentrasi Gerakan Mahasiswa Indonesia—CGMI), affiliated to the PKI, and the Indonesian National Students Movement (Gerakan Mahasiswa Nasional Indonesia—GMNI) had either been banned and purged, respectively, with many CGMI and GMNI activists being killed or arrested. The CGMI and GMNI were absent from the streets while KAMI, and some allies, with logistics supplied by the army, reigned supreme.

Over the course of about a year, the anti-Soekarno student movement assumed the representation of all students. The anti-Soekarno students were simply "the students" despite the fact that they were a small minority compared to the huge memberships of CGMI and GMNI before they had been suppressed by the army. KAMI was seen as the organizational expression of the 66 Generation. This movement's expropriation for itself of the monopoly on representing students was consolidated through the development of a new student press. Key newspapers included the daily *Harian KAMI* and, with perhaps greater prestige, the weekly *Mahasiswa Indonesia* ("The Indonesian Student").

KAMI organized joint seminars and discussions with the army at the University of Indonesia. This "student movement" was then regularly described as the army's partner in establishing the New Order. Even in 2004, in the prize-winning documentary film *I don't think I will ever forget*, by Danial Indrakusuma, people who were student leaders in 1965 as well as key generals confirmed that they worked hand in hand against Soekarno and the left. All of the demonstrations against Soekarno and the PKI during late 1965 and early 1966 were organized by these student leaders, including those demanding the arrest and resignation of cabinet ministers and others. It was student leaders who were used to launch all the frontal political attacks on Soekarno.

The students, the campuses and the 66 Generation intellectuals were allowed the privilege of political mobilization in their role as the main public, civilian allies of Suharto. They were the civilian and "democratic" face of the counter-revolution. They mobilized on the streets, while the army and militias arrested, tortured and killed. Here was the contradiction: the political method of KAMI had been the old method—mobilization! Rallies and demonstrations, leaflets and placards, conferences, congresses and public forums, mass shows of force were the basic methods. During 1966, the student demonstrations even developed some momentum of their own, launching demonstrations not always in accordance with the schedule desired by the army. Confrontations even took place, and students were shot dead.

Paradoxically, the students were depicted as a "moral force" uninterested in the question of power itself, just as they were legitimizing a new ruling power. This depiction, and thereby the restriction of their role to such a "moral force," meant that Suharto could tolerate them enjoying the privilege of mobilization, while everybody else was supposed to be a part of the "floating mass." The campuses became a privileged arena, where political mobilization was possible for at least thirteen years.

The "Anti-Politics" Student Activists

Between late 1965 and 1970 almost all of the KAMI mobilizations were aimed against Soekarno and what Suharto's "New Order" labeled the "Old Order"—the government and politicians of the 1962–5 period. By 1970, many central leaders of KAMI had been absorbed into the regime's political establishment. They became members of parliament or operatives in GOLKAR. Some used their contacts and soon emerged as substantial businessmen. A few went on to be academics. Some remained as "students" or held positions in one or other of the new institutions established as part of the official student movement or in the student press.

Only a few of the 66 Generation of student leaders were not absorbed into the New Order institutions during this period. Between 1970 and 1972, these few student leaders emerged as critics of the Suharto government, however, their criticisms remained confined within the parameters that had been part of the 66 Generation's rejection of mobilizational politics. They still used street protests but projected themselves as a purely "moral" and not a political force.

The anti-corruption campaign that began in January 1970 was the first manifestation of sustained criticism or opposition from amongst the "moral force" students. In mid-January, a group of students at the University of Indonesia issued a statement expressing disappointment in "their professors."[1] The professors were Ali Wardhana and Sumantri Bojonegoro, who both held ministerial positions. The "disappointment" was expressed in relation to the Suharto government's announcement of 100 percent price rises for petrol and kerosene. Within a few days, large student demonstrations began to take place with university students *turun ke Jalan* (going down into the streets), sticking up placards on walls and on passing cars. Although the specific issue was the price rises, in these demonstrations constant and explicit reference was made to corruption. Pamphlets pictured generals and officials feasting on *anggur minyak* (oil wine) but insisting that the ordinary people pay the increases in prices. What was happening to Indonesia's oil income so that a 100 percent price increase was necessary, asked the student protestors.[2]

The same posters also drew a parallel between the oil production and price increase contradiction and the promises of special attention to be given to education and the recent increase in university fees. Thus dissatisfaction with actual conditions of students combined with disenchantment with the government's policies and its attitude to corruption.

As students began to name offenders, including military officers close to Suharto, the official reaction to the student protest hardened. On 24 January, KOPKAMTIB JAYA (Jakarta Security Command) banned all demonstrations and on 27 January a protestor was arrested. Although the ad hoc groups formed during this couple of weeks remained in formal existence for another fortnight, public protest almost completely disappeared.

However, in early February, Suharto took action which gave the students cause to think that they had won some sort of victory. On 2 February 1970, Suharto established the Commission of Four to investigate corruption in Indonesia. It was given wide powers and its members were political and social figures from outside the regime itself. On the next day, a student delegation visited the chairman of the Commission, former 1950s Prime Minister Wilopo, to offer any assistance that might be needed and to publicly claim some credit for the formation of the Commission.[3]

With demonstrations banned but with the Commission of Four as an acknowledgment by the government of the validity of student claims, the ad hoc student group dissolved itself. The group of students behind the

protests had called themselves "Mahasiswa Menggugat" ("Students Accuse"), a title very much reminiscent of Soekarno's defense speech at his
trial in Bandung in the 1920s entitled "Indonesia Menggugat." The leaders
of Mahasiswa Menggugat were Arief Budiman, Ben Manoto, Harry Victor
and Syahrir. Arief Budiman emerged as its most prominent spokesman.[4]
Their announcement of disbandment declared that they were "a moral
force and not a political force."[5] The Soekarno period, of which Arief
Budiman, and KAMI earlier, had been major critics, was seen as being a
period completely overcome by "political fever."

The disbandment of Mahasiswa Menggugat began a period of relative
quiet. Between February and July student protest was confined to some
criticism by medical students of the facilities of the Faculty of Medicine.
However, despite the relatively non-threatening nature of the issue, the
protest was on a sufficiently large scale to cause the authorities to close the
University of Indonesia campus after lecture hours. The intensity of the
protest indicated that general tension within the student community had
not receded.

On 2 July the Commission of Four presented its report to President
Suharto. On 4 July Marie Muhammad, an ex-KAMI leader and student
journalist in the early days of the Bandung student weekly newspaper,
Mahasiswa Indonesia, demanded that the report be made public. When the
government was not able to assure the public that concrete action was
going to be taken, and especially as no commitment was made to publish
the Commission's report, Arief Budiman's student group re-emerged as
another ad hoc organization. This time it was called the Anti-Corruption
Committee (Komite Anti Korrupsi—KAK).

On 18 July Arief Budiman and other student leaders had the first of two
consultations promised to them by President Suharto. They presented
Suharto with documents they alleged proved corruption by one of
Suharto's personal assistants, a senior military officer. Arrangements were
made for a further consultation with Suharto in a few weeks' time. Before
the second consultation could take place, the government was annoyed
even more by another development in the anti-corruption campaign. This
time the initiative was not from the students but from the press: the
prestigious daily newspaper *Sinar Harapan*, connected to the Protestant
churches, leaked the official report of the Commission of Four. Two weeks
after the publication of the report, the second consultation was held with

Suharto. According to Arief Budiman, the first meeting with Suharto gave the students the impression that Suharto was seriously concerned with the level of corruption in the country. However, the second meeting altered that impression. Suharto used the meeting to accuse the students of being manipulated by the politicians. It was clear that no action was going to be taken. Suharto finally did no more than read the report of the Commission of Four to parliament, and with this done, announce next day in his national Independence Day speech that corruption was being tackled.[6]

Government repression of student activities began to harden. On 6 August, two KAK activists were arrested. On 12 August, six more were arrested at a demonstration outside the Prosecutor-General's office. Included amongst these six was Syahrir, the co-founder with Arief Budiman of Mahasiswa Menggugat. A plan for a *Malam Tirakatan* (Night of Meditation) to be held by students in the main streets of Jakarta, Thamrin Street, was condemned by the Governor of Jakarta, Ali Sadikin. The KAK did not go ahead with the *Malam Tirakatan* but another group led by the poet Rendra did go ahead with this action. Rendra and a number of others were detained briefly at the time. Rendra had been associated with the MANIKEBU before 1965 but had not become fully integrated into the 66 Generation because he was out of Indonesia in the USA between 1964 and 1970. Meanwhile the KAK announced that it would disband itself on the 16th.

The next wave of protest was focused on the method of the preparation for and the conduct of the 1971 general elections. Disenchanted at the way the government interfered in the internal affairs of the political parties, and opposed to the use of force in the rural areas to obtain support for the government party, groups of students banded together to urge an informal vote. This group, of which once again Arief Budiman emerged as a leader, was called the Golongan Putih (Golput, the White Group). The name, according to Arief Budiman, referred to the group's recommendation that voters mark the empty, white part of the ballot paper. It could not, however, but leave many people with the impression that moralistic overtones were also implied in the name. *Putih* (white) is sometimes an opposite of *kotor* (dirty). Golput groups were active primarily in Jakarta, Bandung and Yogyakarta. However, the completion of the elections in July and the clear victory of the government party again quickly brought the activities of Golput to an end.

The next issue that appeared on the political horizon concerned the building of the Indonesia Indah Miniatur (Beautiful Indonesia in Miniature) theme park. The project was sponsored by an organization called Yayasan Harapan Kita (Our Hope Foundation). President Suharto's wife, Tien Suharto, was the president of this foundation. Estimated costs ranged from 10.5 billion to 20 billion rupiah. The perceived extravagance of this project and the ease with which it received government support immediately provoked hostile responses from student and intellectual circles.

Throughout December 1971 a controversy raged back and forth between student and intellectual groups on the one hand and Tien Suharto and her main government supporters, Ali Sadikin and Ali Murtopo, on the other.

Arief Budiman, in an article written in 1973, looking back at these events, summed up the main issues with the following words:

> The Indonesian intellectuals reacted. "Is a project such as this necessary? or at least has the appropriate moment arrived to build a project like this? Every year we have to beg for additional loans from other countries to finance our development." The First Lady answered that the money would not be taken from the state budget but would be collected from donations. However, would this not create the impression that domestic funds could be mobilised to finance development if ten and half milliard can be collected to finance such a project. Why couldn't the donations be invested in a more productive venture such as the building of factories? Madam Tien answered that the project would attract tourists and thus be productive. The economists, of course, began to calculate and came to the conclusion that it would not be profitable. It would be more profitable, they contended, to build roads leading to places of tourist attractions or to repair existing roads. Roads, besides being useful for bringing tourist spots back to life, would also be useful for trade. Madam Tien again said that this was a cultural project and should not be viewed from the economic point of view only, for the profit from a cultural project was not materialistic. The artists responded this time and said that it would be better for the money to be used to repair museums and libraries, both of which were in a deplorable condition. In the end,

Mrs Tien said that she would go on with the project for it was her own idea and she wanted to realise her ideas during her lifetime.[7]

Numerous ad hoc student and youth groups formed, amongst which the Gerakan Penghematan (Austerity Movement) was the most prominent. Arief Budiman was involved with this group, as were others from the earlier Mahasiswa Menggugat and KAK groups. Besides the protests of these ad hoc groupings—usually taking the form of visiting the offices of ministers and government institutions—a very important new trend began. This was the active involvement of the official Dewan Mahasiswa (DEMA—Students' Council) in the debate.[8] The DEMA at the University of Indonesia was particularly active in organizing many public forums. On 12 January, the All-Jakarta Body of DEMA and Student Senate Cooperation issued a statement urging the Dewan Perwakilan Rakyat (DPR—People's Representative Council) to struggle for the "people's aspirations" regarding the Mini project.

The same combination of ad hoc student group street protests and office visitations, with university DEMAs holding panel discussions, occurred throughout most of Java and in on Sulawesi and Sumatra. One of the most interesting of the groups that appeared outside the major cities of Jakarta and Bandung was the group centered on *Sendi* newspaper.[9] It also published several important statements regarding the Mini controversy. While the Austerity Movement, as its name implied, concentrated on the economic wisdom of the Mini project and contained its criticism within the usual moralistic framework, *Sendi* viewed the Mini project and the accompanying events from a more political perspective. *Sendi* saw the ease with which Mrs Tien could carry out her wishes, the way in which the military authorities moved to forbid discussion of the issue and disband meetings as well as arrest protestors as simply another indication of the general nature of the government as such, namely, a dictatorship.

Sendi's perspective was considerably different than that of the Arief Budiman-led Mahasiswa Menggugat, KAK, Golput and Austerity Movement groups. These still presented themselves as being generally well disposed towards the Suharto government and acted within the context of a "moral force" to correct the excesses of the government should such occur as a result of the corrupting effect of power, or simply as a result of oversight due to government officials being too busy.

Sendi was formed by a group of students from Gajah Mada University

and a lecturer in *Publisistik* (Journalism and Communications) at the
university. The majority of the students were from regions other than Java.
The first issue of the newspaper was published in early November 1971. In
the first six issues the paper published hard-hitting editorials on (a) lack of
critical and serious research at universities; (b) the farcical nature of the
1971 elections; (c) government neglect in the financing of education; (d)
Pembangunan (Development) as an empty slogan used by the authorities;
and (e) the vulnerability of ordinary citizens to arbitrary arrest and other
maltreatment by the authorities without any possibility of redress. By
January 1972, *Sendi* had established its credentials as a critical journal—
critical of both the student establishment and the authorities. Then, in the
first issue of 1972, in January, it published its first full editorial on the Mini
project, followed by a savage satirical comment. The general approach of
the paper in regard to political criticism can be observed in this latter piece.
It was entitled "Mukaddimah" ("Manifesto"), which is also the title of the
preamble of the 1945 Indonesian Constitution, an almost holy document
in the eyes of the government. The four paragraphs were printed in block
letters and surrounded by a box. The statement, in fact, took the form of a
mock constitutional preamble. It went as follows:

Mukaddimah

Whereas freedom is the inalienable right of just a tiny group in
society, thereby repression and arbitrary rule naturally occur, because
they are in accord with dictatorship and militarism;

And whereas the struggle of the ruler and his wife has reached a
point of happiness where they are able to gouge out all the wealth
they can;

By the grace of Satan and impelled by the desire to be obeyed, the
rulers over the people of Indonesia declare their power;

Subsequent thereto, to form a strong ruling power which shall rule
over all the people of Indonesia and all of Indonesia's wealth; and in
order to promote personal status and prestige while impoverishing
the nation, so shall be formulated the Indonesia Mini regulation
establishing the Our Hope Foundation.[10]

The striking contrast between this outright and unrelenting condemnation
of the government as a whole and the "moral force" concept of "moral

pressure" and persuasion, with its assumption of the persuadibility of the authorities, underlines the *Sendi* outlook as a new one within the context of student dissent in New Order Indonesia. Not that the *Sendi* group can be seen, at this time, as a student group supporting an alternative leadership to Suharto and thus becoming fully involved in political struggle. Rather, the difference lies in its open depiction of the government as a military dictatorship with tendencies to corrupt and undemocratic excesses rather than a genuinely development-oriented government.

The Mini controversy stirred up a wide range of opposition: amongst intellectuals, lawyers, artists as well as students. Suharto began the repression of the opposition with a threatening speech on 6 January 1972. In this speech he accused the anti-Mini forces of being really out to topple the government and remove the armed forces from the administrative and legislative areas. He commented that these activities had been organized by the same old people (*orang itu-itu juga*) since 1968. He also made the most severe threat ever made against civil dissidents, including students, since 1966. He threatened to use the full power of the armed forces to "knock out" the protestors if they continued in their "misuse of democracy."

Although this speech presaged the quick demise of the anti-Mini movement, it also provoked several immediate critical responses from students and other groups. On the day after the Suharto speech, the papers published a statement by Arief Budiman and other Austerity Movement supporters entitled "We Will Be Powerless." Their statement revealed the difference in outlook between the student activists formed out of the opposition to Soekarno, and the new generation, represented by *Sendi*. The statement confirmed the signatories' opposition to the Mini project, but also announced that in the face of the threat of armed forces as made by President Suharto, the students, as but "soft flesh, with eyes full of hope," could do nothing else but remain silent on the issue. The tone of the statement was one of disappointment, but one of still remaining hope in the government. According to Arief Budiman, writing in 1973, the statement was considered "very touching" by many people and was a great blow to Suharto in the eyes of the Javanese.

To pak Harto, in remembrance of our friendship formerly in 1966, we want to convey the message in order to distinguish who are friends, and who are enemies; who truly loves pak Harto and who wants him to trip and fall? We hope pak Harto still remembers our old friendship and still wishes to hear what we are saying. With tears in our eyes we have hands to you pak Harto: Good luck.[11]

A few days later, about seventy students and youth gathered at the graves of three students who had died in 1965–6 actions and swore to maintain the ideals of the early student actions. Among those attending were Arief Budiman, Julius Usman (a former activist in KAPPI, an anti-communist high school students group), Imam Walujo (a signatory of the "We Will Be Powerless" statement) and the Dutch-born civil rights activist, Haji Princen.

On 25 January, a statement was issued by a group of seven intellectuals from the University of Indonesia. These intellectuals—Dr Alfian, Dr Dorodjatun Kuntjorojakti, Mrs T.O. Ichroni, Mardjono Reksodipuro and Dr Juwono Sudarsono—had also been active in criticisms of the Mini project. The intellectuals' statement was primarily one of solidarity with the students and other youth. In Yogyakarta, *Sendi* also published an editorial on the subject of the overnight arrest of several students on the evening of 31 December at a protest against the Mini project—an obvious reflection of the hardline decided upon by Suharto. The *Sendi* writers took the first step towards shifting the attack from the role of individuals and even institutions to raising the issue of opposition to a "system":

It seems that our enemies are not individual persons. We do not need to hate Mrs Tien Suharto and her seizing of the opportunity to push her project forward. Or to see the army that is arresting demonstrators as the enemy. That is all meaningless. Because while we are trapped in this chaotic system, anybody and everybody can act arbitrarily. . . . It seems that our enemy is not WHO but WHAT.[12]

The varying types of protest, however, were met by similar responses from the government. Arief Budiman and other student activists were arrested in late January. *Sendi* finally had its permission to print revoked, and Ashadi Siregar, *Sendi*'s chief editor, was arrested and charged with insulting the Head of State (in the Mukaddimah). He spent almost a year in gaol. Sporadic protesting continued up until early February, the last major event being a poetry reading organized by the students of the Faculty of Letters at the University of Indonesia on 31 January 1972. Some 66 Generation poets, now dissenting, read protest poems. Although all the detainees were released during February, the protest movement was not able to revive. The threat to use the regime's security powers against the movement and the show of force in the arrests silenced most student protest for almost eighteen months.

The Beginnings of the New *Pergerakan*: 1973–4

Between July and November 1973 a new wave of student protest hit Indonesia. The protest movement of 1973–4 developed in a quite different way than that of 1970–2, though many of the issues were the same. This change reflected the different range of social forces that were involved. The sudden influx of significant amounts of foreign capital had forced the closure of thousands of small Indonesian firms, especially textile businesses. The newspapers of Indonesia's indigenous business interests, such as *Nusantara, Indonesia Raya, Abadi, Pedoman* and others, began a sustained attack on government economic policy.

The student movement was operating in an environment where significant sections of the broad ruling layers—small business, the Islamic establishment, significant sections of the press—were potential allies. Moreover, all these groups had their own newspapers. Thus 66 Generation intellectuals, mostly people with PSI links or background, not only controlled some independent newspapers but also had influence in the GOLKAR newspaper *Suara Karya* through its editor, Rahman Tolleng, a former KAMI leader.

The students went into action, therefore, in a climate where discontent with the Suharto government had spread to a number of sections of the original New Order alliance.

Another difference was that the leadership of the student body itself was now in the hands of a new generation of students. The outlook of these students was much more like that of the *Sendi* group than that of the "moral force" group and Arief Budiman. Indeed, in Yogyakarta where *Sendi* was based, students associated with that newspaper played a major role in the 1973 protests. This new 1973 generation never went so far as to openly call for Suharto to be replaced, but its calls for a completely new economic strategy, its attacks on the so-called economic technocrats, its call for the disbandment of the President's group of personal assistants and, most importantly, its alliance with a faction of the military opposed to Suharto, represented a real intervention into the process of the struggle for power.

The University of Indonesia Discussion Group (Grup Diskusi Universitas Indonesia—GDUI) played an important role in developing the policies of the protest movement. This group had been formed much earlier and had been operating as a seminar for academics and advanced students. In late 1973, some of its main figures became very active in criticism of the government's economic policies. Especially active was the former Mahasiswa Menggugat and KAK activist, Syahrir. Syahrir was now an assistant lecturer in Development Strategy at the University of Indonesia. He was assistant to Professor Sarbini Sumawinata, a PSI figure who had been questioning the government's policies since early 1971, mainly on the grounds of insufficient attention being paid to employment opportunities and income distribution.

In Jakarta, one of the main themes that developed amongst the dissidents—dependency on foreign capital—got its first major public exposure through the weekly news magazine *Tempo*, run by one of the most prominent, younger 66 Generation intellectuals, Goenawan Mohammed. On 15 September *Tempo* published a report entitled "Japan Arrives, Sees and Grabs."[13]

In September 1973, Syahrir and another UI academic close to GDUI, Dr Juwono Sudarsono, both visited Yogyakarta. Sudarsono spoke at the Faculty of Social and Political Sciences at Gajah Mada University on the subject of "The international dimensions of Indonesian development." During the discussion the subject of Indonesia's economic dependence on foreign countries was critically discussed. Then in November former *Sendi* activists Aini Chalid, Ashadi Siregar and another Yogyakarta activist, Fauzi Rizal, were invited to Jakarta. They all met with the GDUI group, and Aini Chalid gave a talk at the Faculty of Social Sciences, UI entitled "The process of fermenting a new struggle." In October in Bandung and Jakarta student protests on the same theme, and critical of the development strategy as a whole, began to emerge. Already angered by police harassment of students with long hair, a group of students from the Institut Teknologi Bandung (ITB) protested to the West Java Dewan Perwakilan Rakyat Daerah (DPRD—Regional People's Representatives Council). Posters were stuck up on the DPRD's walls which read "Foreign capital serves the people, or the people serve foreign capital?"; "The GNP goes up, the people's trousers rot"; "A million barrels are pumped out, a million of the people's pockets are emptied" and "A thousand yen are invested, a thousand small businesses fold." In Jakarta, besides the GDUI, the University of Indonesia DEMA, referred to as DEMA UI, also became involved. Its chairman, Hariman Siregar, also a member of GDUI and a medical student, soon emerged as the leading critic among students in Jakarta. The DEMA UI's campaign soon led to the launching of the "24 October Petition."

24 October Petition

To remind the Military Government, intellectuals and technocrats of the following matters:

1. To review the development strategy and to formulate a new strategy with the proper balance between social, political and economic affairs which is anti-poverty, anti-ignorance and anti-injustice.
2. Quickly free the people from the grip of uncertainty, the rape of the law, the reign of corruption, the misuse of power, rising prices and unemployment.
3. Institutions for channeling society's opinions should be strong and function properly and must be given the maximum opportunity and place [in political life].
4. We are those with the greatest stake in the future and so the determining of the future, which cannot be separated from today's conditions, is both our right and duty. May God accompany the Indonesian nation on its journey.[14]

On and off campus a whole variety of other groups began to form. They had names such as National Pride Committee, National Awareness Committee, Anti-Luxury Committee, Debt Paying Generation and Black December Group.

Soon after the 24 October Petition was launched, creating a major stir in the press, J. Pronk, the Dutch Minister for Overseas Development and the chairman of the IGGI, visited Indonesia. Pronk was met by demonstrators both in Jakarta and Yogyakarta.

In Yogyakarta, at a meeting between university students and Pronk on the campus of Gajah Mada, the criticism of foreign aid and investment came from a very active group called GEMIRI, the Indonesian Students Movement for the People. In a pamphlet entitled "Overseas Aid and Our Development," GEMIRI addressed the problem of foreign aid and investment with the following words:

> Overseas aid can give short-term help but it can also become a long-term burden . . . Or it can indeed become the weapon for large countries to gouge out raw materials and produce from developing countries.

Throughout November and December 1973 the number of protests increased. Most DEMAs had issued statements critical of the development strategy or of the extensive political power of KOPKAMTIB or of the power of the President's personal assistants. Street demonstrations occurred every day in December carried out by the various youth and student groups, sometimes aimed at government institutions, sometimes aimed at such symbols of luxury as nightclubs and beauty contests. Actions were also taken against the offices of various companies and it soon became clear that Japanese capital was being singled out as a symbol of foreign capital in general.

Both in Jakarta and Yogyakarta, the next important event in the development of the protest movement was the planned holding of midnight meditation meetings—*Malam Tirakatan*—on New Year's Eve. In Jakarta, before this event, Hariman Siregar, chairman of the DEMA UI, had to confront a revolt from within his ranks. Ten DEMA members issued a statement of no confidence in Hariman Siregar, on the grounds that many of the meetings held in the name of the DEMA UI had not been agreed to by the membership. However, the Rector of the University continued to recognize Hariman as the legal chairman. This revolt came at the time of the planning for the "Night of Meditation," and at the time of the DEMA UI statements opposing the upcoming visit of the Japanese Prime Minister Tanaka and indicating the possibility of demonstrations.

Given reports of a meeting by these ten breakaway students at the house of an assistant to Ali Murtopo, ASPRI (personal assistant) to Suharto for political affairs, it is clear that the attempt to discredit Hariman Siregar was also an attempt to stop the Night of Meditation and any possible anti-Japanese demonstrations in January at the time of Tanaka's visit. In Yogyakarta, the planned *Malam Keprihatinan*—Night of Sadness/Suffering—was greeted with a statement on 31 December by the regional KOPKAMTIB commander that "Every act of violence will attract another act of violence."

The Night of Prayer and Meditation in Jakarta was attended by approximately 300 students, and lasted from 11 pm until 2 am. Attending were representatives from other University DEMAs in Jakarta, as well as delegates from Bandung and Padang Pajang. There were several speakers including Hariman Siregar and the UI Rector Nahar Mardjono. Hariman Siregar delivered a speech examining the role of Japan in Southeast Asia's economy, with special reference to Indonesia, and offering biting criticism of the Indonesian government's own attitude towards development. After analyzing the reasons for the increase of Japanese economic activity in Indonesia, Hariman came to the conclusion:

> The relationship between Indonesia and Japan had put Indonesia in a position of dependency and if we examine the country's position in the international system, we see that because of Indonesia's weakness, we are more a prisoner of the system than a participant.[15]

The economic characteristics of this dependence were pictured by Hariman in his general analysis of the role of foreign capital in Indonesia:

> the economy is now based on five sectors. The first is overseas aid; the second, foreign capital; the third is exports of rubber; the fourth is oil and the fifth, timber. And we know that the increase in rubber, oil and timber output would not be possible without those foreign inputs. So we can see that overseas aid and capital are the central factors in our economy.[16]

It was early in January 1974 that the government began to respond to the rising wave of student criticism. Already in the previous few weeks, several of the members of the smaller ad hoc student and youth groups had been arrested or detained for interrogation. Now the government began to respond to the DEMA. First, Suharto responded positively to a request by the DEMA for a meeting with him. This occurred on 11 January when 100 students from thirty-four student councils of major universities met with Suharto for an hour-long discussion. Two declarations were handed to the President, one signed by the DEMAs from Jakarta universities, and the other signed by universities from other parts of Java, and from Bali and Sumatra.

Two days earlier, on 9 January, a student meeting at the ITB burned effigies of Presidential advisor Sudjono Humardhani and Japanese Prime Minister Tanaka. On the same day UI students organized another panel discussion between Emil Salirn, Minister of Communications, and Dorodjatun Kuntjorajakti, social scientist and GDUI figure, on the topic of foreign capital. On 10 January, another panel discussion was held on the role of Japanese foreign capital, this time with Nurcholis Madjid as moderator. On 12 January, the day after the DEMA-Suharto meeting, twelve DEMAs from Jakarta held a rally in the grounds of the Universitas Kristen Indonesia, where effigies of "Tokyo Dog" Sudjono Humardhani and "Economic Imperialist" Tanaka were burned. At the same meeting, organized jointly by the DEMAs of Universitas Kristen Indonesia, Trisakti and IKIP Muhammidiyah, Hariman Siregar appealed for newspapers to boycott advertisements of Japanese companies. A project officer was also appointed for the student demonstrations planned to welcome Prime Minister Tanaka on his arrival.

The most important pressure on the students to stop the demonstrations was a joint statement on the same day by Generals Panggabean and Sumitro that "the most recent student actions tend towards the forming of forces, and can be interpreted as an act of MAKAR [rebellion, attempt to seize power]." Despite the warning, the demonstrations continued.

On 15 January about 500 student and youth protestors met Tanaka at the airport. At 8 am other students met at the Medical Faculty of Universitas Indonesia and from there marched to Trisakti University. They shouted slogans and carried banners criticizing Japanese investment. At Trisakti University reportedly around 2,000 students rallied confirming the general theme of the protests and also rejecting the accusation of MAKAR.

Meanwhile, in other parts of Jakarta riots and looting was breaking out. By the afternoon, areas of the city up to 10 kilometers apart were being ransacked or smashed up. In the evening a curfew was declared for 6 pm.

Whatever the effect of the demonstrations may otherwise have been, the occurrence of rioting immediately provided the government with grounds to act against the students and their supporters. The demonstrations of the students and the rioting were taken as parts of the same event. Responsibility for the rioting was laid squarely at the feet of the students.

By 19 January, at least eighteen intellectuals and students were arrested, including Hariman Siregar. On 21 January, Yap Thiam Hien, a Jakarta civil rights lawyer, who, along with H. Princen, had been extremely active in protesting illegal arrests and detentions throughout December and January, were also arrested. By 6 February, the Attorney General announced that forty-five people suspected of political involvement in the "Malapeketa 15 Januari" or MALARI (15 January Disaster) were under arrest. In the days to follow, several important Jakarta newspapers and magazines were closed down for having published so-called inflammatory reports of the riots and preceding events. Demonstrations occurred in other cities until General Sumitro ordered the banning of all demonstrations in the regions on 20 January.

The 1973–4 Movement and the Old *Pergerakan*

After only one generational change in the student population and despite the repression of left-wing ideology, ideas very similar to those espoused by Soekarno and the PKI began to emerge. The 1973–4 student leaders were mostly anti-communist, with highly negative and critical perceptions of the Soekarno period and with conventional views of communism as simply a form of repressive totalitarianism. Yet their critiques of political and economic policies sounded very similar to phenomena that the PKI and Soekarno were also campaigning against.

The PKI and Soekarno campaigned for the "retooling" of corrupt *kabir* (capitalist bureaucrats). The 1973 student leaders campaigned for the dismissal of corrupt officials entwined in the struggle for business concessions from foreign interests. The PKI and Soekarno campaigned under the slogan "Go to hell with your aid!" and talked about the need to build an independent economy free from neocolonial domination. The new generation spoke of the foreign domination of the economy and the role of aid as a lever of power over the whole society. Some of the largest student demonstrations were in response to foreign officials—the Dutch Devel-

opment Minister Pronk and the Japanese Prime Minister—who would
have easily been classified as representatives of NEKOLIM (neocolonialism
and imperialism) which Soekarno had also identified as a primary enemy.

The students' criticisms, however, were not underpinned by the same
Marxist political theory that had flourished in Indonesia since the first
decades of the twentieth century. In the 1970s, it was the ideas of the New
Left, coming out of US and Australian campuses, that made its way,
unevenly, into the student movement in Indonesia. Writings about
dependent development and neocolonialism developed in Latin America
were also available. These did not contribute to any Marxist-style left-wing
current. Rather, embryonic ideas of class exploitation, official corruption
and foreign economic domination developed as part of a more general
democratic agenda. Still, it was clear that the terror and repression after
1965 had been effective, within the student movement at least, only in
suppressing the old vocabulary. It could not suppress the recognition by
some people of real, existing phenomena.

These "new" ideas were, interestingly, complemented by another
critique that in some respects was missing, or at least subdued, in the
pre-1965 left's campaigning. Even though just a few years before, KAMI
leaders recognized a student-army partnership, the new movement exhibited an open hostility to militarism. The *Sendi* Mukaddimah as well as
the 24 October Petition both referred to militarism or a military
government. Before 1965, the left had refrained from an open attack
on the military as a left wing was developing within the military itself.
After 1965, left-sympathizing officers were executed, arrested or purged
from the officer corps. This included some senior generals as well as the
Commander of the Air Force, Omar Dhani, who was brought before an
army tribunal and gaoled. The PKI's approach was to attack the "anti-
people aspect of the state" while defending the "pro-people aspect." By
1973, the perception of contradictions within the army had not completely disappeared. Suharto's rival, General Sumitro, had began a
campaign for a "new pattern of leadership" and had even made a trip
to Buru Island to see the communist and other left prisoners and promise
them an approaching release. Sumitro was dismissed by Suharto after the
MALARI demonstrations and riots, ending for the next fifteen years any
serious attempts by senior army officers to portray themselves as more
liberal than Suharto. After 1973 anti-militarism, never such an explicit

part of the *pergerakan*, congealed as a part of the new agenda of the *gerakan mahasiswa* (student movement).

These ideas, this embryonic left critique, developed precisely in the realm of mobilizational politics. Mobilizing students looked for ideas from other arenas of mobilization: the US New Left, Latin America and the Thai student movement, which also launched big anti-Japanese and anti-military demonstrations in January 1974. In academia itself the echo was much fainter, still mediated by the anti-communist sentiments of the pro-Western PSI intellectuals. They were further removed from the arena of mobilization, although several paid the price of a year in gaol for having any connection with the student movement at all. The young economist, Syahrir, who had been the closest to the students, was tried and sentenced to five years for subversion along with two student leaders, Hariman Siregar from Jakarta and Aini Chalid from Yogyakarta who also received heavy sentences.

The impact of this period of student political mobilization throughout 1973 was heightened by an additional separate but parallel campaign of dissidence. This was launched by the poet and dramatist, Rendra. As a writer associated with the 66 Generation who had participated in student movement activities in 1972 and early 1973, Rendra also enjoyed the "privilege" of being able to engage in mobilizational politics. At the same time, being outside the haven of the campus, he was under constant pressure from the security authorities and needed to engage in a series of political maneuvers to protect this "privilege," including a high-profile meeting with General Sumitro.

The initial phase of Rendra's campaign, aimed particularly at the increased repressiveness and role of the military, was a media campaign publicizing a play he was preparing for performance in January 1974. By the end of 1973, Rendra, who was already a celebrity because of his flamboyant lifestyle and love of poetry as well as earlier protest actions, had become the most high-profile critic of the government. This campaign had some elements of mobilization politics: media conferences, high-profile public appointments with officials, participation in open public for a and street protests. It was the climax of Rendra's campaign, however, that was most reminiscent of pre-1965 *pergerakan* activity. Formally, this activity, taking place in Jakarta in January 1974, was a drama performance. Politically, however, it can be marked down as the first use of Jakarta's huge sports stadium for a mass political rally, with the *semangat* (spirit) of a genuine *pergerakan* mass rally, since the stadium was used by Soekarno and the PKI for the same purposes.

The Istora Stadium was packed out with thousands of people for a performance of the play, *Mastadon dan Burung Kondor*. The play described a student-led mass revolt against a military dictatorship set in a fictional Latin American country. One character in the play is a poet who tells why he must speak out:

> I hear the voice
> the scream of a wounded animal.
> Some one has shot an arrow at the moon
> A bird falls from its nest.
>
> People must be awakened
> Witness must be given
> So that life might be guarded
> (Untitled poem in W.S. Rendra,
> *State of Emergency*, 1980[17])

The semi-mystical cry of witness, however, is accompanied by a beautiful poem, *Mastodon and Condor*, throbbing in its original Indonesian language rhythm with the power of a suffering voice, and easily mistaken as a poem from the pre-independence *pergerakan* or the pre-1965 radicalism.

> The mountain wind moves softly through the forest,
> sweeps across the wide river,
> and finally comes to rest among the tobacco leaves,
> Sadly it watches
> the weary pace of the farm labourers
> as they march across the rich earth,
> which offers them only poverty.
>
> The farm labourers work,
> planting seed in the fertile ground,
> bringing in the abundant harvest,
> and lead lives of misery.

They live in shanties without windows
and harvest for landlords
who live in huge places.
Their sweat falls like gold
for the carpetbaggers who run cigar factories in Europe.
When they demand their share of profits,
the economists straighten their ties,
and send them condoms.

My people's faces are lined with pain.
They move like ghosts,
all day,
reaching out,
turning this way and that,
finding nothing.
By sunset, their bodies are pulp.
They lie down, exhausted,
and their souls turn to condors.

Thousands of condors,
millions of condors,
moving to the high mountains,
where they can rest in silence.
Only in silence
can they fully savor their pain and bitterness.

The condors scream.
They scream with rage
as they escape to the lonely mountains.

The condors scream,
and their screams echo among the rocks
and the silent mountains.

Millions of condors clawing at rocks,
pecking at rocks, pecking at the air.
In town, men prepare to shoot them.[18]

Ali Murtopo's fear of mobilization, of involvement in "conflicts of political and ideological interests," proved to have a basis—at least, from the perspective of the counter-revolution. The students' privileged status allowing mobilization had provided the fertile ground for old ideas to begin to grow again, even if using different words. And this was not the only fear that the new *gerakan* heightened: there was also the new activity of the supposedly "floating mass": the "millions of condors clawing at rocks, pecking at rocks, pecking at the air."

The Bitter Fruits of De-organization

The counter-revolution and its policy of enforcing the "floating mass" had the purpose of permanently suppressing mass mobilization activity. In the past, it had been the party system and the system of affiliated mass organizations which had organized these mobilizations. The mass base of these parties, especially those most successful in organizing, had been located not only in the villages, but also in the cities. In the cities also the mass of the population had become de-organized.

Between 1966 and 1973, there was no serious union organizing of any kind. The government had made initial moves to institute the formation of a new union federation, the All Indonesian Labour Federation (Federasi Buruh Seluruh Indonesia) in 1972, which it kept under tight control, excluding workers from any real participation in decision making. But in 1973, even as a "yellow" union, it had virtually no presence among the proletariat and semi-proletariat of either Jakarta or other major cities. The old unions, especially the big left-wing unions, had been smashed, their leaders and key support bases slaughtered and terrorized. *Aliran* political life had been ended. The millions of proletarians and semi-proletarians living in Jakarta *kampung* and surroundings had no organized political life at all.

While organization had disappeared, politics itself cannot just be disappeared. The student mobilizations kept issues of discontent before the population. Dissident voices from the student movement were published in several major newspapers until some of them were closed down in January 1974. The separate campaigns launched by General Sumitro around the theme of a "new pattern of national leadership" as well as the remarkably high-profile mobilization campaign by the poet and dramatist, Rendra, made sure that the general atmosphere, especially in the cities where the media magnified the activities of students, artists and politicians, was increasingly politicized and tense.

The effect of de-organizing the urban "floating mass" was to facilitate the emergence of a new form of political protest in Indonesia: *rusuh*—riot. Mass discontent with social and economic conditions and anger at corruption and the emergence of an elite living an ostentatious lifestyle were no longer represented in a political movement. They simply burst forth onto the streets of Jakarta in mass riots in a phenomenon not seen before in independent Indonesia. Riots, where spontaneous anger manifested in violent attacks on shops selling luxury goods, government offices and other symbols of the alien lifestyles of the enclave economy, became a regular phenomenon in New Order Indonesia. The "floating mass" did not always just float.

Between 30 December 1973 and 14 January 1974, student demonstrations in Jakarta had escalated. These demonstrations, widely reported in the press and by word of mouth, heated up the political atmosphere. The Japanese Prime Minister, Tanaka, was scheduled to arrive in Jakarta on 15 January directly from Bangkok. The large and militant student demonstrations against Tanaka and Japanese investment in Bangkok were also widely publicized in Jakarta. Hariman Siregar had earlier traveled to Bangkok to meet Thai students and this visit was also widely publicized. On 14 and 15 January, thousands of students assembled on the campus of the University of Indonesia and marched into the city center. News of the demonstrations spread quickly over these two days, on the radio and then through the press on 15 January. In tandem with the student demonstrations, riots broke out.

Rioting occurred in the main Chinatown retail center, the main shopping mall complex, the night club center and along the main thoroughfares where motor car and other luxury goods showrooms were situated. It was later reported that at least eleven people died, seventeen were seriously injured, 120 less seriously injured and 775 people arrested. Allegedly, 807 cars and 187 motor bikes were destroyed, mainly set on fire. The same report stated that 144 buildings were destroyed as well as the main Coca Cola bottling factory, at the time a prime symbol of the new and much increased Western presence.[19]

Brian May in his book *Indonesian Tragedy* described what he called the "ferocious" riots during Tanaka's visit:

Leaflets distributed by thousands of students who paraded through the city on the morning after Tanaka's arrival demanded the dismissal of Suharto's three special assistants—Humardani, Surjo and Murtopo—a reduction in prices and an end to corruption. . . . Mobs from the poorer quarters joined the students, and for two days Jakarta was shaken by violent rioting, The showrooms of Astra motor company, a Japanese concern in which Mrs Suharto was believed to have an interest, were heavily damaged; more than 100 shops were burned and looted; 650 Japanese and other motor cars were set on fire or battered; a crowd of several thousand blocked a six-lane road while youths ransacked massage parlours and burned the furniture in the street. In some areas of the city security forces fired on the mobs. By the time the riot had subsided at least eleven civilians had been killed and about 130 injured.[20]

Again and again during the 1970s, 1980s and 1990s, the now de-organized urban "floating mass" was to vent their discontent in the form of *kerusuhan*. During the 1980s, student activity was suppressed and *kerusuhan* broke out as discontent sharpened with no political focus generated by a tandem political movement. As a result, the scapegoat factor became more prominent with attacks on Chinese or Christian shops or houses, as well as symbols of luxury living and government authority. The biggest of these occurred between 20 and 25 November 1980 when the major Javanese towns of Solo and Semarang and scores of other smaller towns were hit by such rioting.[21] So even the small town "floating mass" could be activated in this way. In the 1990s, the MALARI pattern re-emerged as student and other organized mass protests began again. Twice major rioting occurred in tandem with major organized protests: in July 1996 and May 1998, the latter bringing down the country's dictator.

The Counter-Revolution's Last Offensive

Suharto responded to the MALARI events by arresting more than a hundred students and academics and suppressing several major newspapers. His major rival in the military, General Sumitro, was forced to resign and tighter control was instituted over the officer corps. This suppression was not yet total, however, and the protest momentum revived quickly. Most importantly, the campus retained its status as an arena of privileged mobilization. There was no ban on student political activity. Although it took three years for the DEMAs to recover from the arrest of so many student leaders, they continued to exist and were slowly able to resume activity.

Of course, the underlying issues of discontent, especially among the students and the urban and rural "floating mass" had not disappeared. The years 1974 to 1977 were marked by incidents that only served to underline the issues that had been raised by the student movement. The state oil company, PERTAMINA, despite huge windfalls in profits as a result of the rise in world oil prices, almost went into bankruptcy as a result of suspect deals. President Suharto was forced to dismiss its director, an army general, Ibnu Sutowo, who went on to become a millionaire businessman. There was a general sense of the oil profit windfalls fueling an extravagant lifestyle among the elite. Hariman Siregar, Syahrir and the Yogyakarta student leader Aini Chalid, went on trial during 1974 and 1975 and all their trials received extensive newspaper coverage, ensuring all the political issues that had been raised by the student movement continued to be discussed.

After a brief tactical retreat to the performance of Greek tragedies in the aftermath of the suppression of the student movement in January 1974 and the massive success of his mass *Mastodon and Condor* rally, Rendra managed to gain permission to perform a new play in Jakarta and then in Yogyakarta. Again the performance of *The Struggle of the Naga Tribe* was more like a *pergerakan* mass rally than a typical stage drama. It was performed in the large open-air theater in Jakarta's main arts complex to an audience of several thousand people over two nights, who reacted to much of the play as if they were listening to fiery popular orators. The performance was also a national event with extensive media coverage. The performance, the mobilization of an audience through prior media coverage, the response of the audience, the reviews and controversy all told a fundamental story: this was again another real manifestation of the methods of mass political mobilization, even if carried on in a limited basis, in the absence of the broader organization of the "floating mass." With almost all of the 1973 student leaders and their intellectual allies in prison, Rendra also emerged as the most prominent opposition spokesperson.

Naga Tribe itself raised all the issues of the 1973 movement: arbitrary rule by a military government, corruption and an economic policy based on surrender of the development of the national economy to foreign interests. The play depicted a conflict between a village community as yet untouched by these phenomena and a government in an unnamed country with remarkable similarities to Indonesia at that time. This rather non-"floating" village community confronted, including in direct polemics and near physical fight, a coalition of a corrupt queen, Her Majesty; Colonel Srenggi; a chorus of drone parliamentarians; Mr Joe, the US Ambassador; and Big Boss, the foreign mine company owner.

There are a number of indications that these and other activities kept the issues raised in 1973 on the agenda and widespread in society. In September 1976, the government announced that there had been a secret attempt to replace the government in what the head of KOPKAMTIB called a "palace revolution." This "palace revolution" was apparently being carried out by a low-level Agriculture Ministry official, Sawito, who was also a mystic. He had prepared documents calling for Suharto to surrender power to the elder statesman and conservative figure, former Vice-President Mohammad Hatta. The whole case, and later Sawito's trial, once again kept all these issues in the public mind. More than this, however, the depth and extent of feeling around the issues of corruption and arbitrary rule was reflected in the fact that one of the statements written by Sawito was signed by Cardinal Darmoyuwono, the head of the Catholic church; Dr T.B. Simatupang, probably the most senior intellectual from the Protestant churches; Prof. Dr Hamka, one of the most respected Islamic teachers and R. Said Sukanto Tjokrodiatmojo, a former police chief and head of the Secretariat for Cooperation among Mystic Groups and former Vice-President and "founding father" of the Republic, Mohammad Hatta himself. These very senior figures would not have signed Sawito's statement if the sentiments it expressed were not widespread in society. The statement was presumably meant to be used to force Suharto to resign. A part of the statement read:

> . . . if the current progress in national development is evaluated in the context of the way in which it has really benefited the Indonesian people as a whole it is clear that a part brought about an obvious deterioration in the standard of human dignity. This [deterioration], already in its critical stages, is leading us into the valley of gross indignity and has endangered both national life and the Indonesian

national Character to the extent that the very unity of the society and the process of national development are threatened. The danger of this threat is already quite apparent in the throttling of the sovereignty of the law.[22]

That discontent was also reflected, for the first time during the New Order, in a wave of worker and farmer protests. Between 1967 and 1977, there had been an increase in the size of the factory workforce, particularly textiles, and between 1977 and 1980 there was a wave of strikes as this new generation of factory workers attempted to win wage rises and better conditions, in particular the right to strike. International Labour Organization figures show a jump from six strikes a year to several score each year by 1978–80. The pioneering documentation *Indonesian Workers and their Right to Organise* recorded details from more than sixty of these strikes and protests, mainly among textile workers.[23] There was also another wave of protests by plantation workers in Sumatra where thousands of rural laborers came into conflict with the military. These developments (which petered out after a series of repressive steps followed by a recession in 1982–3) also drew attention to all these issues during the last years of the 1970s. All these developments—the student leader trials, the *Naga Tribe* event, the Sawito affair, the strikes and plantation worker protests—both reflected and deepened the impact of the 1973 protests. By 1977, a new generation of students were leading the student councils and preparing another wave of protests following very tame May 1977 elections, where the "simplified" parties "competed" and delivered a massive 66 percent victory to GOLKAR.

The 1977 student protests were again occurring: demonstrations, mass leafleting, sit-ins, public forums and conferences all featured again. The student press also revived. The students pursued the same themes as in 1973: military power, arbitrary rule, unjust economic strategy, and foreign dependence and debt. The repression of the students in 1974, the heavy sentences handed out to Siregar, Syahrir and Chalid, and the refusal of the regime to make any concessions to the students' demands had also hardened the movement's militancy. Demonstrations increased in size and number between October 1977 and January 1978. By January 1978 student councils from more than sixty universities around the country were coordinating. Leafleting and postering spread throughout Jakarta and

Bandung, with students at the Institute of Technology in Bandung (ITB) taking the lead. Newspaper coverage of the student actions, occurring daily by January 1978, was also extensive, in both the mass circulation and elite dailies.[24]

On 20 and 21 January the regime launched the last battle of the counter-revolution's offensive, thirteen years after it began. Six newspapers, including three prestige dailies and a main Jakarta tabloid, were banned. All student councils were frozen, that is, they were banned from continuing activity. One hundred and forty-three student leaders were arrested along with fifteen non-student activists. Widespread protest activity continued despite the arrests until the sitting of the People's Consultative Assembly (MPR) in March, which re-elected Suharto. However, after the MPR finished, the regime continued its repression. The privilege of mobilization that it had granted to the campuses when the KAMI students were allies of the counter-revolution was now completely withdrawn.

Student councils were banned on all campuses under a new policy called Normalization of Campus Life (Normalisasi Kehidupan Kampus—NKK). Murtopo's concept of the "floating mass" was applied now in this arena as well. Students were to study and that's all, just as the "floating mass" was to remain "wholly occupied with developmental efforts." Key student leaders were put on trial and sentenced to between one and four years' gaol.

Following the two waves of suppression, in January 1974 and then January 1978, NKK was to remain more or less effective in ending mobilizational politics on campus and off for the next eleven years, until 1989. After the banning on dissolution of the student councils and the announcement of NKK, there were some final protests. A protest statement was issued by eleven prominent academics, intellectuals and artists, including Rendra. The last real mobilization action was a mass poetry reading by Rendra in the open-air theater in the Jakarta Arts Center before thousands of Jakartans cheering every attack on the government in his poems. Provocateurs attacked the poetry reading, running up to the stage and throwing ammonia bombs, which forced Rendra and others off the stage as the fumes dispersed. But the reading resumed. The next day, Rendra too was arrested for "reading poems that provoked violence," that is, by the provocateurs. Rendra spent almost a year in gaol. His arrest was a last repressive foray in the battle to end mobilization.

One poem that captured the essence of this fiery mass rally, and which

Rendra declaimed with all the *semangat* of a *pergerakan* activist was "Poem of an Angry Person":

> Because we eat roots
> and flour piles up in your warehouses . . .
> Because we lived all cramped up
> and you space is so abundant . . .
> So we are not allies.
>
> Because we are soiled
> and you are shiny bright . . .
> Because we feel suffocated
> and you lock the door.
> So we distrust you.
>
> Because we are abandoned on the streets
> and you own all the shade . . .
> Because we endure floods and you party on pleasure boats . . .
> So we don't like you.
>
> Because we are silenced
> and you never stop nagging . . .
> Because we are threatened and you use violence against us . . .
> So we say to you NO.
>
> Because we may not choose
> and you are free to make your plans . . .
> Because we have only sandals
> and you are free to use rifles . . .
> Because we must be polite
> and you have jails so NO and NO to you.
>
> Because we are the current of the river
> and you are the stones without heart . . .
> So the water will erode away the stones.[25]

Rendra's *Naga Tribe*, his other plays of 1975–7, and the poems he read and declaimed as part of the student protest—which he called "A Poet's

Pamphlets"—not only captured the spirit of the whole *gerakan*. They also attracted the ire of those intellectuals and artists who still had the KAMI spirit of 1965. They attacked these works in the same spirit that the left-wing literature of 1965s had been attacked. For them, the kind of descriptions found in *Mastodon and Condor* and "Poem of an Angry Person" were "caricature" without nuance. Echoing the cries of these intellectuals in 1966, such "propaganda" constituted "tyranny."[26] Rendra's pamphlet poetry began to be accused of taking literature back to the PKI's LEKRA writing.

Work continued throughout the 1980s by students and ex-students (as they left campus and found jobs) in developing the critiques begun during 1973–8, but no longer within or connected to a mobilizational framework. It was the period when the "NGO politics" of "civil society" began to develop, often—though not always—hostile to mass action and mobilization. The student movement between 1973 and 1978 had continued the political methods of before 1965—but with no organizing together with workers or peasants—and had reintroduced some of the old critiques, set out in a different vocabulary. But the adoption of these methods had never amounted to a conscious embrace of the pre-1965 political culture. Mass action or mobilization politics did not develop again until the late 1980s but this time as a conscious strategy of a section of a new generation of activists. But, for this to develop, another very key aspect of the initial counter-revolutionary offensive by the Suharto regime—the attack on historical memory—needed to be subverted.

4

Memory

The suppression of the student movement in 1978 meant that the "floating mass" policy now applied to all social sectors without exception. The counter-revolution withdrew privileges from the campuses. The battle with students between 1973 and 1978 was the last episode of the counter-revolutionary offensive that had begun in 1965. The New Order had also successfully managed its first general elections using the fully "simplified" party system. After 1978, for at least a decade, the counter-revolution's work was that of maintaining itself and the stability of the new system.

The New Order's political programs had also been strengthened after 1973 as a result of a windfall gain in the economic field: petrodollars. As a result of the formation of the Organization of Petroleum Exporting Countries (OPEC), oil prices rose dramatically in 1973. Taxes and royalties on oil as a source of revenue for the government increased from 19.7 percent of government revenues in 1973 to 48.4 percent in 1974–5. While the oil boom had no dramatic impact on increasing growth in GNP: "The most immediate effect of the oil boom on the Indonesian economy was greatly to expand revenues accruing to government from the royalties paid by extracting companies, . . . Between 1973–74 and 1974–75 budgetary revenues from this source almost trebled, and in the latter part of the 1970s, oil revenues accounted for close to half of all government revenues from both and external sources."[1]

These extra funds were used to finance an expansion in government-contracted infrastructure development as well as to subsidize cheaper credit for small and medium business and cheap credit for small farmers wanting to take advantage of the green revolution in rice agriculture. Politically, this meant a decrease, for at least a decade, in political discontent from small and medium business and small rice farmers. Discontent from small and medium business, which had suffered considerable collapse in competition with new Japanese capital, had been important in heating up the political atmosphere in 1973.

With all the most important work of the counter-revolutionary offensive finished, and petrodollars buying off previously discontented sectors of society, the government felt confident enough to make a decision that brought immediate, and probably unexpected, consequences. In 1979, it released the 12,000 prisoners on Buru Island prison camp. Leading intellectuals and activists from the pre-1965 left and the Soekarnoist movement were released back into society.

It is likely that the regime calculated that the reorganization of the new "floating mass" society, the terror of the late 1960s, combined with the disorientation suffered by the 12,000 prisoners who had been excised and alienated from society over the previous fourteen years, would mean that these former activists and intellectuals would present no real threat. On the whole, this assessment turned out to be correct. Most of these prisoners returned to society and did not become involved in any political activity that represented a threat to the New Order or the new political situation that had stabilized in 1978. However, there was one important exception. The activities of just three revolutionary Soekarnoists during the 1980s had an enormous impact on the political atmosphere by starting the process of subverting the regime's falsification of history and its erasure of collective historical memory.

The student *gerakan* of 1973–8 had used many of the methods of the *pergerakan* and the pre-1965 left's campaigns. It had generated many ideas very similar to those of the Soekarnoists and the left. The movement, however, had never questioned the New Order's version of Indonesian history, including, indeed beginning with, its version of the last years of Soekarno and the events of 1965. No matter how critical of the New Order the 1973–8 students became, nobody ever questioned the demonization of Soekarno, the PKI and the pre-1965 left that was part of the New Order's propaganda. The main reason for this was overwhelming monopoly on ideological discourse of the 66 Generation, the army and younger intellectuals trained or influenced by them. This included figures from the PSI and MASYUMI, who were long-term opponents of the PKI. Of course, this monopoly was based upon the physical absence of any institutions or individuals able to present an alternative version of history.

Throughout this period, the regime carried out a continuous program of propaganda demonizing the PKI and Soekarnoism. The essential symbol of this demonization was all the propaganda surrounding Lubang Buaya, the location of the well where the bodies of seven executed generals and other army officers were hidden on 1 October 1965. These generals and officers were executed by their captors, other army officers, when Colonel Untung's unilateral "retooling" action started to collapse. These executions were depicted as an act perpetrated by frenzied communist women, who were accused of torturing the generals and mutilating their bodies, including their genitals. Despite the fact that the army's own autopsy showed that the only injuries sustained by the bodies were those resulting from being dropped in the wells after execution, these horror stories were not withdrawn from the media. Later, a museum in memory of the generals was built at Lubang Buaya and these events were mythologized in the schools, media and in popular film. On top of this demonization was the formal ban on Marxism and Leninism.

Then, when the political prisoners were released, they were also systematically stigmatized. Their identity cards were marked with a code, "ET," which identified them as political prisoners. It was made public that they also were required to report regularly to military or police authorities. These political prisoners were banned from employment in the civil service and "vital enterprises." Meanwhile, the school curriculum was written to institutionalize the regime's version of the 1965 events as an act of conspiratorial "treachery" by the PKI against the nation. By 1978, the labeling of the PKI as "traitors" and evil was the only public discourse, embedded through thirteen years of school and 66 Generation media monopoly. The demonization was complete and total.

In April 1980, three "demons," defying the ban on political prisoners' writing or publishing, established a new publishing company, called Hasta Mitra. The three individuals concerned were Hasyim Rachman, Pramoedya Ananta Toer and Joesoef Isak.

They had been leading figures in the world of journalism and literature before 1965. Politically, they stood in the revolutionary wing of Soekarnoism. Hasyim Rachman was editor of the mass circulation Soekarnoist tabloid, *Bintang Timur*, affiliated to the small, radical Partai Indonesia (Partindo).

Bintang Timur was the highest-selling newspaper in Jakarta. Despite its close ties to President Soekarno, the paper had also been banned by the military on occasion. The newspaper also published a cultural page edited by Pramoedya Ananta Toer, which carried essays by him, especially on Indonesian history. It also serialized his novel. In 1960 Pramoedya himself was detained by the martial law authorities after he had published polemics, including in *Bintang Timur*, against policies announced in 1959 that were discriminatory against the Chinese population.

Although Pramoedya was elevated to membership of one of the plenary bodies of the Indonesian Cultural Institute (LEKRA) which was tied to the PKI, *Bintang Timur* was his main political vehicle during the 1960s rather than the PKI newspaper. He too was a strong supporter of Soekarno and a leading polemicist against those writers opposing the campaign by left-wing writers to place art and culture within the general mass mobilization behind the demands of the social revolution: land reform, workers' control of state enterprises, nationalization of foreign companies, and "retooling" of corrupt and conservative officials, among others. Between 1962 and 1965, a bitter struggle developed between the left and right among intellectuals and artists. At stake was which perspective was to have access to state and social resources to publish and promote works of art and culture. Pramoedya emerged as one of the most effective spokespersons for state and social resources being prioritized for cultural mobilization, envisaged as part of the general political and social mobilization and radicalization. He was a savage critic of what he called cosmopolitanism, that is, a perspective on culture and society that was based on Indonesian history as written by the Dutch and which looked subserviently and uncritically at Western societies. He called for the "rooting out" of all such attitudes.

Joesoef Isak had been editor of one of the other major daily newspapers in Jakarta, *Merdeka*. As he took the paper ever further to the left, fully supporting President Soekarno, the newspaper's owners, Mohammad Diah and his wife, sacked him. However, after this he was elected unanimously as chair of the Jakarta branch of the Indonesian Journalists Association and later also became the Secretary General of the Asia Africa Journalists Association, where Hasyim Rachman was also active.

Hasyim and Pramoedya were arrested in 1965 and not released until 1979. Joesoef was arrested in 1967, after being detained and released several times in 1965 and 1966, he was released in 1977.

Heavy with History

The arrival of Hasta Mitra and the publication of Pramoedya Ananta Toer's books were developments heavy with history and evocative of historical memory in different ways. Even before Hasta Mitra began publishing books, its first political action resonated continuity with the national revolution. Hasyim Rachman and Joesoef's first open political act was to seek a meeting with Adam Malik, vice-president of Indonesia at the time. Malik was a long-term anti-communist and opponent of the PKI and allied himself with Suharto in 1965. He was soon after appointed Suharto's foreign minister. However, at the same time, Malik was a real figure from the *pergerakan*. He was one of the *pemuda* activists who had "kidnapped" Soekarno and Hatta in August 1945 to pressure them to proclaim independence immediately, rather than wait for agreement from any foreign power. That Adam Malik was willing to meet them and give a blessing for the publishing plans, despite official policy, represented an incursion of the old *pergerakan* into the New Order's counter-revolutionary "floating mass" society. Malik, despite his anti-communism and his opportunistic willingness to collaborate with Suharto, was an anachronism within the regime: somebody who had been a genuine nationalist revolutionary. He was later to receive the three Hasta Mitra men again, after their first book, *This Earth of Mankind*, had been published. The three Hasta Mitra former political prisoners and the vice-president—on different sides of the class divide within the Cold War framework—stood side by side for a photograph in the vice-presidential palace declaring a solidarity as national revolutionaries. Malik called on all of the nation's youth to read Pramoedya's novel. Defying the official ban on all Pramoedya's work issued in 1966, Malik also called for it to be compulsory reading in the schools. Malik, like Soekarno himself, was also a collector of Indonesian art and also ensured he obtained the works of PKI painters for his collection, allowing them to be exhibited.

The presence of Vice-President Malik in the Hasta Mitra story was an early indicator of the impact that the publishing project would have on the historical memory of at least some sectors of Indonesian society. It is hard to say which other factor was the more important: Pramoedya's books themselves or the fact that it was revolutionary Soekarnoists who were publishing them, in defiance of state repression and political taboo.

The first four books published by Hasta Mitra were all by Pramoedya and they were all historical novels. The first to come out was *This Earth of Mankind* in 1980. The novel was set at the turn of the twentieth century in the Netherlands Indies. According to a public statement by Malik in September 1980, just two weeks after the book's release: "I have read this entire book. It is very good and its historical value is extremely important. Through this book our children can come to know how their fathers faced colonialism."[2] The book caused an enormous furore. First, of course, there was shock that political prisoners, banned from publishing, should dare publish. There was an immediate questioning of whether this was allowed and whether the books would be banned, although Vice-President Malik's protection seemed at least to guarantee a delay.

But this shock was accompanied by the appearance of many positive responses. Reviews quickly appeared by all the prominent literary critics in the major daily and weekly media. *This Earth of Mankind* became the main political and cultural discussion point all through the latter months of 1980 and early 1981. It was the post-1966 Generation critics who were the most positive and who delved more deeply into the novel's content.

Adhy Asmara's book, *Analisa Ringkas Kemelut Roman Karya Pulau Buru Bumi Manusia Pramoedya Ananta Toer* ("A short analysis of the controversy surrounding *This Earth of Mankind*, Pramoedya Ananta Toer's Buru Island work"), lists thirteen reviews, some by prominent witers such as Rendra, Yakob Sumarjo, Parakitri, S.I. Peoradisastra and Goenawan Mohammed. The essayist Parakitri ended his lengthy review in Jakarta's most prestigious morning daily with the words:

> This novel, with great power, tells the story of the wretchedness of the native people, not just humiliated by the arrogance of the Dutch but also by the remnants of their culture—symbolized by a whip made from the genitals of a buffalo!
>
> This book, the first to be published by Hasta Mitra, in Jakarta, 1980 is the first of a series of four with the remaining novels to follow. If these books are published too in Dutch, English and French then *This Earth of Mankind* will will become part of world literature. And it will stand there no less in stature than the novels that have won the Nobel Prize. (*Kompas*, 28 August 1980)[3]

This Earth of Mankind presented itself as the semi-fictional account of the teenage years of a person who later became one of the pioneers of the Indonesian national revolution, Tirto Adhisuryo. Quite a lot is known about his political career as a young adult until his death or, according to Pramoedya, his assassination. However, there is little known of his teenage formative years, except what could be imagined—and was imagined by Pramoedya—based on some short stories about a teenager of the time written by Tirto himself. Pramoedya wrote *This Earth of Mankind* in Tirto's voice, as a first-person narrative, but making it clear that it was semi-fictional, by having his narrator protagonist state clearly that he was mixing his diary and other notes with his "imaginings." The novel tries to explain how a young Javanese man, in his late teens, brought up in a backward, aristocratic family, and given an elite education in a snobbish school for mainly Dutch children, could become a nationalist revolutionary. As there was no nationalist revolutionary movement at the time and the word and idea Indonesia were not yet in existence, this story was then not just the story of how one more individual became convinced of the need for an anti-colonial struggle for liberation but how "the first" such individual came into being. It is therefore a story of the very conception of the revolution.

There could be no more potent journey into history than this: it was a genesis story. Vice-President Malik's responses were typical of those who were conscious of this and not frightened of what the genesis story showed. As one prominent literary critic, Yakob Sumarjo, wrote in a major news-paper, Pramoedya was showing people:

> An era inhabited by our fathers whom we have never known. The fathers of our nation who laid down the basis of the great struggle against colonialism and human oppression, whose fire later flared high and burned down its massive and filthy house of oppression.[4]

Of course, even the New Order's version of the history of the colonial period told a story of anti-colonial struggle, but its version was that of a military struggle. Pramoedya's story, however, was of political struggle, of a student and a writer, and of popular mobilization and protest. The fictionalized teenager, called Minke, created through Pramoedya's imagin-ing of how Tirto may have seen his own teenage years, relates a very personal story of oppression: not economic oppression, but oppression of personal rights in family and love. In this sense, the genesis is located in the theft of dignity and the strength of character shown in response; of those who fight back against the odds.

The story of the revolution's gestation which unfolded over the next three volumes recounting a decade of Minke-Tirto's life, was even more subversive of the New Order's sterilization of history. The initial struggle against suppression of personal rights and dignity connects Minke with the mass of people around him. It is to the ordinary people he appeals, through one of their languages—Malay—and through the new medium of the printed word. It is these people outside the elite world, the enclave world, who begin to intrude on his consciousness: peasants, plantation workers, villagers. There is a whole odyssey that unfolds, back and forth, between enclave and the outside world of the people, both in its concrete reality and the world of ideas. At the end of the odyssey is a mass organization, the Sarekat Islam; a popular newspaper, *Medan Priyayi*; and men who were among the first radical national revolutionaries. These included the red Haji, Misbach; the fiery woman agitator of the railway workers, Siti Sundari; and the communist novelist and party leader, Mas Marco, just to name three real figures of the *pergerakan*.

Every possible element of the *pergerakan* method is depicted in the novels: street protests, leafleting, strikes, boycotts, mass rallies and public meetings, congresses and conferences, campaigning newspapers, peasant uprisings and political confrontation, and most fundamentally mass organization. Tirto Adhisuryo was a founder of the Sarekat Islam which became a mass organization with more than a million members. In Pramoedya's novels Indonesia was the *pergerakan*, even before either word came into being. What could be more subversive?

This Earth of Mankind, and the sequel novels, *Anak Semua Bangsa* (*Child of All Nations*), *Jejak Langkah* (*Footsteps*), and *Rumah Kaca* (*House of Glass*), are themselves, as a history of the genesis of Indonesia, also a history of the genesis of the *pergerakan* itself. But that was not the only impact on the collective historical memory in Indonesia at this time. The contents were one historical reminder; the author and publishers were another. Even before the regime reacted with its banning of *This Earth of Mankind*, the 66 Generation reacted in a way which revived discussion of the Soekarno years and the events of 1965. This subject had not been discussed in the media for more than a decade. A new round of discussion put the issue of how to assess the Soekarno years back on the agenda.

Goenawan Mohammed was one of the signatories of MANIKEBU in 1962 and a part of the movement to overthrow Soekarno and Soekarnoism. After 1965, he won permission to publish the country's first news weekly magazine and soon developed one of the biggest publishing companies in the country. He was one of the first of the 66 Generation to bring the old history back onto the agenda again. In November 1980, in his magazine, he opened his first major response to the revived presence of Pramoedya with a direct reference to the old conflict. But he also framed this with an acknowledgment of the existence of what he called "historical amnesia."

> See: my friend still talks about "us" and "them." "Us" refers to the writers of the 60s, who were the object of hostility from the communists and whom Pramoedya said must be "rooted out." "Them" refers to the writers like Pramoedya, who during Guided Democracy had the wind in their sails, controlled the mass media and were close to power—and they went after whomever they considered "contra-revolutionary." . . .
>
> But we must admit: there is something lacking and an injustice if we look back at the past in a one eyed way. Especially when we are talking about the 1963–65 period—almost two decades have disappeared.
>
> Anyway, in the 17 years since then, children who were aged between 5 and 13 then would be aged between 22 and 30 today. What do they know? There are no notes about the political and cultural problems of the years of their childhood. So given that there is such a large number of inhabitants in this young age group, we are threatened with historical amnesia.[5]

Nowhere in Goenawan Mohammed's article does he ask the question as to why there are "no notes" about this period. With the leftist writers dead or in gaol, the power to suppress information was fully in the hands of the 66 Generation itself. Mohammed dates the period of controversy as that of 1963–5, but strangely, though revealingly, he also says that the climax of this period was 1963, the first year of the period he names.

I have used the word "hostility," I have used the word "conflict."
What actually did happen then—that involved Pramoedya and his
opponents?

The climax of the hostility was reached in 1963. On one side were
the artists who supported the Indonesian Communist Party (PKI).
Standing with them, though not in the same organization, were the
other "revolutionary" writers and artists, especially those in the
National Cultural Institute (LKN), the organ of the PNI.

On the other side, were those writers and artists who did not join
up anywhere. Some of them, because of the pressure to group
together, joined the cultural organization protected by the NU,
Lesbumi. Others wanted to remain independent—just at a time
when such an attitude attracted hostility.

In 1963, under pressure to take some kind of position, a grouping
of artists formulated together what they called the Cultural Manifesto. Many people did not understand this manifesto, especially if
they could not read between the lines, given the limits on the freedom
to speak during the "Guided Democracy" period.[6]

Mohammed's essay repeated the MANIKEBU grouping's complaints of
the 1960s. The "terror" came from reading the polemical attacks on them
in the press, especially Pramoedya's "brutal" attacks in *Bintang Timur*. He
also listed again the three instances of MANIKEBU figures losing their
jobs. The literary critic H.B.Jassin left his job at the University of Indonesia
following a series of student demonstrations against him. The main
formulator of the MANIKEBU and contact person with their army
supporters, Wiratmo Soekito, lost his job on state radio. The poet Taufiq
Ismail, who later published the *Tirani* collection, was dismissed as a
lecturer at the Bogor Institute of Agriculture.

In any case, this essay, along with several others by leading 66 Generation writers as well as Rendra, served to inject an awareness of the whole
period of 1963–5 into the public discourse. This was a partial remedy to
the "historical amnesia" that Mohammed spoke about. As the quotes above
show, Mohammed saw 1963 as the climax, something which in itself also
helps explain the historical amnesia. The launching of the MANIKEBU
document was the climax, not the actual resolution, of the conflict in the
form of the establishment of a military-backed government in 1965 and the

mass killings and arrests of 1965. In fact, in all the 66 Generation essays this aspect gets no or only passing mention.

In his essay, "From *This Earth of Mankind*" Mohammed comments:

> Because of all this [the actions against MANIKEBU people], when on the morning of October 1 1965 I heard over the radio that a seizure of power had taken place—and could guess where the move had come from—I felt that a dark ending to all this was about to befall us. At that time I was 24 years old.
>
> But suddenly things turned out different. And the darkness that I thought would befall me, befell Pramoedya instead—and hundreds of other communist and "revolutionary" artistic people. As for myself, I was grateful. But I saw Pramoedya and the others later on Buru island in 1969. The layer upon layer of the past has convinced me even more deeply: fate can be strange, but human suffering is the same. It would be a waste to repeat this.[7]

So both recent and earlier history were back on the agenda because of the publication of *This Earth of Mankind.* Without the emergence of Hasta Mitra, it is possible that both aspects of history would have remained totally lost, a part of the "historical amnesia."

Impact

The controversy and debate did not let up. Hasta Mitra published other books edited or compiled by Pramoedya, mainly essays, short stories and novelettes by the early Malay-language writers publishing at the beginning of the twentieth century. Pramoedya also compiled a collection of the short stories of Tirto himself, including a biographical essay on Tirto. All were banned. There is little doubt that the combined effect of the revival of writing about the period of national genesis and the discussion of 1963–5 did have an important impact on the historical amnesia that had been induced by the New Order and the 66 Generation.

The impact is difficult to quantify and took some time to work its way through the political culture and to find its place. There was also a massive counter-attack by the New Order which tightened its grip on its version of history. Pramoedya's novels were reprinted several times before the ban robbed Hasta Mitra of the capital needed to continue their publication. In total more than 60,000 copies were printed. There were also an unquantifiable number of photocopies made, even before the printed version came out. Somehow copies of the typescript version circulated. There are myriads of anecdotes that indicate that a wide range of people read them, even the families of the state prosecutors themselves. Joesoef Isak tells one such revealing story. Joesoef bore the brunt of the interrogations of the publishers that followed the ban, having to report to the Attorney General every day, from early morning until evening, for a month. A prosecutor interrogated him for hours on end about the contents of the books and about Pramoedya. "What has Pramoedya written?" he was asked, exasperating him with the level of ignorance that the New Order had created. Pramoedya was one of the country's most well-known writers during the 1940s, 1950s and 1960s. After explaining, Joesoef also suggested that the attorney check in an encyclopaedia: "What is an encyclopaedia?" Suharto's law officer replied, "Can you spell it for me, please." (Later though, at the end of the interrogations when he told Joesoef that the book would be banned, he slipped a piece of paper under the table saying he would like a copy—a free copy of course—because his wife wanted to read it.)

It was among university students, however, that the impact was felt most strongly. It started to show up in the late 1980s and early 1990s with the circulation in photocopied form, and sometimes the publication of booklets, based on the university theses of students who had chosen to write about the *pergerakan* period. There is little doubt that these young intellectuals had been influenced by Pramoedya's writing. They wrote on the labor movement, on early radical writings and the early *pergerakan* media, on the history of the Sarekat Islam and how it gave birth to the Indonesian Communist Party in the 1920s. They reprinted materials from the period or other books on these topics. While this work remained on the fringes of establishment academia and did not gain a place in the establishment media, it did produce its own institutions and play a role in helping form new institutions. The overt signs that new groups had been established by young people influenced by Pramoedya's writings, or by the revival of historical memory generated by the publication of his books first emerged around 1990.

The most significant signal of a change within the student movement on attitudes towards the pre-1965 left was the emergence of an organization called INFIGHT (Indonesian Front for the Defense of Human Rights).

INFIGHT, founded in 1990, was the first open political group in Indonesia to campaign in defense of the political rights of detained members of the PKI. It launched a campaign in 1990 opposing the Suharto government's decision to proceed with the execution of several PKI members who had been on death row since the 1960s. Such a stance was unheard of during the 1973–8 student movement and, of course, anathema to the 66 Generation. The 1980s had been a period more of discussion and study than movement building and it was through that discussion and study that the new attitude to the old left had been formed.

INFIGHT in 1990 also took up the cases of Bonar Tigor Naipospos, Bambang Isti Nugroho and Bambang Subono. In 1989, these three active discussion group members were arrested and charged with distribution of Pramoedya's *The House of Glass*. All three were sentenced to more than seven years in prison.

Many members of INFIGHT were also actively involved with the first large-scale mass mobilizations that were organized in 1989 and 1990, mostly of peasants in West and Central Java who were campaigning for restoration of land ownership lost to various commercial developments (including golf courses). There were many of these mass actions, sometimes involving over ten thousand peasants in a single action. These were the first attempts at mass mobilization of non-students—of workers or peasants— since 1965 and they represent a qualitative turning point in the history of the New Order.[8] It was, in fact, the same students who began serious attempts to organize and mobilize at the mass base and who took up the cause of the rights of the pre-1965 left and the issue of censorship of Pramoedya's books. The timing, also coinciding with the publishing of Pramoedya's books between 1980 and 1989, is also indicative of the influence of the Hasta Mitra events and the impact of even a modest revival of the historical memory.

Another organization that was a reflection of this post-Hasta Mitra consciousness was Yayasan Maju Bersama (Advance Together Foundation—YMB). Several history and politics students from the University of Indonesia in Jakarta, including some who had pursued interests in the history of the 1920s *pergerakan*—the period immediately following the events depicted in Pramoedya's *House of Glass*—helped to form YMB. For these students and others like them, Pramoedya's novels had inspired them not only to look back and study history but also to become actively involved in political action. *Footsteps* and *House of Glass*, which told of the trials and tribulations of the Sarekat Islam organization and of the politics of the *Medan Priyayi* newspaper, acted as virtual handbooks on how to build a mass political movement. The YMB was a small grouping of students and ex-students taking the first steps in the direction of mass organization.

YMB oriented itself mostly towards the new factory working class that was expanding at the end of the 1980s. Its student and ex-student members made contact with workers in the *kampung* communities around clusters of factories and urged workers to organize themselves. They held educational courses on Marxism and Indonesian history, where Pramoedya's books were often used. YMB published a magazine, called *Cerita Kami* ("Our Stories"), which recorded long dialogues between the student activists and workers, reflecting a return to the pre-1965 idea of attempting to directly reflect the experiences of the working class and peasantry. YMB itself went through a split in 1992 with a number of its members forming a new organization, the Jaringan Kerja Budaya (Cultural Work Network—JKB), in 1993, which remains active today. Others became active in the current that later formed the People's Democratic Party (PRD).

JKB emerged as a small but active intellectual center, leading the development of academic Marxism in Indonesia. In 1999 it began publishing the journal, *Media Kerja Budaya* ("Media Work Culture"— MKB). Pramoedya himself gave the keynote lecture entitled "The Importance of History" at the launch of MKB. Throughout the 1990s and also since the fall of Suharto, JKB has promoted the writings of Pramoedya, the rights of political prisoners arrested as part of the 1965 counter-revolution, and promoted Marxist approaches to historical and political analysis and an interest in the history of the *pergerakan*. Between 2002 and 2004, JKB members helped compile an extensive oral history of the experiences of pre-1965 leftists. Through MKB, public forums and interventions in the press, JKB has helped ensure that the revival of interest in a left-wing approach to Indonesian history has remained alive. The leading figure of JKB is Hilmar Farid, a history student at the University of Indonesia in the 1980s, who mainly works outside the formal educational sector. JKB has also attempted to adopt an overt political stand by issuing two major political manifestos: *Agenda Rakyat: Mengatasi Krisis Ekonomi* (*Peoples Agenda: Overcoming the economic crisis*), published as a pamphlet in 2001 and *Agenda Rakyat: Menegakan Keadilan* (*Peoples Agenda: Fighting for Justice*), published in 2002.

JKB has not developed in a similar vein, however, to either LEKRA or LKN. Although having a strong empathy and solidarity with the pre-1965 left tradition, JKB has remained separate from any political party or political movement organization. It has confined itself to primarily intellectual activity, although frequently lending its name to various campaign coalitions throughout the 1990s. As a result, its political manifestos have had little impact compared to its role in providing continuity in left-wing intellectual approaches, building on the efforts to revive historical memory.

By 1998 consciousness of the question of historical amnesia and political liberalization had spread beyond the initial pioneers who had been directly influenced by the Hasta Mitra books in the 1980s and had begun to organize in 1990. A new generation of students and intellectuals, radicalized by the heightened political struggle in the last years of Suharto and inheriting the legacy of Hasta Mitra and the initial works of the early 1990s generation, took up the struggle to remember history. In September 1998, a new organization was formed called Masyarakat Indonesia Sadar Sejarah (Indonesian Society for the Awareness of History—MESSIAS). The motto of the organization was *Perjuangan melawan kekuasaan adalah perjuangan ingatan melawan lupa* ("The struggle against power is a struggle against forgetting"). MESSIAS draws its active members primarily from young academics and journalists who graduated in the 1990s. It presents itself as less activist than JKB but its publications, including its website, have played an important role in furthering public discussion around issues of forgotten history. Like JKB, it has concentrated its publications and forums on the history of the working class and peasantry and of the organized left. Unlike JKB it has invested more work into the rescue of the historical memory of Soekarno, and not only the PKI and its affiliated organizations.

One of its patrons is the historian Dr Asvi Warman Adam, a graduate of the Ecole des Hautes Etudes en Science Sociale (EHESS), Paris. Since the fall of Suharto, Adam has become one of the most widely quoted intellectual figures in the Indonesian press on the issue of the need for a rewriting of Indonesian history. Adam has been at the forefront of those calling for a revision of the history of the events of 1965, including some form of rehabilitation for the hundreds of thousands of victims of the New

Order's violence. He has also promoted the publication of two volumes of previously unpublished speeches made by President Soekarno after 30 September 1965 and during the period of the slow coup against him by General Suharto. These speeches were published by MESSIAS under the title "The Revolution is Not Yet Finished."

In some respects, the efforts of Adam and MESSIAS have had a more overt impact than that of JKB. Adam was for a while a senior historian in the state-sponsored Indonesian Academy of Science and several MESSIAS' members are academics in major universities or journalists and writers with regular access to the mainstream media. Adam is also a member of the team of historians appointed by the Indonesian government in 2000 to write a new official history of Indonesia. As a result of their activities, the anniversary of 30 September 1965 in 2003, became a major moment for widespread public discussion of the need for the "straightening out of history."

Both JKB and MESSIAS activities have been primarily located in the intellectual or academic sphere, even though both have had important impacts on the general political atmosphere. Hilmar Farid, along with other JKB activists, represented one section of the YMB group when it split in 1992. Others from the YMB joined forces with students and a few workers from around the country to form a low-profile grouping that was essentially a pre-party formation. This grouping went on to found the Persatuan Rakyat Demokratik (People's Democratic Union—PRD) in 1994 and the Partai Rakyat Demokratik (People's Democratic Party—PRD) in 1996.

Several different factors contributed to the formation of the PRD—and these will be looked at in later chapters—but the revival of historical memory provoked by Pramoedya's books was one of these factors. Most PRD documents and writings look specifically at the political and economic situation in the country at any one point and possible tactics that the party can pursue to advance the struggle against the dictatorship and for the winning of power by an organized workers' and peasants' movement. Direct reference to Pramoedya's books and the revival of interest in the history of class struggle in Indonesia are less central. The continuity with the pre-1965 traditions, as represented by Hasta Mitra, was symbolized, however, by the presence of Pramoedya, Joesoef Isak and Hasyim Rachman at the press conference in 1994 which announced the formation of the

PRD. Pramoedya himself formally joined the PRD in 1999 in a public ceremony. He drew attention in his speech to the connection between the formation of the PRD and the breaking down of the hold of the New Order's version of history:

> I assess the Young Generation, I mean the PRD, as being of higher quality than the generations that have gone before. Let's go straight to the core: since you were children you have been educated with the political lies of the New Order, painting the New Order as angels and depicting all those layers of society who refuse to defend it as devils. From primary school to university. And you all have seen through those lies.

If JKB was the "academic" manifestation of the beginning of the revival of the memory of the national revolution, the PRD was its party manifestation. Several founding members of the PRD were also members of YMB and participated in discussions of Indonesian history, including Pramoedya's works. Similar discussions were taking place in other groups throughout Indonesia during the 1980s and their members helped found the PRD. A key feature of the PRD's outlook was the assertion of continuity not so much with the PKI of the 1960s but with the *pergerakan* of the 1920s and 1930s. Key essays by PRD leaders emphasize the necessity to revive the political culture of the *pergerakan*. Sometimes the language of the *pergerakan*, such as the use of the term *vergardering* (mass gathering), has been deliberately introduced into the PRD's writings and agitation.

Central to this continuity, however, has been the concept of mass action itself. The PRD's adoption of a mass action approach to politics does not only stem from the renewal of study of the *pergerakan* and the period of national awakening that was provoked by Pramoedya's books. A critique of the dead end of student politics, of a study of the movement against Marcos in the Philippines during the 1980s and of a return to classical left writings were also important (see next chapter). But there is no doubt that Hasta Mitra's publication of Pramoedya's books and the recovery of historical memory were also crucial. One of the first major documents that the PRD produced was entitled "Indonesian Society and the Indonesian Revolution." This document took as its starting point an analysis of the *pergerakan* period.

Historical Memory at the Mass Level

As soon as the counter-revolution finished its final offensive and ended mobilizational politics on the campuses, the counter-revolution faced a counter-offensive, first by the Soekarnoists of Hasta Mitra and then by the new generation of radical intellectuals and political activists that followed. This new generation had a massive impact on the course of Indonesian politics during the 1990s, in particular through the building of student, peasant and worker mass protests, called *aksi*. In terms of the specific phenomenon of revival of historical memory, however, the impact was more limited. Goenawan Mohammed's "historical amnesia" remained relatively intact at the mass level.

The New Order wasted no time in launching an intensified campaign to strengthen the hold of its version of history as soon as the whole issue began to loom as a subversive specter. In 1984, the government launched a new subject to be taught from kindergarten to high school—the *Pendidikan Sejarah Perjuangan Bangsa* (Education in the History of the National Struggle—PSPB). The material for all the courses was written by historians from the History Center for the armed forces headquarters. Brigadier General Nugroho Notosusanto, the head of the History Center, was appointed Minister for Education and Culture during this period.[9] The new course had specific political goals, namely that:

a) students would understand that the Dutch colonization caused the suffering of the Indonesian people;

b) the students would come to believe in the justice of the struggle of the heroes in the expulsion of the Dutch;

c) students will understand that it was political and territorial unity that brought Indonesia to the doorway to independence;

d) students will understand that the Dutch were able to implement a divide and rule tactic because there was no political and territorial unity;

e) students would believe that the absence of political unity and the putting of personal and group interests first resulted in a government that strayed from the 1945 Constitution (material about the Republik Indonesia Serikat);

f) students would believe that the PKI unilateral actions [peasant occupations of land] were the PKI's attempts to unilaterally enforce its will in order to destroy the Unitary State of the Republic of Indonesia;

g) students would believe that the actions against the PKI were driven by the courage to defend independence and justice,

h) students would believe that the New Order's priority interests are those of the State and Society.[10]

New textbooks were written for this compulsory subject to be taught at every year in school. The material was to be learned by heart and with no alternative versions presented in school, or available anywhere in the city *kampung,* towns and villages—only in student activist circles. PSPB was taught unchanged from 1984 through to 1994, when the material was reorganized into two separate subjects, history and citizenship—but with the same content.

Throughout this period a key element in the history content was to strengthen the Suhartoist version of events during 1962–5. The textbooks, structured for rote learning, were meant to consolidate a stereotype of Guided Democracy and the PKI and the basis for the coming to power of the New Order. *Sejarah Untuk SMU Kelas 3* ("History for Senior High School Class 3") was published in 2001 and based on the 1994 curriculum "perfected" in 1999.[11] It retains the traditional reference name for Colonel Untung's retooling action: 30 September 1965/PKI—"PKI" is still incorporated in the reference.

The text provides a standard list of the "preparations" that the PKI was allegedly making for the events of 30 September. At the top of this list— meant for rote learning—was the following: "Mobilizing workers, farmers, fisherpeople, small traders and lower civil servants in the interests of the party." (p. 52)

Second on the list was: "Launching unilateral *aksi* [referring to the peasant land occupations]."

Not surprisingly it is the manifestations of mobilizational politics that are targeted for attack and delegitimization in the curricula. The other two items on the list of "preparations" were "Creating the politics of conflict and mutual distrust" and pressing for the mass organizations to be armed as militia.

All the texts repeat the official version of events on 30 September and 1 October itself with no reference to the questions that have been raised regarding Suharto's own role and knowledge of events. The demonization of the PKI and the holding of the whole movement as collectively responsible for the murder of the generals was a central part of the high school education. There is no change in this aspect of the curriculum post-Suharto.

In the period immediately after the publication of Pramoedya's books, the pumping of the Suhartoist version of history through the school system was buttressed by a program of feature films reinforcing this message. One of the most prominent 66 Generation dramatists—Arifin C. Noor—was commissioned to write and direct a film entitled *Perkhianatan G30S* ("30 September Movement Treachery"). The film, which used top celebrity stars, was based on the Suhartoist version of the events of 1965. It set out to convey the specific impression that the PKI was evil, sadistic, cunning and its leaders hungry for power. The film was not only screened in the cinemas in the normal commercial sense. Almost all school children were herded to see the film every year on the anniversary of 30 September for the next twenty years. Again the screening of these films took place in an environment of a total absence of criticism, critiques or alternative versions of history.

This film was further reinforced with other Suhartoist films, especially those promoting the personality of Suharto himself. These were mainly films presenting the hero mythology around Suharto's involvement in the armed struggle against Dutch colonialism between 1945 and 1949—always leaving out his role as a sergeant in the Dutch colonial army used to suppress Indonesians before 1942.

The 66 Generation monopoly of the media and the universities, the New Order's systematic totalitarian policies on historical demonization in the school system over two decades, and the use of the cinema have ensured that the subversion of the New Order monopoly on historical memory that began with the Hasta Mitra books did not penetrate deep into the mass of the population. Even today, knowledge—memory—of the Indonesian national revolution and its full history of rebellion, radicalism and popular empowerment is very weak, even non-existent among the mass of the population. It is even weak among university students and student activists. However, the debates generated by the Hasta Mitra publications and the public discussions and writing organized by the generation of young intellectuals influenced by those books has not been without some impact, even if still limited.

The new curriculum now mentions the mass killings of 1965 and refers to it as a "tragedy." The new texts have felt the need to refer to the fact that there are different versions of how many people were killed—a break from the era when there was only one version for everything. A text such as "History for Senior High School Class 3" tries to explain the killings as a result of clashes between pro- and anti-PKI forces:

> anti-PKI youths in several regions start to carry out similar actions [occupations of PKI offices, etc.] Direct clashes with the PKI and its supporters could not be avoided. In some areas, especially Jawa, Bali and North Sumatra a situation developed resulting in the loss of life to violence among members and supporters of the PKI, including members of supporting organizations. This violence was also used by people for their own interests with the result that people who had no connection with the PKI or supporting organizations were also victims. (p. 62)

In this version, the military plays no role in the mass killings which are depicted as a result of "clashes"—although the text also acknowledges that the victims came from only one side of the "clash."

This kind of small amelioration of the old propaganda in official government texts was facilitated by the presidency of Abdurrahman Wahid. Wahid had often spoken out on the need to come to terms with the killings of 1965, especially in the 1980s when the atmosphere was already changing after the Hasta Mitra events. Significantly, Wahid decided to make a public visit to Pramoedya's house for consultations during his presidency.

By 2006, however, conservative elements in the bureaucracy and the academe seemed to be trying to seize back the initiative from critical historians. Historians and Education Ministry officials involved in a 2004 history textbook came under criminal investigation in September 2006 because their textbook had no longer insisted that the Communist Party of Indonesia (PKI) was the mastermind of an attempted left-wing coup in September 1965—in line with a new 2004 history curriculum.

On 19 September, Education Minister Bambang Sudibyo told journalists that the government of President Susilo Bambang Yudhoyono, a former Suharto-era general, had decided to abandon the 2004 curriculum. The 19 September issue of the London *Financial Times* reported that

Sudibyo said he had also asked the country's attorney-general to investigate the historians and other officials responsible for textbooks derived from the 2004 curriculum that failed to blame the PKI for the coup. According to the attorney-general's office an investigation was under way into the publication of the history books, saying "they had caused 'restlessness amongst the people'."

The 20 September *Jakarta Post* reported:

Education Ministry curriculum center head Diah Harianti had argued that the 2004 curriculum more comprehensively explained the events surrounding Sept. 30, 1965. Instead of associating the tragedy only with the PKI, it blamed the social conflicts on ideological and political differences among citizens. Now, with no explanation, the Education Ministry had decided to reinstate the PKI as the main culprit, he said. "Members of the police, attorney general's office (AGO) and State Intelligence Agency questioned Diah and one other official at the curriculum center recently about why 12th-grade history books based on the 2004 curriculum did not blame the PKI for the violence."

In March 2007, the Attorney General moved to ban these textbooks. In response, scores of intellectuals began a petition to oppose the measure. Former President Abdurrahman Wahid called on the Attorney General department's officials themselves to be arrested for violating the freedom to publish.

Soekarno

There is one other chink, however, in the New Order's armory against the country's revolutionary past that needs to be discussed and that has a different origin than the subversion of the old hegemony initiated by Hasta Mitra. This is the memory of the figure and personality of Soekarno. The main evidence of the existence of this memory is the rise in popularity of Megawati Soekarnoputri, one of Soekarno's daughters, between 1991 and

1999. Megawati was a virtually silent member of Suharto's parliament during most of the 1990s. Then she began a meteoric rise, primarily pushed by support from local-level business elites aspiring to go national and who felt held back by the dominance of Suharto crony capital in Jakarta. She was elevated to the position of Chairperson of the Indonesian Democratic Party (PDI) by this base of support, with some assistance from individual army generals looking to their own futures.

While it was a section of the regional business that propelled her to the chairpersonship, it was her name, Soekarnoputri, which appeared to be the main lightning rod for popular support. She offered no alternative economic, social or political policies whatsoever to Suharto, always speaking in very general and abstract terms on every policy issue. When Suharto started to maneuver to remove her as chairperson of the PDI, she further strengthened her popular appeal by refusing to concede. Her defiance of Suharto on this one issue, combined with her name, drew massive popular support. In the 1994 elections, millions turned out for her rallies, although the GOLKAR and state machine were able to ensure that GOLKAR still delivered a massive vote for itself. In the 1997 elections, when the protest momentum was on the rise, millions turned out to support the call for an alliance between Megawati and the Islamic parties to oust GOLKAR. Megawati herself, by then removed from chairpersonship of the PDI, called for a boycott of the elections. In PDI support areas the boycott was implemented almost totally.

It is difficult to identify the mechanisms by which the Soekarno name has remained a symbol of proximity to the *rakyat*, the *marhaen*, the *wong cilik* (little people). Official history simply stamped Soekarno as "Proclaimer" of independence but also as a part of the rottenness of the PKI-dominated Guided Democracy era. However, there were always cheap, popular pamphlets being published about Soekarno. While they often avoided the 1960s, they contributed to maintaining a sense of him as a political leader close to the people. Word of mouth from an older generation who supported Soekarno to the next generation is also one explanation. There are many stories told about Soekarno informally among the people. Over time they have become less and less political, emphasizing primarily his cultural affinity with the masses: his affinity for popular food, for sneaking out of the palace and mixing with the people and so on.

Soekarno's charisma—that is, his massive popularity—is also a key fact of

Indonesian history that has been impossible to ignore. Here and there, in this report and that, in this reference and that, in any reference to the period before 1965, it is not possible to avoid a mention of "Bung Karno." The term "Bung Karno" itself nails the memory of Soekarno in people's minds as somebody close to the people. "Bung" is only used in reference to leaders, members of the elite, who are perceived as having no feudal pretensions and are close to the people. After 1965, "bung" went out of usage in Indonesia, to be replaced by the feudalistic "Father" and "Mother" when speaking of leaders or members of the elite.[12]

The memory of Bung Karno as an enormously popular leader among ordinary people has proved impossible to eradicate completely. In fact, although vague in its content, the memory retains enormous emotional hold. This memory is also connected to the awareness that the Western powers were hostile to Soekarno and that he stood up to them. That Soekarno once told the West: "Go to hell with your aid!" is also remembered. Official history has also been unable to eliminate from the historical record that Indonesia hosted the 1955 Asia Africa Conference, the meeting that began the non-aligned movement, and that Soekarno was the primary figure at this conference. The memory of the popular leader, close to the people, is also connected, as a result, to a memory of a period when national pride was strong.

The real content of Soekarno's political thinking and political history has been separated from this memory which is now vague and ill-defined. But even so, it remains a subversive memory, a reminder of a time when there was a leader whom a huge number of people felt was close to them, and who did want to mobilize them in political participation. During the 1970s, when Rendra's theater group, Bengkel Theater, was acting as the vanguard of opposition to the regime, the groups' musicians, performing as the Kelompok Kampungan, released an album that began with excerpts from a fiery speech by Soekarno.

In this sense, the memory of Soekarno is connected to the fact that there is one word from the national revolution which has been impossible to eliminate from mass political consciousness: *rakyat*. Soekarno's memory—vague and ill-defined—is connected to the continuing prevalence of strong populist sentiment, a strong sentiment that leaders should respect the *kedaulatan rakyat* (people's sovereignty). Everybody still wants to speak in the name of or for the *rakyat*, even the New Order leadership. This should not be shrugged off with an "of course, all politicians like to speak in the name of the people." As discussed earlier, in the Indonesian national revolution *rakyat* is essentially a class term, it refers to the poor and exploited people specifically; it is a term of contrast with the *pembesar* (person of influence), *orang kaya* (rich person), *penguasa* (ruler) and *pejabat* (official). The continuing use of the term *rakyat* by all political actors throughout the period of the New Order is because, of course, in real life the *rakyat* do exist as such a real, material class(es), a class visibly separate culturally and economically from the elite and the enclave world. Politically, the historical reference point for this pro-*rakyat* sentiment has been the figure of Soekarno.

During the 1990s, this resilient populist sentiment, the Soekarno name and the new post-Hasta Mitra generation of activists came together to give rise to the revival of another word, concept and activity from the national revolution: the Dutch word *actie*, but this time in Indonesian: *aksi*.

5

Plans

On 2 May 1994, about forty activists from around Indonesia met at the offices of the Jakarta Legal Aid Institute (YLBHI) to announce that they had formed a new political organization, the Persatuan Rakyat Demokratik (People's Democratic Union—PRD). The new organization brought together local student, worker and farmer activists based in Jakarta, Bandung, Yogyakarta, Solo, Semarang and Surabaya in Java, Medan in Sumatra and Menado in Sulawesi. This was the first attempt to form these local activist groups into a national organization, at least openly, above ground. Sugeng Bahagijo, who had been elected chairperson of the PRD after a three-day meeting of over 100 delegates from around the country, welcomed "everybody as members, farmers, workers, students, intellectuals and others, as long as they are concerned about the development of democracy in Indonesia."

In its founding declaration, the PRD called for a restoration of full democratic rights and freedoms, a return to civilian rule and redistribution of the wealth of society to the poor.[1] The PRD declaration also went much further than any previous pro-democracy group in Indonesia in the 1970s and 1980s by publicly calling for the restoration of full civil rights to the tens of thousands of former communist and Soekarnoist political prisoners and also calling for self-determination in East Timor.

Present at the launch of the PRD were a range of prominent figures in the democratic movement. These included Adnan Buyung Nasution, Director of the Indonesian Legal Aid Institute. Other figures present included Mohtar Pakpahan, head of the recently formed union SBSI (Indonesia Workers Welfare Union), Dede Triawan from the environmental organization WALHI and Mulyana Kusuma from YLBHI.

After the launch of the PRD on 2 May 1994, the Indonesian regime threatened it with sanctions should it engage in any political activities. At the same time, many figures from the more liberal wings of a number of mainstream organizations, for example Jakob Tobing from GOLKAR and Aberson Sihaloho from the Indonesian Democratic Party, defended the PRD's right to engage in political activity.

Soon after the launch of the PRD, Soesilo Soedarman, the Minister for Politics and Security, stated: "The PRD is not legal. There are only three political vehicles recognized by the government, PPP [Partai Persatuan Pembangunan, United Development Party], Golkar [Functional Groups] and the PDI [Partai Demokrasi Indonesia, Indonesian Democratic Party]. The government will take firm action."

The Director General of Social and Political Affairs of the Home Affairs Ministry, Sutoyo, also announced that if the PRD put up resistance, the police would "disband them forcibly".

This hard-line position was countered by Harsudiono Hartas, former armed forces general and then deputy chairperson of the Supreme Advisory Council, a state advisory body appointed by President Suharto. Hartas was reported in *Media Indonesia* on 5 May: "The PRD was formed because the political culture and mechanisms are blocked. The youth and students are looking for another way to struggle for their aspirations."

At the same time, Jakob Tobing told the press that the government shouldn't act too hastily in condemning the PRD as outside the law. On the other hand, Agung Laskono, Chair of the National Council of Leaders of GOLKAR, stated sharply that the formation of the PRD was "unconstitutional."

Aberson Sihaloho stated his strong approval of the founding of the PRD by calling it a manifestation of current frustrations with the political infrastructure.

Beyond Students

The formation process of the PRD was partly in reaction to the failure of the 1978 student movement and the dead end reached by the NGO and student movements in the 1980s. However, in the 1990s there were still other opposition political groups that the PRD needed to assess. A report

on the national situation delivered to the PRD founding conference
provided a tentative analysis of these opposition forces:

> The first [group] that must be noted is the Petition of Fifty. This
> group has been the opposition since the New Order but has always
> been only half-hearted. It has no mass base or newspaper and has only
> weak international support. They have demanded that Suharto be
> brought before a special session of the People's Consultative Assem-
> bly to give an accounting [of his crimes and abuses]. Their recent
> relations with Minister of Technology Habibie, reflecting Suharto's
> attempt at reconciliation, has lost them credibility in the eyes of the
> people. Their main agenda is for a multi-party system, minus any left-
> wing parties.
>
> As a political grouping, FODEM has failed to develop into a
> strong and broad formation, because it has not wielded any effective
> political tolls: it has no newspaper which openly and clearly advocates
> its political program, holds no real discussions, and no other pub-
> lications let alone mobilizes any masses under its banner [Forum
> Demokrasi (FODEM) was a small group of intellectuals who
> regularly made public statements critical of policies seen to be
> restricting democracy.] As Suharto has been expanding his own
> forces, FODEM should have been clearly telling the masses what
> FODEM wants to achieve. FODEM has the biggest potential to
> obtain international support.[2]

Commenting on the student movement, meaning the trend represented by
FAMI, that is, students who were not allying themselves in political activity
with workers and peasants, the report states:

> The increase in the scope and level of issues raised by the student
> movement leading up until the arrest of the 21 proves that the New
> Order regime has been unable to silence it. This proves the pre-
> paredness of the student movement to overcome the repressive
> measures taken against it, so that it can turn itself into an agent
> of democracy. It is true that so far there has not been the ability to
> maintain persistence in some campaigns, such as the campaign
> around the 21 students. But the mass student movement can become

a force that can effectively demand democratic change if it can overcome some political and organizational problems. These include the problems of inter-regional and inter-campus rivalry.[3]

The PRD's criticism of the 1980s opposition groupings of the Petition of 50, FODEM and FAMI reflected its emphasis, indeed its central prior-itization of, the necessity to engage in mass mobilization in direct defiance of the "floating mass" policy. The PRD emerged out of a process of debates and splits based on a rejection of any strategy that did not put mass mobilization at its center. Perhaps the first published outline of this rejection—an early manifesto for this new political current—was an article published in the English-language version of the social sciences journal *Prisma* (no. 47, September 1989) under the pseudonym Fazlur Akhmad. Fazlur Akhmad was, in fact, Danial Indrakusuma, one of the founding members of the PRD in 1994 and a leading figure in all of the pre-party formation activity that led to the formation of the PRD. The article was entitled: "The Indonesian student movement—a force for radical social change?". Indrakusuma identified what he saw as the strategic weakness of the student movement up until the late 1980s:

> Before 1970 the first activists to become aware of the shortcomings of this alternative [linking up with the military] were Soe Hok Gie of GEMSOS (Socialist Student Movement) and Ahmad Wahib of HMI (Muslim Students Association). However, like others in the genera-tion of new activists in the 1970s who decided that this strategy was wrong, they made another strategic mistake; *separated from popular power, they had no strong or broad mass base.*[4]

This weakness—separation from popular power—was also identified as the key weakness of the two major forms of student activity after 1978: study groups and non-government organization (NGO) activity. Indrakusuma continued later in his article:

> Until now, those students who have looked to this alternative in study groups have not been aware of their decay. A comparison with the *Studieclub* of the 1920s shows that they were in fact superior to the study groups of the 1980s. Historical analysis clearly shows how

the *Studieclub* responded to and stimulated objective political-eco-
nomic conditions. . . . In the political and economic conditions of
the New Order, however, the study clubs are not transforming
themselves: they more closely resemble apolitical debating clubs in
their activities. They wallow in theoretical issues and cannot act
dialectically, responding to and stimulating objective change. . . .[5]

He critiques the earlier generations of student leaders for consistently
avoiding mass mobilization. Referring to the student leaders of the early
1970s, he states:

Their strategy is moral action—to change the system from within
(mostly by using the ideology and institutions of NGOs). No
political action can strengthen their bargaining position [because]
they see mass organisation for political pressure as taboo. They often
shelter behind the word (it is only a word) tactical, but in reality they
never take political action on the ground to mobilise the masses.[6]

On the 1973–4 and 1978 leaders, he writes:

Their political ideal was to take political power, but they lacked the
political boldness to become involved in mobilising people from all
sectors of society. . . . In the case of Malari, the masses were told to
retreat. In the 1978 movement . . . mass mobilisation was even less
well prepared.[7]

Indrakusuma also criticizes the NGOs as having become bureaucratized
and unable to transform their political agenda, therefore unable to initiate
political action.

In fact, by 1987, a small number of activists had already grouped
together and decided to begin a campaign to revive mass mobilization
politics. In this, they remained a tiny minority among the whole student
sector who had been either drawn into the scores of mushrooming
discussion groups or the NGO community development and issue advocacy groups that had on the basis of foreign funding during the 1980s.
Indrakusuma himself was not totally negative about the experience of the
1980s. His article also commented:

Many factors have . . . provided the student movement of the 1980s with valuable experience in understanding and organising: discussions, the distribution of campus media, informal relations with youths in the ·cities and demonstrations, leading to continual reconsideration of tactics and strategies.[8]

Indrakusuma was right. Although the suppression of the student sector in 1978 ended mass mobilization politics for a whole decade, the regime could not stop political discussion and other kinds of political experience. The whole of the 1980s was an intense period of political discussion and learning, beginning with the publication of Pramoedya Ananta Toer's books. It is no accident that Indrakusuma's 1989 article itself includes a historical review of the student movement during the colonial period and makes historical comparisons of political struggle.

But it was not just more engagement with past historical experience that seeped into the world of political activism during this period. It was also the period of the first re-engagement of political activists from the student sector with elements of society outside the student sector. As students graduated or dropped out of studies, many shifted into the NGO community development organizations. Indrakusuma noted how "social research, and . . . social action for charity and 'income generation' [projects]" became major activities of the NGOs.[9] All these activities brought them into direct contact with social sectors outside the student sector: labor, peasants, fishermen, *kampung* women and so on. A period began of documenting the social conditions of all these sectors. By the end of the 1980s, the libraries and publications of NGOs encompassed an enormous amount of data on the conditions of life of ordinary people.

The documentation of economic and social inequality by the NGO sector did impact on the kind of public discussion that seeped into the media, as well as the political discussion among student and former student activists. This change happened very quickly. Even by the early 1980s, it had influenced discussion so much that the most influential NGO—the Indonesian legal aid foundation, YLBHI—began issuing annual human rights reports which went far beyond looking at the violations of civil liberties. The conditions of farmers, workers and women were surveyed in every report. Furthermore, the director of the YLBHI in the early 1980s, Todung Mulya Lubis, developed the concept of "structural human rights," theorizing the need for structural change in society if these basic rights were to be met.

In the 1981 YLBHI human rights report, its editors, Mulya Lubis, Fauzi Abdullah and Mulyana W. Kusumah, opened with the following analysis:

> One thing is clear: the structures and the processes producing the violation of basic human rights are becoming increasingly integrated, strengthening each other, as time goes on . . .
>
> The Indonesian economy appears every day to become more integrated with the world capitalist system extending its reach through the giant multinational corporations and the international financial institutions. Our increasing dependency on them seemingly results in the implementation of policies that are not beneficial to the majority of people. And this dependence too appears to press the repressive and ideological apparatus to give further protection to the dominant economic interests, so that the scooping out of profit on a national scale is made secure, while the majority of people feel it is harder and harder to live.
>
> With the increasing large-scale entry into Indonesia of large capital and of the international financial institutions, a dialogue has opened up between the international and national elites who are able to determine policy. Alongside this, we see the majority of the *rakyat* left behind, struggling with increasing poverty.
>
> This pattern of economic growth requires a pattern of political policies that does not tolerate participation. There has been a systematic centralisation of power and a systematic weakening of any alternative centres of power. The political parties, as legal channels for the aspirations of the *rakyat*, weaken every day with every new internal conflict and the emergence of figures whose personal and political integrity is highly dubious. Outside these formal channels, surveillance becomes heavier with every passing day. What is clear are the political mobilizations—especially in the case of the electoral democratic festivals—purely for the purposes of legitimizing the rulers.[10]

The report—like those before and after it—provides a devastating picture of the inequalities that had developed in the education and health sectors, as well as conditions for workers and peasants. It included a thirty-three-page appendix listing cases of labor protests over wages, conditions and violations of the right to organize. The YLBHI was viewed in this period as more or less a mainstream organization. Its access to the media was extensive. Its building was used by almost every other NGO and student group in Jakarta and surrounding areas for press conferences, seminars and other events. The spirit of its analysis, linking the violation of rights (defined to encompass social and economic rights) to structures of dependence and subordination to the world capitalist system, big foreign capital and international and national elites, permeated the whole of the dissident sector throughout the 1980s.

This spirit, this general outlook, prevailed in all NGOs and student groups by the end of the 1980s, when Indrakusuma wrote his essay for *Prisma*. The 1990 YLBHI report, under a new director, Hendardi, was even bleaker, illustrated with stark cartoon illustrations depicting the suppression and exploitation of an impoverished and malnourished *rakyat*. The social and economic deprivation being suffered by every sector—labor, peasants, fisherpeople, teachers, the urban semi-proletarian informal sector, teachers and women—was documented. This report concluded with a document, "Joint Declaration on Basic Human Rights in Indonesia," signed by nine of the major NGOs in Indonesia, including civil liberties, women's rights, health rights and consumer organizations. It was a comprehensive critique of economic inequality, political repression and social oppression affecting all sectors of society (see Appendix to this chapter). In terms of a critique of the nation's socio-economic and political situation, these popular classes—proletarians, semi-proletarians and peasants—were well in the picture. Indrakusuma's critique was that the NGOs and discussion groups did not see them as an active part of the solution.

Active Engagement

All the same, for such ideas to develop and spread, some elements among the activists had to see the need for an engagement with these sectors that went beyond seeing them simply as victims. More and more groups were formed whose orientation included a "live-in" approach, whereby students would spend time with peasants and workers, in their homes and communities. The "live-in" approach was pioneered by activists who had spent some time in the mid-1980s with the anti-Marcos movement in the Philippines. These few students had left Indonesia and sought to be integrated into the mass organizations campaign against Marcos. They had sought to learn from the Philippines experience, after concluding that students alone could not win change. In the Philippines, they had learned the techniques of community organizing and mobilization.

By 1989, there were many such organizations active throughout the country, wherever there were university campuses. The engagement with non-student sectors went beyond either "social research" or "income generation" projects, such as cooperatives—although these aspects were often preserved. There were two new types of engagement. The first was political education and the second was mobilization. Students began taking radical political ideas, as well as information about existing legal rights, to the worker and peasant communities with whom they were engaging. Discussion groups, although not called that, spread to workers and farmers, wherever students could reach them. But protest actions, involving mobilizations of workers or peasants alongside students, also began to take place. It was peasant protests that dominated in the first phase of this development, from about 1988 until 1992.

The peasant farmer protests that achieved national prominence were those carried out by the Kedung Ombo peasants, backed by student activists. In 1985, the World Bank approved a US$156 million loan to the Indonesian government for the construction of the Kedung Ombo Multi-purpose Dam and Irrigation Project in Central Java. The purpose of the project was to flood 59,654 hectares of wet rice fields to generate 225 MW of electricity. The project required the resettlement of 5,390 families (around 20,000 people) in thirty-seven villages.[11]

According to INFID data, only a small percentage of families had freely accepted compensation for their lands and were actually willing to move. Up to 3,391 families had refused to accept compensation, primarily because the rates offered were far below the market value of the land and they were not adequately consulted. Typical land prices in 1989 outside the project area were between Rp. 4,000 (around US$2.60 1989 exchange rate) per square meter. Yet the compensation rate offered to the affected people by the local authorities was only Rp. 250–750 (around US$0.28) per square meter.

Farmers had protested the inadequate compensation since 1987 and by

1988 students began to join the protests and help organize visits by the farmers to nearby cities, and eventually to Jakarta. Some of these demonstrations were very large and the campaign soon became a national cause. The major weekly news magazines carried stories on the front covers. The case gained increasing legitimacy, and the mainstream NGOs, such as YLBHI, also became involved in helping about 50 farmers take the case to the Supreme Court. With several thousand farmers involved, there were many opportunities for activist groups to make links with different groups of farmers at different times. No permanent alliance between specific farmer groups and activist groups developed. The Kedung Ombo farmers lost their struggle; they were flooded out and never received adequate compensation. At the height of the campaign, Suharto himself charged them with being "stubborn," later increasing the threat by stating that the region was known in the past as a PKI support base.

But the Kedung Ombo case, by becoming nationally famous over the 1988–90 period, helped legitimize and popularize *aksi*—street protest, actions, demonstrations, mobilization. By 1991, *aksi* involving peasants had become increasingly prolific. The spirit of *aksi* was exemplified in many of the songs and anthems adopted by the activist groups, such as that adopted by the most active group in Yogyakarta, the Yogyakarta Students Communication Forum (Forum Kommunikasi Mahasiswa Yogyakarta—FKMY):

> Rise up all you who struggle for democracy
> Spirit and blood aflame
> Unity solid like rock with worker and peasant
> and patriotic student
>
> Wipe out the robbers of the people's land
> Wipe out all the enemies of the people
> Advance with fists held high
> Welcome a tomorrow of prosperity and dignity
> national democracy
> in Indonesia.

At the national level, one group of activists played a particularly central role in promoting this trend. This was SKEHPI (Sekretariat Kerjasama Pelestarian Hutan Indonesia—Indonesian NGOs for Forest Conservation). It was established at a meeting of NGO activists in Lembang, West Java, in August 1982. During the 1990–1 period, SKEHPI's activities went beyond the forest conservation issue. SKEHPI activists were involved in promoting and helping organize a series of large peasant *aksi*—sometimes involving over 10,000 farmers. Most of these actions were by farmers who had lost their land to major commercial development projects—golf courses, commercial market gardens, cattle ranches and so on. SKEHPI also hosted the transfer to Jakarta of such peasant protests from around the country. (Most SKEHPI activists were connected to INFIGHT, which had also pioneered the 1990 protest actions against the execution of PKI prisoners.)

The more media coverage these protests attracted, the more similar protests occurred in other parts of the country. There is no study that gathers together all the data on these actions however a magazine appeared in 1990 which began to record many of these actions. This was *Progres*.[12] It was initially edited by two leading figures from SKEHPI, Indro Cahyono and Danial Indrakusuma, the author of the 1989 *Prisma* article. Australian sympathizers helped the publication by providing an editorial address outside Indonesia and a former MALARI activist helped in raising funds for the magazine. Later a split occurred within the INFIGHT and SKEHPI leadership grouping and Indro Cahyono ceased to be a part of the editorial group. *Progres* published views from the full spectrum of the political opposition, but specialized in material documenting the burgeoning protest actions taking place around the country. During its three years of publication *Progres* documented protest actions by farmers and workers throughout Java, Sumatra, Kalimantan, Sulawesi, Lombok and others of the eastern islands. A single issue of *Progres*, covering two months of activities, would on average document forty to fifty cases of strikes, workers' protests and peasant mobilizations. *Progres* drew its documentation from a combination of newspaper reports and chronologies describing actions, written by those involved. The forty to fifty actions reported each issue were just the tip of the iceberg.

By the end of the 1989–92 period the techniques of street protest activity, including strike activity and land protests, had become very widely generalized. The widespread familiarity among workers, peasants and others of the techniques of protest activity was due to two key factors. It should be noted, of course, that one factor that was not operative was educational activity by large trade unions. The only large trade union was the government-controlled All Indonesia Workers Union (SPSI), used as an instrument to ensure that the working class stayed a passive "floating mass."

One factor was that despite tight control over the media in reporting explicit political opposition to the Suharto dictatorship, there was little censorship of reporting worker and peasant protest activity. This was true in the 1970s and 1980s as well as the 1990s. There are large collections of news clippings on worker protests in the 1970s and 1980s gathered by the Leiden-based INDOC project and also large collections of such clippings—involving thousands of cases—gathered by myself for the 1980s, now held by the library of the Australian National University.[13] There are also several such collections in various NGO libraries in Indonesia. The widespread press reporting helped legitimize these protests and integrate them into urban popular culture. News reports of strikes, for example, were an important element in the tabloid press, such as *Pos Kota, Terbit* and other dailies aimed at the popular readership in Jakarta. In Java, newspapers like *Bernas* also gave considerable coverage to protest actions. Moreover, they were mostly not hostile reports, unlike most of those in the mainstream Western media. The reports usually did report in some detail on the conditions of the workers, and often had short interviews with the workers.

However, the press reports operated at a very general level, giving a general legitimacy to labor and peasant protest. They only provided minimal information on the techniques of worker protest. In an environment of increasing spontaneous activity, buoyed by the public and press sympathy, the more organized sectors of the movement had from the beginning decided to produce what turned out to be a very popular and useful document. This was the *kronologi*.[14] The *kronologi* was a detailed account, often by the minute or every five or ten minutes, of all the stages in the preparation and implementation of a protest action or strike. All aspects of the activity were covered: where workers gathered; how they were organized; the division of labor; how they approached the employers; how they dealt with factory security; what they did when the police or army arrived; who gave what speeches and when; and so on and so on. These very detailed documents were widely circulated among activists. Between 1990 and 1992 *Progres* also used these chronologies as a source. The production of these *kronologi* has remained an institution of the activist movement.

Although it was banned by the Attorney General's office on 16 June 1992, *Progres* continued to publish and circulate until 1993, when its funding source ran out. The magazine was always distributed at minimal cost and never made a profit. The Attorney General's banning order stated: "The aforementioned publication published things not in accordance with the facts, with the result that it gives rise to mistaken opinions within society about the nation's leadership."[15]

The emergence of new institutions arguing for a strategy of mass mobilization was opening the way for a new political element to be added to the previously spontaneous tendencies of worker and peasant protest. *Progres* and the *Progres* editorial group were the first such major visible institutions. But there were others being formed around the country in a quite complex process. *Progres* had been a tool for intervention among the layer of activists who had become more seriously engaged with non-student sectors, either in helping to organize the protest actions or in carrying out political education among workers and peasants—although by 1993, the emphasis was on engaging with factory and transportation workers. In the Central Javanese university city of Yogyakarta and the South Sumatran city of Lampung, where there was less industry, activists also maintained contacts with farmers.

In Jakarta, two groups played a central role in developments. These were Yayasan Maju Bersama (YMB—Advance Together Foundation) and Forum Bebas Belajar (FBB—Free Study Forum). Both groups comprised student activists and some longer-term activists who were organizing "live-ins" with workers, educational programs and some strike actions. They were also centers of intense discussion over political theory, drawing on a wide range of sources, including all variants of radical political theory. The historical novels of Pramoedya Ananta Toer were also widely read. Each of the groups had also succeeded in recruiting a small number of factory workers as organizers. *Progres* was widely read among these groups, who also operated as a center for distribution for *Progres*, after the split between SKEHPI and INFIGHT, and after Danial Indrakusuma became active in YMB.

The split between SKEHPI and INFIGHT occurred in 1992. The split resulted from a clash between two fundamentally different approaches to building a political movement in order to challenge the New Order. There was a very basic consequence of deciding on an *aksi*-oriented strategy of mass mobilization: there needed to be a structured organization to develop the skills, understanding and consistency to successfully pursue such a strategy. The strategic orientation to *aksi* was not simply about activism, about being more active, but about building a whole movement based on this strategy. Those orienting to this approach, including Indrakusuma, started to build a core of people working in this direction. This core building, based on seeking a tight consensus on political approaches and a certain level of discipline, came into direct conflict with the traditional form of organization among student activists, which was loose, informal and often relied on *pemimpin–anak buah* (leader–client follower) relationships.

It was a bitter split, with the group led by Indro Cahyono leveling all kinds of charges against Indrakusuma, including the red-baiting charge of having spent time with the leftist movement in the Philippines. In any case, after the split INFIGHT gradually receded into inactivity and SKEHPI gradually returned to become an established NGO working in traditional conservation spheres. FBB and YMB were essentially post-SKEHPI organizations, in that they both had adopted theoretical approaches, incorporating mass action as a central element of strategy. The crystallization of the organized *aksi* current as a party organization, the PRD, was connected to another split, this time in the YMB.

YMB was only a small organization, with between ten and thirty activists, mainly students, but one or two full-time workers as well. Most were students from the University of Indonesia. They had concentrated on political education and had published several issues of a magazine called *Cerita Kami* ("Our Stories"). *Cerita Kami* comprised mainly transcriptions of extended dialogues between factory workers and activists concerning worker conditions, often attempting to incorporate Marxist concepts of surplus value, exploitation and class into the dialogue. FBB was also comprised primarily of University of Indonesia students. In both cases they were mostly from history or literature faculties. Among the YMB activists were Danial Indrakusuma and Wilson who went on to become leaders of the PRD. YMB also included Hilmar Farid, who later emerged as the central figure in academic Marxism and the Jaringan Kerja Budaya (JKB) group. FBB members included Dita Indah Sari, "Wahyu" and several others, all of whom became early leaders of the PRD and of the first trade union connected with the PRD.

In January 1993, activists from YMB and FBB joined with others from similar groups in Yogyakarta and Surabaya to participate in a joint action with farmers in East Java, in the village of Blangguan. Farmers in the poor village of Blangguan were involved in a conflict with a local marine detachment which had begun in December 1992. The marine base wanted the farmers' land. They had even driven tanks into the village and flattened their houses and crops, mostly corn. Individual farmers had been approached and told not to plant their corn; others who had planted had their crops torn out. The farmers had decided to resist and had made contact with activists in Surabaya, who had then communicated with Jakarta and Yogyakarta. More than twenty FBB and YMB students from Jakarta and Yogyakarta headed to Blangguan. As the village was under tight surveillance, the activists were to infiltrate into the village by different routes during the evening and were to participate in a mass planting of the fields the next day.

But the farmers' huts were raided and most of the students captured. Others came out with the farmers and a head-on clash occurred. Around fifty villagers and students were arrested. Some students did escape through the fields and were able to make their way back to Jakarta. Those who were arrested were subjected to electric shock torture, beatings and having their heads submerged in the toilet bowl. This was the first time since 1965 that students had been subjected to torture. It was the Blangguan incident that provoked the split in the YMB.

Blangguan was a traumatic event. Activists slowly made their way back to Jakarta after being released from detention. None were ever charged with any crime. But some returned in shock. Torture was a new experience, not just for the individuals but for the movement itself, and especially for students. Some argued that the direct confrontation with the military was unwise, but a general issue arose. Was it premature to embark on a strategy of open mobilization in confrontation with the New Order? The YMB split and its members dispersed into a range of different activities. However, within a few years the pattern and character of the split had become clear. The pro-*aksi* activists, a minority, started to merge with the majority of FBB activists and other pro-*aksi* elements that were emerging from other splits in Yogyakarta, in particular from the

FKMY. Most of the others gravitated to the JKB, the center of the academic Marxist current.

One of the first organizational manifestations of this merging process was the formation of an underground group called the Front Pemuda Nasional (National Youth Front). *Progres* published an interview by an Australian journalist, Mike Carey, with a FPN spokesperson, in its March 1993 issue. This was the first publicly printed statement by the FPN. *Progres* also editorialized to welcome the formation of the FPN. The FPN spokesperson stated that its eventual goal was to establish socialism in Indonesia. It stated its medium-term goal as achieving a "multi-party political system." Answering a question about what the student movement had achieved, the FPN spokesperson answered:

> There are six doors to democracy that have been opened. First. issues of relevance to the *rakyat* have begun to grow in society. The old culture of silence is being broken down by the people. Now many people speak about the problems of the people. Second, there is a militancy among the people now. There are many, many mass actions now, both organised and unorganised. Third, the propaganda and agitation work of the students has succeeded; this is reflected in the wide recognition by the people of the bankruptcy of the government and the desire for an alternative. Fourth, the struggle has borne fruit already in the form of new alternative institutions and organisations that the regime cannot fully control. Fifth, there is a much greater sense among the people, workers and farmers, of their rights. Sixth, at the individual level there are more and more people, a majority now in the movement, who have come to more radical, alternative views.[16]

The FPN, in its 1993 or later forms, did not emerge into the public arena again. However, other new *aksi*-oriented organizations did emerge. These were the Students in Solidarity with Democracy in Indonsia (SSDI) and the Indonesian Labour Struggle Center (Pusat Perjuangan Buruh Indonesia—PPBI). It was the leaders and activists of the SSDI and PPBI who initiated the formation of the PRD in July 1994. SSDI and PPBI were joined by the National Peasants Union (STN—Serikat Tani Nasional) and the People's Art Workers Network (Jaringan Kerja Seni Rakyat). Even taken together, this PRD current was quite small, but its formation represented a new stage in the course of Indonesian political development. There was now an agent of conscious political intervention into the rising worker and peasant *aksi*, actually promoting *aksi* as a strategy. This agent had organization and ideology. The impact of its interventions was to accelerate the popular acceptance of *aksi* as a form of political struggle laying the ground for a more general radicalization of Indonesia politics.

Appendix: Manifesto of the People's Democratic Party

[This manifesto was issued on 22 July 1996 at a ceremony to announce the formation of the People's Democratic Party.]

There is no democracy in Indonesia. Democracy, meaning people's sovereignty, should be the basic principle and foundation for the formation of any state. As long as this sovereignty has not been given its rightful place in the political, economic and cultural life of a nation and people, history will continue to throw up resistance.

The state authority during the thirty years of Suharto has become an institution which shackles and obstructs the opportunity for the development of popular participation in the process of determining social and political life. Executive power has become enlarged, is oppressive, uncontrollable and overrides the authority of the legislature and the judiciary.

Oppression Under the New Order

The history of the Indonesian nation is actually the history of a people's struggle, a struggle famous for its tenacity in resisting all forms of exploitation and oppression with the aim of achieving humanism and peace. However, the coming to power of the New Order regime in 1965 has meant backward steps for Indonesian society when compared to Indonesian political life in the period of 1950–59. Basic rights of popular participation have been shackled, limited and cut off by the implementation of the five political laws and the dual function of the military (ABRI). The aim of independence, that is freedom to choose, to supervise and to determine the course of the political life of a country, has moved further and further away from everyday political life. Systematically, the authorities of the New Order regime dominate the political arena through brutal, cruel and unconstitutional methods. They do not value differences of opinion or criticism and do not want to hear the people's aspirations.

The rise of the people's resistance—that is of civilians—is greeted with intimidation, terror, arrests, jailing, bullets and even with slaughter. Newspapers, magazines, books and other tools of education which are critical and dare to differ from the point of view of the authorities are banned and closed down. Journalists who do not favor one-sided reporting of the government's point of view are sent to jail. The working class, who are economically oppressed, are intimidated, terrorized and even killed. Peasants find it increasingly difficult to keep their land and defend their rights, as they are confronted by the military when they resist capitalist encroachment into their land. All these authoritarian strategies are logically employed, implemented, enacted and maintained with one aim in mind, to ensure the stability of capital accumulation.

Economic Injustice

Till now, we have witnessed the widening of the gulf between the rich few and the poor majority. Workers are promoted by the Suharto dictatorship and sold cheaply to invite investment and capital accumulation for the rich. Indonesia's economic growth of more than 6 percent per annum is only enjoyed by a small minority group. Economic assets which are vital for the quality of life of the people are privatized with concessions traded amongst Suharto's cronies and their families. Monopolies and oligopolies that exploit the people are protected and facilitated by the powers that be. Economic hardship increases when the government is filled with corrupt people who are in collusion with bureaucrats working for private interests and their respective business groups. Imperialist organizations such as the World Bank and the International Monetary Fund continue to prop up its growth by pouring in millions in the form of foreign loans. As a result, Indonesia's foreign debt has now reached US$10 billion. This means that we occupy the third highest rung on the foreign debt ladder, beneath Brazil and Mexico.

Indonesian economic development, which benefits the few owners of capital, and exploitation by foreign investors in Indonesia, have resulted in a society which has become more brutal and further away from the aim of the people of reaching prosperity and justice.

The People Resist

After thirty years, eight months and twenty-two days of the New Order government, the Indonesian people can no longer accept and tolerate this government, economically, politically or socially. There are many examples that prove this: workers are striking in many industrial estates, peasants are actively resisting eviction, students are demonstrating against militarism, intellectuals resist attempts to stifle academic freedom, indigenous people in Kalimantan and West Papua are fighting back against Jakarta's exploitation. In East Timor, the Maubere people have never stopped fighting against the military invasion and occupation by the New Order. Forms of resistance taken up by the people continue to increase—from mass actions, where many sectors of the population work together, occupying Parliament, invading police and military headquarters, confronting the military—to mass production of leaflets. The essence is this: popular dissatisfaction is everywhere, the people are no longer content to live under the New Order regime. The socio-economic and political system that is now safeguarded by the regime has proven to be unable to articulate, let alone resolve, the concrete problem faced by the people.

The current system is bankrupt. This is the time for the five political laws to be repealed and the time for the military, currently sheltering under the dual function of ABRI doctrine, to return to the barracks.

Political Reforms

The package of five political laws is the government's justification for limiting the people's rights to political participation. The role of political parties as a channel for the people to become involved in politics, as the birthplace of popular sovereignty, needs to be established immediately. Fair and democratic elections, those which do not limit the participation and the political aspirations of people as given rights in a modern civil society, have never existed. The structure of the Upper and Lower Houses of Parliament reflect the tactics used by the regime to maintain power. Those belonging to cliques and the military have the special privileges of being appointed by Suharto and have never had to subject themselves to elections. Laws governing mass organizations do not allow them to have political affiliations and their formation is often obstructed. Lastly, laws governing referenda are such that they have never been enacted to decide important questions, for example the appropriateness of the 1945 Constitution given the changing socio-economic and political world context. Instead the constitution has become something sacred. People who are sovereign are people who can learn about and have the opportunity and the ability to understand their sovereignty and can understand their ability to engage in politics. If we are to achieve these aims, there is no alternative but to repeal the five political laws of 1985.

The military encroaches on civil life. In a modern society civilians who don't carry weapons should have absolute control over the military, turning the military into the "giant mute" (to borrow the French term *La Grande Muette*). Not one word on power or politics should be communicated through the barrel of a gun. Therefore, the people have to demand the repeal of the dual function of the ABRI doctrine.

The subordination of the New Order regime to the world capitalist system means that the Suharto government has been unable to escape from international scrutiny over the oppression which exists in this country. The fall of authoritarian regimes in Latin America, Africa and Asia has taught the regime and the democratic movement that no authoritarian power can last forever. Everything has its end, just as it has its beginning.

Oppose Neocolonialism: Self-determination for East Timor

Foreign economic policies should have an anti-neocolonial character, as opposed to the policies of agreements, such as those embodied in NAFTA, APEC and AFTA. International must abide by the principles of peace and humanism. For that reason, the end of the Indonesian occupation of East Timor has to be part of our political program, not merely of us extending solidarity, but of fighting alongside them for their right to determine their own destiny and to be independent. The Indonesian people's democratic struggle will not be complete and genuine unless it joins with the Maubere people's demand for independence. PRD opposes national chauvinism and considers internationalist links as the mainstay of the people's struggle. The

integrated nature of global capitalist power, with the support of governments who have no respect for democracy, necessitates an international
resistance. For that reason, PRD will actively support all international
forums and actions which are of a grassroots character and are opposed to
oppression.

The Way Forward

Efforts to resist the New Order's authoritarian nature cannot be separated
from the program of the PRD. As a political party, we feel we have the right
and the obligation to participate in the political process to determine social
and political life. The opposition to popular participation cannot be
allowed to continue. In the present conditions, people's sovereignty in
this system does not need legal and formal recognition from the authorities,
when they don't even value the active participation of people in scrutiniz-
ing and criticizing it. The problems in Indonesia that are brought on by
capitalism need to be resolved. This has to come about through wider
involvement of the people, through democratic participation. The many
forces that are capable of bringing about political improvement need to
unite their programs and activities immediately to form a popular democratic government based on the grassroots.

A government that is democratic and people-oriented needs to have a
clear vision for the future for the Indonesian people. It needs to have a clear
vision of the way out of the economic, social and political problems we
have, problems which have existed for thirty years, eight months and
twenty days. To achieve clarity in direction towards a democratic society,
we need to seek the forces from the people, who have the strength to push
towards this goal. Because of this, questions of strategy and tactics need to
be formulated based on the potential existing inside the people themselves.
Of all the potential present, we see the resistance put up by workers as the
most significant force that will be harnessed and organized into the
democratic struggle. Their increasing numbers, their continuing fight back
and their strategic position in the capitalist system of the New Order will
make the working class a stronghold for democracy now and in the future.
The second strength we see is that of students and intellectuals. This social
layer have become the pioneers in the political resistance against the New
Order. Their ideological, organizational and political ability are important

contributions to the democratic struggle. The adventurism of the students' movement, and the resulting loss of power of organized students, can only be avoided if it is linked in with the people's democratic struggle as a whole. The third proven force that is still continuing to develop is the urban poor. Their increasing numbers and marginalized state as a result of the attractiveness of the city and the uneven development between city and countryside form the basis of the urban masses.

In actions supporting Megawati, we can see how this sector militantly and tenaciously defended their rights. The last sector that is also important is the peasant sector. Brutal capitalism has impoverished them and robbed them of their land which is their means of subsistence. It is not surprising that it is this sector, spread throughout Indonesia in large numbers, which will be an important supporting force in the democratic movement.

To unify and mobilize the existing democratic forces, a common platform is necessary, one from which we can act in unity. It is not enough for unity in action to be represented by a common program and method, it needs also to have the ability to decipher the political situation in order to force the widening of popular participation. For the sake of that momentum, we need to respond to and anticipate [the effects of] the general elections in 1997. The elections will be a time when mass consciousness will be focused on politics, a time featuring mass mobilizations by the contestants. The democratic movement must monitor this mass consciousness, so that it can intervene and contribute towards the raising of people's awareness about the political motives of the New Order. We should not isolate ourselves from the consciousness of the masses, much less to look down upon it. We have an opportunity to take advantage of the coming elections. A tool for organizing and broadening the opposition networks and taking advantage of the elections is provided through the formation of KIPP [independent election monitoring committee].

KIPP is intended not only for monitoring the elections but to assist in raising the consciousness of the people around their daily problems. KIPP has already become popular. Because of that, we expect that KIPP can break the illusions of the masses and can be used to campaign to educate and mobilize the people to say that the issue of elections is related to the issue of people's sovereignty. This sovereignty will always be related to the five political laws of 1985 and the dual function of ABRI. That is where

KIPP should be anchored. KIPP should not just be a concept merely for the monitoring of the election process from voter registration to vote counting. Instead, it should monitor how far popular sovereignty is being taken into account in the election in order to assess its legitimacy.

United Front

The most important and urgent step that must be taken is to create a united front based on a common platform to reach strategic aims ultimately designed to achieve popular sovereignty. These strategic aims would include the repeal of the five political laws and the dual function of ABRI. This front must have its roots deeply in the masses or it cannot exist and will never grow strong. Because of this, the type of organizations inside a front must be at the level of political parties or mass organizations. A front for struggle that is serious and genuine must have programs, tactics and strategies and slogans that are based in the masses. A front is a body to mobilize the masses, not a vehicle for campaigning on political issues. Previously we had not realized the meaning of "political front" and could not differentiate between an "action committee" and a "political front." In future, we need to build a democratic political front and this needs to be done as soon as possible.

There is no point maintaining the existence of an organization if it cannot understand and resolve the strategic issues under the New Order. PRD considers that a front that is structurally supported by the masses needs to be built. As long as these mass "pockets" have not been mobilized into the democratic struggle, this front will be incapable of confronting the militaristic and domineering power of the New Order. With all the problems of Indonesian society we have looked at above, we should also be able to envisage and articulate what a future democratic society might look like. PRD considers that it is more important to come up with political solutions to ease the way towards economic solutions for the problems of an Indonesia that has been exploited in a wholesale manner under capitalism. PRD sees that it is important in the future to build a modern civil society that respects popular sovereignty and institutionalizes democratic practices with their own legislative, executive and judicial structures. The structures of true democracy must be subservient to the sovereignty of the people. For that reason, a popular democratic coalition government must be created for the future, in order to channel the aspirations of the people. This channeling of aspirations needs to be able to respect various ideologies and their respective methods without military intervention.

The development of a modern civil society in Indonesia that is based on popular sovereignty will depend on how we build a democratic movement now. Strategy and tactics need to be formulated now with the concrete state of the people in mind. Because of that, PRD believes and is confident that the organizing of the masses is the only way to bring about popular sovereignty. The founding of the PRD is one manifestation of and an answer to the dysfunction of extra-parliamentary institutions. Its formation also aims to provide a clear goal for the people's struggle, towards a multiparty and peace-loving popular democratic society.

Jakarta, 22 July 1996

6

Aksi

The "floating mass" policy of the New Order gave a special character to the whole of the political life of Indonesian society: disorganization, de-organization. The 1980s was the decade of student discussion groups, NGO critiques and, in the late 1980s, the beginning of more spontaneous protest actions as well as the beginning of the formation of a conscious political current promoting mass action as a current. It was also the period during which Central Java was hit with scores of riots when hundreds of buildings and shops were set alight or destroyed in scores of towns. The "floating mass" never really did simply float. A political life—atomized and without any national format or vehicles—always continued. This was fostered by the impact of the *rakyat* sentiment, especially in the media, which continued to report the real life of the ordinary people, including their restlessness, in the pages of the tabloid press.

The period 1988–94 was a period in which the political atmosphere radicalized quickly. The de-organized character of political life can disguise this fact. There was not the rise of a big, well-organized mass movement under a single or a few banners, nor the emergence of any powerful new political figures. Instead, there were hundreds, perhaps thousands, of small protest actions, scattered around the country. There was much organization and many organizations, it was just that they were almost all ad hoc. The populist sentiment around the idea of the *rakyat* never dissipated. There was also by then a new group, small but with activists in several cities, agitating for the people to get rid of Suharto using mass protest.

There was an incipient radicalization of political discourse as the ideas of the NGOs, students and critical artists crept into the media, often indirectly. Critical and populist lyrics crept into pop culture. Two of the most popular musical groups with millions of youthful fans, one around the singer Iwan Fals and another the group Slank, incorporated sentiments of dissent as early as the late 1980s. Probably Iwan Fals' most famous stanza is that from the immensely popular song, "Bongkar" ("Tear apart").

> Oppression and arbitrary rule
> Too much of it, too much to be able to describe it all
> Hoi! stop it, stop it now
> We are fed up with this uncertainty and greed
> We hoist our ideals on the streets
> because at home there is no one we can trust!

The dis- and de-organized character of all this politicization, the fact that it did not manifest itself in permanent organizational form—in big parties, trade unions or political movements—meant that the depth of radicalization taking place was often underestimated. In many ways, by 1994 there was already an incipient radicalization everywhere. This was very vividly shown when a new variant on the MALARI demonstration-plus-riot syndrome occurred in Sumatra's biggest city, Medan, in April 1994. On 14 April, 20,000 workers from twenty-four factories went on strike and held a peaceful demonstration in the Deli Serdang industrial zone of the city. The strikes were held in response to the discovery of the body of a leader of an earlier strike floating in the river. The striking workers organized a long march from the industrial zone into the city where they rallied at the Labor Ministry and Governor's office. Later in the day, after the rallies at these sites, when the marches were heading towards a major thoroughfare in Medan, military anti-riot troops attacked the demonstrators. The workers fought back and the street fights broadened into general rioting. Further demonstrations of several thousand people took place again on 18 April while smaller strikes, clashes with the security apparatus and rioting continued to flare up throughout the city and the industrial zone for more than a week. One of the demands being raised by the demonstrators—apart from an investigation into the death of the strike leader, Rusli—was for the right of the workers to join a newly established independent trade union, the SBSI. As a result, both local and national leaders of the SBSI, including its national chairperson, Mochtar Pakpahan, were arrested, tried and gaoled.[1]

In 1999 a team of researchers from the Yayasan Insan Politika (YIP), some of whom were also academicians in the Academy of Social Sciences, gathered material from newspapers to try to get a picture of just how much *aksi* activity, in particular student demonstrations, had taken place between 1989 and 1998.[2] It was a limited survey using only a few, mainly Jakarta- or Java-centric, newspapers. All the same, they were able to issue a three-volume listing, rich in data.

Their data list between thirty and forty student protest actions, mainly in Jakarta and Java, each year between 1989 and 1992. Strikes and peasants' actions are not covered, although the 1989 data do include several actions by students in solidarity with the farmers of Kedung Ombo. Issues ranged from campus democracy, solidarity with peasants and workers, protest over the arrest of activists for distributing the books of Pramoedya Ananta Toer, protest over demolition of heritage buildings, the first Iraq war, press freedom, school fees and many others. The thirty to forty protests for each year that the listing gives was just a sampling of the protests occurring at the time.

After 1992, their sampling shows a sudden increase in the number of protests. In 1993, it gave 71; in 1994, it gave 111; in 1995, it (probably inaccurately) shows a drop to 55;[3] then in 1996, up to 143; and in 1997, it listed 154 protests. Again these were very limited samplings from a few newspapers, and they still excluded worker and farmer protests, as well as many of the protests in 1996 by members of the Indonesian Democratic Party (PDI) in revolt against Suharto's refusal to recognize Megawati Soekarnoputri as chairperson of the PDI. For most of the period after 1992, protest actions of one kind or another were happening almost every day, somewhere or other in the country. Newspaper coverage, activist bulletins and word of mouth meant that the sense of protest was spreading everywhere. Still, these actions were mostly local, spontaneous initiatives. The YIP listing gives, wherever possible, the name of the organizations connected with the protest actions. All the data for the almost 800 protest actions listed show that the vast majority were organized by ad hoc, impermanent organizations reacting to local issues and conditions. There was only one organization or network that appeared repeatedly, and in different cities, and that was the SSDI (later called SMID[4] when it took an Indonesian-language name) and the rest of the network associated with the PRD.

There was a stiffening of repression starting at the end of 1993. In December 1993, twenty-one students from FAMI were arrested in Bandung during a demonstration demanding that Suharto be put on trial by a special session of the People's Consultative Assembly. Then in June 1994, following a three-year period of relative tolerance of political criticism of the regime in the media, three major weekly news magazines, including the leading *Tempo* and the hugely successful *Detik*, were closed down. This represented a major clampdown and shocked many people, especially those in the NGOs and the media. Students and journalists held several actions to protest the closures but were met with violent dispersals. There was a general hardening of regime statements against opposition. In March 1995, Tri Agus Susanto, a founding member of the activist group PIJAR, was arrested and imprisoned for publishing material campaigning against the clampdown. There can be little doubt that this hardening was itself a reaction to the increasing combativeness of the de-organized "floating mass." The PRD decided to confront the repression with a radicalization of its actions.

The first action was one of the biggest worker demonstrations organized since 1965, mobilizing around 10,000 workers. The PPBI activists, including Dita Sari (ex-FBB) and Wilson (ex-YMB), had forged contacts with workers at the Great River garments factory as early as 1991, when there had already been some strike activity. In 1995 conditions had still not improved at the factory, which produced Triumph women's underwear as well as men's shirts with the brand names Arrow, Kenzo and others. The owners in 1995 were Abdul Latief, the Minister of Labor and retired Admiral Sudomo, a previous Minister of Labor. This was the first large-scale, open mobilization where banners appeared declaring a worker–student alliance. It is perhaps worth reproducing the *kronologi* that the activists issued at the time.

Chronology Great River Industries strike, 18 July action.
06.00–0700 hrs
Students and workers began arriving at the Great River Industries Pty Ltd factory at Bogor. The factory security units were waiting ready.
07.00
Posters, banners, headbands were readied under the direction of the field commander. The military arrived and came in amongst the masses. The posters read:

"SPSI: where is your devotion to us?"

"We want to live decently."

"Lower prices, increase wages, freedom to organise."

"GRI shirts are luxuries, our wages are cheap."

"7000 ok, PPBI Yes."

The main banner was unfurled which read: "Worker–Student Alliance: PPBI–SMID"). This was followed by speeches by representatives of SMID and PPBI.

07.42

One truckload and three hardtop landrovers full of military police arrived and approached the crowd.

08.00

Speeches continued by PPBI and SMID representatives from the factory bridge. The crowd was then about 6000. Soon afterwards, representatives from the Department of Labor and the SPSI (Serikat Pekerja Seluruh Indonesia—All Indonesia Workers Union) arrived and began to appeal to the workers. But when SPSI representatives spoke they were met with shouts from the workers of "SPSI is impotent" and "You take bribes!"

08.30

The field leader gave directions for the worker comrades to tighten their ranks. The aim was to march in formation from the factory to the Bogor Regional Council of Representatives (Provincial Parliament).

08.45

The workers, now about 13000 and mostly women, moved off towards Bogor about 6 kilometers away. As the demonstration was now so large, it was divided into two columns on either side of the road. About 50 military aided by several score of plain clothes intelligence operatives began harassing the marchers, especially those on the eastern side. Many on the eastern side ran across to join their comrades on the western side. Military vehicles also began pushing workers to the edge of the road. The marchers sang songs of struggle and chanted slogans.

10.15

The marches reached the Provincial Parliament which was blockaded by the anti-riot squad which was armed with canes. They also had two fire engines. However, the marches got through the blockade and entered the parliament grounds. The same troops established another blockade inside, reinforced by a further company of anti-riot troops.

10.17

Because the masses defied the blockade and entered inside the grounds, the military brutally seized six participants in the action. These were Dita Sari (Secretary-General, PPBI), Kelik (Central Council, SMID), Lukman (Central Council PPBI), Haryo (SMID Jakarta), Margiyono (SMID Yogya), Akbar (SMID Semarang) and Sandy (SMID Yogya). Several of those detained were injured in the process of arrest. The military also seized the megaphone and banner.

10.25

The masses maintained their own blockade. The military attacked a worker (Edi, from the cutting section) injuring his head, which was covered in blood.

10.30

The worker comrades began handing out a leaflet entitled "Great River Industry shirts are luxurious, our wages are cheap."

10.50

The military became increasingly brutal, attacking and hitting the demonstrators, dispersing the demonstration. While demonstration marshals were handing out bottled water to the demonstrators, two boxes were seized by the military who began drinking it and using it to wash their faces. Meanwhile the dispersed crowd reformed and shifted to the main square.

11.00

The demonstration formed marching lines on the road as all negotiations had failed. Meanwhile the military had also occupied the main square.

11.05

The workers began marching home. At the same time, the military continued provocation and harassments.

11.20

The demonstration left the vicinity of the parliament in order.

11.30

As the main body of the demonstration marched off, several students and workers were still at or near the main square. At that point the military attacked Nasrul, who was kicked and stamped upon. Several worker comrades began screaming hysterically and shouting insults at the military. The military turned upon them and detained a worker comrade, Nuraini.

11.55

The demonstration left the area and marched home. At the time of this report, the detainees are in two groups. Seven students have been taken to Bogor police headquarters, while the Great River Industry workers have been detained to be forced to negotiate with the Department of Labor, SPSI management and parliament members.

At the moment, those detained are:

Dita Sari (Secretary-General, PPBI),
Kelik Ismunanto (Central Council, SMID),
Lukman (Central Council PPBI),
Haryo (SMID Jakarta),
Margiyono (SMID Yogya),
Akbar (SMID Semarang),
Sandy (SMID Yogya),
Nasrul (PPBI),
Nuraini (GRI Pty Ltd worker),
Umi (GRI Pty Ltd worker).

(Chronology attached to press release
issued by YLBHI, 19 July 1995.)[5]

The activists and workers were released the next day but were formally charged in August.

The strike lasted three days and the workers and students launched other protests outside the factory compound in addition to the march to the regional parliament. This included a picket and occupation of the lobby of the Ministry of Labor by about 250 students. They were also dispersed with violence and more were arrested. The chronology travelled widely through email and the strike was reported in the media.

The Great River strike, a milestone in the history of the movement, is not recorded in the YIP list. The YIP researchers seemed to rely on just one Central Java newspaper for data on actions during June and September 1995 and only occasionally included worker actions. In November, the list records a 3,000-strong strike in the medium-sized East Javanese town of

Jombang, involving factory workers, university students and students from religious schools. Three hundred university students occupied the Ministry of Labor's office. Three students were arrested and charged with spreading lies. YIP also recorded a demonstration of 1,000 students on a Yogyakarta campus where students and military clashed.

A second PRD initiative was astounding, given the political conditions in Indonesia and was clearly meant to increase the level of defiance of the regime. Since 1975, one of the most sensitive and taboo issues in Indonesia had been Suharto's decision in 1975 to invade and occupy East Timor. The East Timorese themselves had launched a revival of their own mass action campaign with demonstrations during the papal visit to East Timor in 1990 and then in Dili in December 1991. The December 1991 demonstration was attacked by Indonesian military and hundreds were killed. After this act of repression, the center of the Timorese *aksi* campaign shifted to Jakarta in the form of occupations by Timorese youths of foreign embassies. The Timorese youths would normally seek asylum overseas. The campaign of embassy occupations served to help internationalize the issue of the occupation in Europe and North America. Up until 1995, very few Indonesians had spoken out against the invasion. The PRD's founding congress in 1994 had declared its support for an act of self-determination and another student organization, PIJAR, had also expressed its solidarity with the East Timorese.

Then, on Human Rights Day, 10 December 1995, the PRD launched the first ever high-profile protest action in support of East Timorese self-determination.[6] Furthermore, the action was carried out jointly with East Timorese activists. More than 100 members of the PRD, including SMID and PPBI, joined with a similar number of East Timorese activists to occupy the Dutch and the Russian embassy compounds. The media had been alerted. The action was a direct affront to the regime and it retaliated by mobilizing "pro-Jakarta supporters" who demonstrated outside the Dutch Embassy. Then, in contempt of all diplomatic conventions, they climbed over the fence into the compound and attacked the PRD and East Timorese activists, as well as the Dutch Embassy staff. The Dutch Ambassador himself suffered an injury to the head. After negotiations between the embassies and the Indonesian government, the activists were allowed to leave the embassy without being arrested. They immediately went into hiding, although one PRD leader, Petrus Haryanto, was later picked up at a medical clinic where he was being treated for wounds, detained and terrorized for several days.

Aksi involving various ad hoc groupings—though with at least one PRD member or PRD-influenced activist present[7]—continued to be organized around a broad range of issues. The YIP list, using just five of the scores of Indonesian dailies, gives three for January 1996; ten in February 1996 in six cities in Java, Sumatra and Bali; and thirty-two actions in March in twelve different cities in Java, Sumatra and Sulawesi. Then on 23 April 1996, *aksi* exploded onto the front pages of the newspapers as the 1974 MALARI pattern of student demonstration and urban rioting resurfaced. A student demonstration in Ujung Pandang, the provincial capital city of South Sulawesi, over increases in public transport costs imposed by the provincial government turned into a riot.[8] The next day a follow-up demonstration by students from at least three campuses turned into a clash with the military and police and was also accompanied by widespread rioting throughout the city. Six university students were shot dead and more than 100 injured. Thirty-five were arrested and charged.

On 26 April, 10,000 students held a demonstration demanding the lowering of the public transport prices, the dissolution of extra-legal repressive institutions and the end of military violence. The Governor eventually revoked the price rise.

The YIP list then notes forty-eight actions during May, more than half of which were protest actions over the violence in Ujung Pandang. During May these listed actions, based on just six newspapers, took place in Bandung, Jember, Jakarta, Semarang, Solo, Surabaya, Yogyakarta, Salatiga, Purwokerto—all on the island of Java—and Medan, Padang, Pekanbaru, Lampung and Palembang in Sumatra as well as in Ujung Pandang itself.

In the aftermath of the arrest of PRD leaders in 1996, a human rights organization in the USA collated a chronology of such protests organized specifically by the PRD. The list read as follows:

April 17, 1995, Medan: Students demonstrate at the local parliament (DPRD) against President Suharto's statement that protesters who confronted him on his state visit to Germany earlier that month were "crazy, fanatic." Ten of the demonstrators are subsequently arrested, nine from Medan and one, the SMID national coordinator for international relations, from Yogyakarta.

April 25, 1995, Yogyakarta: Some 300 students gathered near Gajah Mada University, to protest the arrest and beating of their colleagues in Medan. Andi Arief, then head of SMID-Yogyakarta, appears and says the "crazy fanatics" are the corrupt military. The protest is broken up by the district military command.

May 1, 1995, Jakarta: PPBI and SMID activists, led by Dita Sari (head of PPBI), lead several dozen workers and students to the Ministry of Labor as part of the commemoration of International Labour Day. They demand a minimum daily wage of 7,000 Rupiah (US$3.50), an end to corruption, the right to organize, an end to military intervention in labor disputes, and freedom for labor leader Muchtar Pakpahan (previously arrested in 1994 in connection with labor demonstrations in Medan). Five people are arrested and later released, including Dita Sari, Nasrul (PPBI-Bogor), Fitri (PPBI-Tangerang), Ruchiat (PPBI-Cakung, North Jakarta), and Wignyo, (PPBI-KBN Industrial Estate, North Jakarta).

May 1, 1995, Semarang: Some 400 students and workers gathered at Diponegoro University in Semarang for International Labour Day and try to march toward the Central Java governor's office. Police and military block their way, clashes take place, and sixteen students are arrested and briefly held, including Petrus Haryanto, the general secretary of SMID, and Lukman, national director for PPBI. Garda Sembiring, of SMID-Jakarta, is also arrested. The demonstrators carry banners in English reading "Demand Minimum Wage" and "Militarism Go to Hell."

July 18, 1995, Bogor: PPBI and SMID activists organize 13,000 workers from PT Great River Industries, a garment factory that produces Triumph underwear and Arrow and Kenzo shirts and that is partly owned by Indonesian Minister of Labor Abdul Latief and former coordinating minister for politics and security, Admiral Sudomo. As the workers marched toward the Bogor parliament, demanding a minimum wage of 7,000 Rupiah, menstrual leave for women workers and an end to the government-controlled union, SPSI, the military set up a blockade to prevent them from going inside the grounds of the parliament building. Six activists, who had broken through the blockade, were arrested, including Dita Sari and Lukman of PPBI, and five SMID activists from Yogyakarta, Semarang and Jakarta. They were held briefly and released.

December 7, 1995, Jakarta: SMID and PRD activists join East Timorese students in the occupation of the Dutch and Russian embassies to protest Indonesia's occupation of the former Portuguese colony.

December 11, 1995, Solo: Some 14,000 workers take part in a strike and rally organized by PPBI at Sritex textile factory (PT Sri Rejeki Isman) in which President Suharto's eldest daughter, Tutut, and Minister of Information Harmoko are both shareholders. Among other things, the factory makes Golkar uniforms and shirts. Fifteen PRD organizers are arrested by the military just before the program for the rally begins on the grounds that they did not bring their identity cards. Among them are Garda Sembiring, Herman of PRD-Surabaya, and Kelik Ismunanto of PRD-Jakarta. Edy of PRD-Solo leads the workers on a march to the local parliament where they demand the minimum wage with a separate food allowance, a monthly paycheck calculated on thirty rather than twenty-six days, menstrual leave for women workers and an end to the system of setting production targets.

February 5, 1996, Menado: Activists of SMID-Menado and the Indonesian Peasants Union (Serikat Tani Indonesia), an affiliate of PRD, help organize a rally for peasants from the village of Kaneyan, Minahasa, North Sulawesi, who are protesting the construction of high-voltage power lines across their land. The protest has been going on since late 1994 and both the police and the village head have told peasants that opponents of the project will be considered "obstructors of development" and communists.

March 11, 1996, Jakarta: Fifty students from the industrial area outside Jakarta SMID (SMID-Jabotabek) led by Buyung H. march to the Ministry of Labor to demand free and fair elections and hold an "open forum" in front of the ministry. Garda Sembiring reads their demands for repeal of five 1985 laws that restrict democracy. The demonstration is peaceful.

March 23, 1996, Solo: Meeting of KIPP, Solo, led by students from Serikat Rakyat Surakarta, an affiliate of KIPP [and PRD], broken up by the subdistrict military command.

March 26, 1996, Lampung: Establishment of KIPP-Lampung, with executive committee composed of SMID, Forum Diskusi Mahasiswa-Lampung (Student Discussion Forum), LBH-Lampung, SBSI, and various Protestant and Sukarnoist student groups. Bambang Ekalaya, coordinator for KIPP-Lampung [and SMID leader], arrested and interrogated for nine hours at the regional military command (Korem 043) following the opening of the meeting.

April 25, 1996, Pemalang: Over 100 students organized by the Indonesian People who Support Megawati (Masyarakat Indonesia Pedukung Megawati) and PRD hold an "open forum" to discuss democracy, election-monitoring and events in Ujung Pandang. Twenty-three students are briefly detained.

April 22–26, 1996, Ujung Pandang: Demonstrations to protest increase in transportation fares. The first, on April 22, was coordinated by the Student Pro-Democracy Alliance (Aliansi Mahasiswa Pro-Demokrasi) with one group marching to the local parliament and another to the office of the governor of South Sulawesi. Both took place without incident. On April 23, the demonstrations grew in size, and riot police were out in force. On April 24 the first violence took place, with several minibuses being overturned. Security forces then began striking out at students and lecturers alike. By the end of the day, armoured personnel carriers enter the campus of Universitas Muslim Indonesia and troops storm the campus. At least three students die, according to officials, from drowning after jumping into the river to escape the army. More than 100 are wounded. The next day was even more violent, with students from virtually every college and university in the city involved. Following the army action, demonstrations in sympathy for those killed and wounded erupted all over Java and Sumatra. [Members of a preparatory committee for SMID participated.]

May 2, 1996, Solo: SMID-Solo organizes demonstration to protest Ujung Pandang in front of the literature faculty of Universitas Sebelas Maret (March 11 University.) Demonstrators are blocked by three trucks of KOSTRAD troops and one from the district military command. SMID leaders urge marchers to defy them. Some fifteen people are detained briefly, including Prijo Wasono, head of SMID-Solo and Dadang Kosasih, of the latter's advocacy bureau.

May 8, 1996, Yogyakarta: SMID-Yogyakarta organizes march and demonstration in solidarity for those killed in Ujung Pandang.

May 9, 1996, Bogor: PPBI helps organize a work stoppage at PT Indo Shoes in the industrial zone in Citeureup, Bogor. More than 7,000 workers take part.

May 14, 1996, Yogyakarta: Bigger demonstration to protest Ujung Pandang deaths organized by SMID-Yogyakarta. Participants estimate that marchers grew from 120 people to some 900, demanding an end to repressive military actions, such as those in Aceh (1989–91), Lampung (1989), East Timor, Tanjung Priok (1984), Nipah (1993), and Timika (1996). Yanti, a SMID-Semarang leader, reminds people that they have no political rights. The marchers head for the Yogyakarta parliament, but the military blocks their way. The SMID leaders decide on confrontation; several are wounded in clashes and taken to local hospitals.

June 14, 1996, Semarang: A rally of over 100 PDI representatives and activists from PRD-Semarang to support the candidacy of Megawati takes place in front of the literature faculty of Diponegoro University.

June 17, 1996, Surabaya: Close to 1,000 supporters of Megawati from PDI and PRD calling themselves the Megawati Supporters Front march in the streets.

June 17, 1996, Yogyakarta: Hundreds of SMID and PRD activists have a pro-Megawati demonstration.

June 18, 1996, Salatiga: Hundreds of students organized by PRD call for the end of the military's "dual function" [political-military role], the repeal of five 1985 laws regulating politics and support for Megawati. Demonstrators occupy the local parliament until almost midnight.

June 18–19, 1996, Jakarta: Some 5,000 workers from PT Indo Shoes, PT Ganda Guna and PT Kingstone, organized by PRD and PPBI, hold a rally at the national parliament building. Budiman Sujatmiko of PRD gives a speech about how important it is for workers to have their own party so that they can pursue the struggle for their economic and political rights. He asks them to support Megawati Sukarnoputri. Dita Sari of PPBI urges them to make political demands and fight oppression. A delegation of workers and

PRD/PPBI is received by four representatives of the Indonesian Democratic Party (PDI) including Sabam Sirait, Marcel Bleding and Aberson. Police and army try to arrest some of the workers as they come out. Garda Sembiring of PRD is beaten. Many of the workers are brought back to Bogor by the mobile police brigade in trucks. The work stoppage at PT Indo Shoes continues the next day.

June 19–20, 1996, Jakarta: A pro-Megawati demonstration organized by an alliance of different groups, including the PRD, starts with about 4,000 people on June 19 and builds to some 15,000 people by the next day. The marchers tried to move from the National Monument in the center of the city to PDI headquarters but were stopped at the Gambir train station by police and military. Four people were reported to have died and dozens were injured when demonstrators and security forces clashed.

June 21, 1996, Lampung: 350 people gather in Lampung for a pro-Megawati demonstration, broken up by military.

July 8, 1996, Surabaya: An estimated 20,000 workers from ten factories march on the streets of Surabaya demanding the minimum wage. Twenty-four activists from PPBI are arrested and brought to metropolitan Surabaya police headquarters; all but two, Dita Sari of PPBI and Coen Hussein Pontoh, are released. Those two are charged under article 160 of the criminal code with "incitement to violence." Others are arrested later for involvement in the same incident.[9]

Soekarnoputri Conjuncture

Even the modest data from the YIP list show the dramatic increase in protest actions from 1989 onwards. This was met with more arrests, the banning of major news weeklies and the ending of all media liberalization and the steady increase in the use of violence in dealing with the protests, including torture, kidnappings (such as that of Petrus Haryanto) and the firing with live bullets on demonstrators. The regime's political crisis was well and truly developing. The crisis was developing separately from another front of trouble for the Suharto regime, namely, its inability to continue to keep one of its previously tame parties under its control, the Indonesian Democratic Party (PDI).[10]

After June 1996, there was a fusion, for almost a year, of the protest movement that had developed since 1989 and political protest around Suharto's moves to regain control over the PDI. But it should be noted that before June 1996, the issue of the PDI had not featured in any protest actions anywhere. The conflict between the PDI leadership and the Suharto regime had not been a factor driving the protest movement—it had, until June 1996, just been background noise.

The conflict between the PDI leadership and Suharto had been brewing for some time. The PDI, a fusion of the old (but purged) PNI and various Christian and other small parties, was one of the three parties permitted under Suharto's electoral and political party laws, the other two being GOLKAR, Suharto's own party, and the United Development Party, a fusion of some Islamic parties. It is not clear exactly when or how, but at some point in the mid- to late 1980s processes began within the PDI oriented towards asserting some independence from the regime. In 1987 Megawati Soekarnoputri was approached to become an election candidate, presumably by the new PDI leadership under Soerjadi. Soerjadi, apparently encouraged by rivals of Suharto from among his former officials, also sought to recruit other relatively high-profile personalities, such as the film star Sophan Sophian, the economist Kwik Kian Gie and the banker Laksamana Sukardi. All of these figures represented a layer of businessmen and celebrities who were already wealthy and relatively independent of the Suharto franchise machine. However, the PDI had long lost most of its old PNI membership base. They had been purged or frightened away after the massacres of the majority left leadership and activists in 1965. The PNI's pathetic state was shown when it only scored 6.9 percent in the 1972 elections.

Megawati's recruitment as an election candidate for the 1987 election campaign and her repeat participation in 1992 served to revive a mass base for the PDI—at least on a temporary basis. She attracted hundreds of thousands of people to her rallies outside Jakarta and up to 3 million people at rallies in Jakarta in 1992. As she traveled through the country, although espousing only the most abstract of policy visions, the PDI started to recruit again, especially at the local level. Soerjadi started appointing local party commissioners—and not party branches—to get around the "floating mass" legislation. It appears that this period helped revive very old PNI networks among the country's poorer layers of the middle class and bourgeoisie. Ed Aspinall describes this aspect:

To account for the strength of Megawati's challenge, therefore, it is necessary to look beyond formal politics, toward an array of more humble informal networks and patterns of organization which assisted to maintain the tenacity of the old Sukarnoist mass base. For example, many members of the old PNI and its affiliates, right through to the 1990s, remained organized in arisan groups (a kind of communal money-saving). Former PNI members used arisan meetings to maintain group cohesion and facilitate political discussion and communication. In former PNI base areas, like Central and East Java, supporters of the old party similarly regularly gathered for slametan (thanksgiving feasts) on auspicious dates, such as the anniversaries of the birth and death of Sukarno. Such practices remained widespread: according to one participant in 1993, there were as many as fifty PNI-oriented arisan groups operating in the Jakarta area alone. Networks mediated by informal community leaders—small business-people, Javanese mystics, martial arts teachers, artists and the like—similarly assisted in maintaining the party's coherence at the local level. Nationalist or PDI-aligned *preman*, semi-criminal elements, played a role in mobilizing young people for PDI rallies in the cities. Many former civil servants retained emotional attachments to old PNI symbols and networks. From the late 1980s there were numerous reports of retired village heads, ABRI officers and other officials returning to the PDI fold.[11]

Aspinall also gives a good sense of the kind of less organized support base Megawati's PDI attracted at election time:

The mass support base of the party, who supplied the crowds at the party's 1987 and 1992 elections rallies, were from even more humble origins. These were the petty traders, owners of small "kiosks," un- or under-employed youth and the myriad others who constituted the urban informal sector. Many were not particularly attached to the PDI but were simply looking for an avenue to protest.[12]

The conflict between Suharto and Megawati developed into confrontation in June 1996, when the government decided to recognize a PDI congress organized by an anti-Megawati, pro-regime faction. They thus moved to withdraw legal recognition of the Megawati PDI, outlawing her from the formal political system. She and her supporters refused to accept this and maintained their stand that her leadership and her PDI were the legitimate parties. This was a level of defiance from within the formal system which had never been reached before.

This happened in the direct aftermath of the Ujung Pandang demonstrations and the escalation in protest actions throughout the country. The momentum of the protest movement which had been underway since 1989 and a new momentum brought into play by this confrontation merged. Beginning on 14 June in Semarang, protest actions against Suharto's refusal to recognize Megawati's leadership began. There followed actions in Surabaya and Yogyakarta on 17 June, in Salatiga on 18 June, in Jakarta on 19 June of about 4,000 people and then the largest action of 15,000 people in Jakarta on 20 June. All of these actions up until 19 June were joint actions of the PDI and PRD, where the banners of both parties were prominent. The 20 June action was organized by a broader coalition of organizations. The demonstration made its way towards Monas from the PDI headquarters, but was intercepted at Gambir station by the military that beat the crowds with rattan batons, kicked them and pelted them with stones. An army tank also drove into the crowd. Five people were killed and around seventy seriously injured. About fifty people were arrested and taken to the nearest offices of the Army's Strategic Command Headquarters.

There were more protest actions the next day in Jakarta as well as other cities around the country, including a large demonstration by the group ALDERA, in Bandung, which was also attacked by troops. In Yogyakarta on 25 June, a demonstration of 7,000 people broke through a military blockade outside the Gajah Mada University campus and made its way to the local parliament. In Jakarta, on 28 June, 3,000 rallied at the national parliament in support of Megawati. On 12 July, 5,000 rallied at the Proclamation Memorial in Jakarta.

The merging of the two momentums, however, did not mean that the mobilization of workers and other sectors around separate issues stopped. Demonstrations protesting over the violence in Ujung Pandang continued through June. The YIP list also notes demonstrations against university fees, corruption in the Indonesian Development Bank and the mysterious escape from prison of a corrupt state oil company official.

In addition, on 18 June—one day before the protests against Suharto's moves against Megawati began in Jakarta—the PRD organized a demonstration of 2,000 workers from Indoshoes Pty Ltd, a company based just outside Jakarta. The 2,000 workers went on strike and came to Jakarta to rally outside the national parliament building, where they were joined by about 3,000 other workers and students. Three thousand of the workers returned to the national parliament the next day but this time they were blocked from entering the parliamentary complex by a military blockade. They then marched to the Ministry of Labor.

Just two weeks later, on 10 July, between 10,000 and 20,000 workers from ten factories in one of the industrial areas of Surabaya went on strike and demonstrated, engaging in running street fights with the military. Scores were injured and more than twenty detained, including two PPBI leaders, Dita Sari and Coen Pontoh. They were both tried in 1997 and sentenced to five years in prison. They were not released until after Suharto fell. The strike was organized under the banner of the PRD and PPBI, who distributed thousands of leaflets among the workers which included the following demands: end the interference of the military in workers' affairs and in the PDI; end the armed forces dual functions; for the nomination of Megawati Soekarnoputri as a presidential candidate.

The date of 27 July 1996—when another round of demonstrations combined with riots of the urban "floating mass" exploded with huge fury in Jakarta—is most frequently given as the beginning of the end of Suharto's rule, as the start of his "long fall." But the momentum of escalating and spreading protest actions was already well under way. The events of 27 July 1996 just spurred things on. Megawati, the PDI membership and those forces mobilizing in solidarity with Megawati's PDI were refusing to be outlawed by the regime. Several score of members were occupying the official PDI national headquarters in a building supplied by the government. The government ordered them to leave the building. They refused. The headquarters became the meeting place for a broad coalition of anti-government forces known as the Majelis Rakyat Indonesia (MARI—Indonesian People's Assembly). While the rallying point for the MARI coalition was defense of the Megawati PDI, it issued a broad range of general demands. These included wage rises for workers, civil servants and soldiers; better prices for farmers' produce; defend the exchange rate at a fixed point; provision of free education and an end to corruption; and repeal of all repressive laws.

In fact, the PDI headquarters was becoming a possible launch pad from which the momentum of the previous twenty-three years since MALARI, and the immediate past seven years since the *aksi* process began, might be propelled onto a higher phase. Not surprisingly, the regime moved to end the PDI headquarters' status as this rallying point. The military and police arrived and cordoned off the general area. After stoning the building for a few houres, forces declaring themselves members of the officially recognized PDI, but made up primarily of hired thugs, and perhaps soldiers, attacked the offices and took them over. Many claim that more than twenty people were killed. More than twenty of the PDI people in the headquarters were arrested and later tried and imprisoned and only released after Suharto fell. Aspinall gives a good summary of the immediate aftermath:

> Meanwhile, a large crowd had gathered beyond the military cordon. As rumors spread that many in the office had been killed, stone throwing began. Although PDI leaders appealed for calm, sporadic clashes continued, with sections of the crowd at one point chanting "ABRI are killers" and burning a nearby police post. The crowd grew for some hours, swelled by residents of nearby slum areas, high school students and other passers-by. Around 2 p.m. troops made a concerted attack, using tear gas, water cannons and batons, but not firing. The crowds scattered, and from this point running battles and widespread rioting took place through a large part of Eastern Jakarta. Many thousands of poor *kampung* residents joined in. The activists from opposition groups among them were able to exercise little control. Eventually, some 56 buildings were destroyed, more than 200 people were arrested, and four (according to official figures) were killed.[13]

In fact, 27 July was another example of the MALARI syndrome: mobilizations where organized protest by a specific political sector is accompanied by widespread rioting among a de-organized section of the population.

A Political Initiative from Below

The July 1996 demonstrations and riots marked another point in the escalating political crisis for the counter-revolution: "floating mass" politics was unraveling. Not surprisingly, the regime launched a direct attack against the main agent promoting *aksi*: the PRD. The PRD was accused of organizing the rioting. A propaganda campaign began labeling the PRD as communist and as a new version of the PKI. Orders were issued for the arrest of all leaders and members. Thirty PRD leaders and members were arrested and detained. The PRD was forced underground—except that during 1997 several PRD leaders appeared "above ground" in their trials. None were released until after the fall of Suharto.

While the organization systematically promoting *aksi* was hounded, protest actions themselves continued to increase, mutating into a wider range of activities. Actions initiated by PRD groups receded for a few months until the organization regrouped underground and relaunched its own campaign of actions at the beginning of 1997, under different banners in different towns. Spontaneous, locally organized actions by students, workers and farmers continued, although for a while the media were slightly more cautious in reporting them. The YIP list recorded about forty student actions between September and December 1996 using six newspapers.

But a new form of *aksi* started to occur: actions by the newly recruited membership of Megawati's PDI. Megawati continued to refuse to accept the legitimacy of the government's recognition of the rival PRD under Soerjadi. Megawati opted to challenge in the courts the legal status of every PDI local branch set up by the Soerjadi party. While litigation appeared as the announced tactic adopted by the Megawati PDI against the regime, almost every single one of scores of court sessions was accompanied by a local PDI mass rally, march or demonstration. Sometimes PDI members would demonstrate at electoral commission or other related government bodies. These were relatively non-militant—except occasionally when dispersed violently; then PDI members fought back—but effectively spread the mobilization method of politics throughout the country. Occurring in parallel with the spontaneous actions, it meant that the country began to enter into a permanent state of *aksi*.

"Floating mass" political culture was truly dead and buried. But de-organization still dominated. While probably tens of thousands of people did join the Megawati PDI between 1993 and 1996, there were millions more who had no organization—at least no permanent organization. Before 1996, riots usually occurred in conjunction with a specific large *aksi*, usually initiated by students, but which escalated political sentiments to a higher level. After July 1996, PDI and spontaneous actions kept so many issues on the public agenda at once that the political mood was approaching a state of permanent anger and dissent and even rebellion.

By November 1996, the PRD had also regrouped and formed new action committees in several cities which began to organize actions. In the four months leading up to the May 1997 elections, the number of protest actions continued to escalate, raising a broad range of issues. However, what was to hit Indonesia in May 1997 was hinted at by new levels of defiance and new kinds of alliances that took place in the south Sumatran city of Lampung in December 1996. Over 10 and 11 December 1996, the city of Lampung was paralyzed by a combination of a strike by mikrolet[14] and bus drivers and demonstrations by university and high school students. The merging of university and high school student and transportation worker protests into a single action took place more or less spontaneously.[15]

In this new climate, riots began to occur separately from any specific organized protest. Riots occurred in the East Javanese town of Situbondo in November, in Tasikmalaya in December, and then on 30 January, in Rengasdengklok, in the ethnically Sundanese part of West Java. There were also more riots in Ujung Pandang, West Kalimantan and West Papua. In all cases, it was reported that a conflict incident between Chinese and non-Chinese, or Christian and non-Christian individuals, sparked the riots. But inevitably the rioters—this time drawn from a more rural sector of the de-organized—attacked government buildings and symbols of consumer prosperity, as well as churches or Chinese-owned buildings.

By the time of the May 1997 elections there was an atmosphere of heightened political tension. There were demonstrations somewhere in the country almost every day opposing the government on some issue or another. A PDI mobilization also took place before the elections in Jakarta where 20,000 people rallied outside a courthouse in Central Jakarta, completely blocking the major thoroughfare of Gajah Mada Street. The country had been rocked by riots in Jakarta just nine months earlier, followed by destructive rioting in other parts of the country. There had also been Lampung.

The legitimacy of the elections was also being challenged in a way that they had never been before. Megawati and her followers, who were clearly the largest party group with an active membership base, were excluded from the elections. Megawati effectively indicated that she wanted her followers to boycott the elections. Several national religious and community figures also indicated that they favored a boycott of the elections. For example, a pre-Easter apostolic letter by the Indonesian Bishops' Conference told Catholic believers that it was not a sin to refuse to vote in the 29 May general elections. Almost all of the various pro-democratic NGOs and activist groups, such as the PRD, PIJAR and others, advocated a boycott. An election monitoring group, itself comprising a coalition of activist groups, including PRD members, also used protest actions to draw attention to the anomalies in the election procedures, most of all the absence of Megawati's PDI, now called the PDI Struggle (PDIP), from the elections.

The call to boycott the elections, coming from so many directions, was not effective, except in the areas where Megawati's PDI was strong, and even there it tended to be more a boycott of the voting and not always of the campaign. The escalating momentum of the protests was not conducive to people staying at home and doing nothing active about a state of affairs in the country that they were increasingly agitated about. Instead the tendency was to mobilize. The May 1997 elections saw the largest mobilizations in the history of the New Order. They were also, perhaps, the most militant in the history of post-independence Indonesia. These mobilizations also took a form which nobody predicted at the time: the *aksi* had become truly politically independent.

Predictions that the GOLKAR campaign would be large and well financed but lackluster and that the Soerjadi PDI campaign would be a flop did come true. Predictions that the PPP would run its usual more or less pro-New Order lackluster campaign also proved true. With the New Order seeking the biggest ever majority for GOLKAR, the PPP pulled back on its campaign efforts, canceling, for example, plans for campaign activities at the village level in many areas on the three days set aside for its campaigns. The regime itself was, however, very sensitive to the possibility of mobilizations. The election laws banned rallies and marches altogether. Strict regulations were put in place to ensure that the police could maintain control over all campaign activities. The parties had to notify the police and other election-related authorities of their full, integrated campaign plans and for every individual activity. Activities were classified as "monologic" and "dialogic" depending on whether the public

attending the activities would also be allowed to speak or not.[16] The
campaign period was to last twenty-seven days, with each party having
turns to campaign—nine days each.

What nobody predicted were the huge, militant mobilizations that
occurred spontaneously on all the days set aside for PPP campaigning in
Jakarta, as well as in several other cities. In Jakarta, on the days set aside for its
campaigning, the PPP had several activities planned for different parts of the
city. Tens of thousands of people streamed out of the densely populated
kampung areas to make their way to the sites of PPP activities. These were,
however, not actual PPP mobilizations but spontaneous mobilizations by the
Jakarta poor giving vent to their anger. They did not carry placards and
banners provided by the PPP or call for support for the PPP, as would usually
be the case. Instead, surprising everybody, they carried their own banners
proclaiming their support for "Mega Bintang," literally "Mega Star." The
"Mega" referred to Megawati and the "Star" was the star and crescent of
Islam. Jakarta's urban poor, whether practising Moslems or more secular
Moslems, united in an angry rejection of GOLKAR and the New Order.
Banners read "A Coalition of Mega-Bintang-People for Democracy," "A
Coalition of Mega-Bintang-People to Refuse Absolute Majority for Golkar"
and "A Coalition of Mega-Bintang-People for Change" as well as "GOLK-
AR is corrupt," "GOLKAR cheats" and other anti-government slogans.

Neither the PPP national leadership nor Megawati had promoted the
idea of such a coalition or battle cry. The idea appeared to have first been
raised in the Central Javanese city of Solo where the chairperson of the local
PPP branch, a maverick by the name of Mudrick Setiawan Sangidoe,
announced that Megawati's PDI was giving its votes to the PPP. In early
May Mudrick met with Megawati, who did not state any support for such a
coalition. The PPP national leadership also made it clear that it was
opposed to such an idea—which would have been tantamount to supporting an alliance with an outlaw, outside the electoral system. The issue was
not raised again by any of the leadership.

The masses had adopted their own political line, calling on the two
major camps in the mainstream opposition to unite against the government. The election campaign was organized so that each party had a day
where it alone could hold activities—although not rallies or marches. By
the fourth and final round, the scale of mobilizations on the street—
defying the government ban on outdoor rallies and defying the urgings and

cancellations of events by the PPP itself—had grown enormously and had become increasingly angry and militant. It is difficult to make an exact estimate of the number of people on the streets on 14 May, one of the later days set aside for campaigning by the PPP. Calculations by PRD leaders put the figure at over 1 million mobilized throughout the city in different locations.[17] There is no consolidated listing of the mobilizations that took place throughout the city as people poured out of the *kampung* heading for different meeting points. However, all descriptions of the campaign point in the direction of massive and extensive mobilizations. Academician Syamsudin Harris referred to the "teeming campaigns of the PPP, which had 'greened' the whole city of Jakarta."[18] Eyewitness accounts and newspaper reports all underline the massive scale of the PPP day turnout in Jakarta, of people *berjubal-jubal*—massing out in crowds—onto the main roads.

The dynamic of this mass-initiated new political line—calling for a united opposition to oust GOLKAR—not only startled but also frightened the regime and the elite generally. Immediately after the first round of PPP day demonstrations when the Mega-Bintang phenomenon appeared, the government banned the use of any placards which used the "Mega-Bintang" slogan, and any other paraphernalia related to Megawati, including any pictures of her or her father, former President Soekarno. These bans, which came on top of the most heavy handed pre-election pro-GOLKAR maneuvering ever implemented by the government, only further infuriated an already mobilized and angry population. The bans tested the militancy of the popular mood. The results of this challenge to the Mega-Bintang masses was an escalation of mobilization and defiance of all attempts to prevent the carrying of Mega-Bintang paraphernalia. This was despite the chairperson of the Jakarta branch of the PPP issuing instructions for party members not to take part in any marches or rallies. His instructions held no sway over any significant section of the previously "floating" masses. The acts of defiance by marching crowds of *kampung* dwellers included attacking and burning down police stations when the police tried to order the handing over of placards or posters, and chasing away the police or military. Other government offices were also attacked and ransacked. Military and police barricades attempting to stop demonstrators were stoned and attempts were made to break through. In many cases, the police and military personnel used force to disperse these

marches. Street skirmishes were common throughout Jakarta. The report
by the Centre for Strategic and International Studies (CSIS) in Jakarta
described it well:

> As an example of the disaffection of the masses, which directly or
> indirectly reflected the "rejection" by the masses of the "leadership"
> of the parties, of the "legal competency" of the election authorities
> and the "authority" of the security apparatus was the case of the
> explosion onto the streets of the greater Jakarta area on the PPP
> campaign days during the last three rounds of campaigning. Even
> though the Jakarta regional Council of the PPP stated that they
> would not carry out any campaigning on those days and the election
> authority had banned rallies and motorcades and the security
> apparatus declared that they would take harsh action against anybody
> violating the campaign rules, the masses and sympathisers still came
> out onto the streets to rally, and in motorcades [with motorbikes],
> shouting banned slogans and ignoring all calls from the security
> apparatus and the PPP officials for them to stop their activities, and
> indeed resisting these authorities in increasingly "violent" ways.[19]

This report also gave some statistics pointing to the level of physical clashes:

> Up until and including the final round of campaigning there were
> more than 200 people who died (mostly in crashes or burned alive in
> buildings during riots as in Banjarmasin), more than 100 seriously
> injured and 400 with lesser injuries. There were 4 policemen
> seriously injured and 15 with lesser injuries; and 3 members of
> the other branches of the Armed Forces who lost their lives; as well as
> 3 seriously injured and 6 with lesser injuries. There were 5 police
> stations, 1 district military headquarters, 26 civil district government
> offices, 110 houses, 6 political party offices, 4 mosques, and 3
> churches damaged as a result of actions by the masses. There were
> 208 vehicles, including 18 government service vehicles damaged.[20]

Another writer, Kees van Dijk, in his book, *Country in Despair, Indonesia
between 1997 and 2000*, using newspaper reports to put together a picture,
described the atmosphere in his chapter "Violent Campaigns":

Not a day passed without crowds somewhere running amuck and taking possession of the streets, fights erupting between groups of supporters of the different parties, and individuals being beaten up. All over Indonesia mobs turned violent. Barricades appeared in the streets where people were urged to resist the security troops or to prevent gangs supporting another party entering their neighbourhoods, and shops remained closed. Stalls selling food or drinks were plundered, and free petrol was demanded at petrol stations. Drivers and passengers of passing cars were forced to hand over money and cigarettes, or had stones and bottles hurtled at them if they did not make the appropriate sign: one, two or three fingers in the air, to indicate their support of, respectively, PPP, GOLKAR or PDI.[21]

Van Dijk's vivid description presents a picture of a society descending into anarchy, which certainly seemed to be the case for a while. But his description also reveals the political nature of the unrest and the role that the PPP campaign days played:

> . . . most clashes broke out around the PPP campaign, which appeared to have turned into rallying points to unleash slumbering hostility against the government and all that it represented. For ordinary citizens, PPP campaign days became days to dread.[22]

Of course, it was mostly "ordinary citizens" who were in fact mobilizing and they had been awakening from the "slumber" or their "floating" for some time beforehand.

Similar mobilizations—almost always outside the control of the PPP—took place in many other cities, especially on Java, in both the Sundanese and Javanese ethnic areas. By the last day of campaigning, the 1974 MALARI syndrome took over. Mega-Bintang mobilizations voicing their clear political line, demanding a democratic coalition against GOLKAR, were being accompanied by outbreaks of rioting. As one group of Indonesian researchers described in their report: "There is no other word to describe the PPP campaign at the end of the campaign period (Friday May 23 1977): RIOTS. The rioting spread from the tip of West Java [Sunda] to East Java."[23] This report, for example, describes how "hundreds" of people were beaten down by rifle butts until tear gas was used on the Javanese town of Tegal, how police stations were burned down in the large city of Cirebon, mass street fighting with GOLKAR members in Semarang, attacks on the police and government offices in Tangerang, and several other examples. In some cities, even military posts were attacked. In the CSIS report, the writers include figures showing that just six of the Jakarta dailies carried reports of at least 250 incidents of so-called violent clashes during the twenty-seven-day campaign period.[24] Their report emphasizes that even these figures are an underestimation, as many incidents went unreported.

The ban on Mega-Bintang placards and paraphernalia, justified on the basis that "there was no registered Mega-Bintang party," was maintained throughout the campaign but could not be effectively enforced. The regime had suffered its first major defeat at the hands of popular defiance. The fear generated by this was felt throughout the elite. While the regime banned it, the PPP dissociated itself from PRD activity completely. An additional worry to the regime and the elite generally was that, despite the PRD being forced underground, PRD activists had been able to intervene to heighten the profile of the political demands of the masses. Under the name of a Mega-Bintang-Rakyat coalition, they started distributing leaflets at marches and rallies with several specific political demands, under the general demand of "Get rid of Suharto!" These included: repeal of the five political laws; repeal the dual function of the armed forces; a cabinet comprising political parties; eliminate corruption and conglomerates; and investigate the wealth of the children of the President, ministers and other officials and lower prices.[25] The PRD activists estimate that they distributed around 600,000 of these leaflets with the help of volunteers from the people joining the mobilizations.[26] These were small leaflets, typed on cheap newsprint paper and stencilled or printed.[27] As one PRD leader explained:

> We in the PRD had a fantastic experience. We distributed 600,000 leaflets with our demands and our ideas for resistance in the midst of the strict control by the military (remember what they were capable of in 1965 and in East Timor!) And the leaflets were taken up by the people enthusiastically. There was not one leaflet to be seen on the ground anywhere. Many housewives took them away and made more copies. When we started chanting: "Mega, Star, the people!" the mass

chant in reply was "The people are on the rampage!" The people really fought back with all their might, trying to break through the barricades the military had set up between different suburbs. They knew, and this is what we were saying in our leaflets also, that if they could break through the barricades so that all the masses from the whole Jakarta-Bogor-Tangerang region could link up, then who knows what could have been achieved. Most of the mass media published the demands in our leaflets. It surprised us at first that reports of our leaflets got through the regime's control over the media. But later we realised that it was the regime itself that engineered the media space because they felt it was necessary to launch counter-propaganda against us.[28]

The PPP leadership itself announced that it was reporting the Mega-Bintang-Rakyat leaflets to the police, although there were no names or addresses on the leaflets. Suharto's Minister for Home Affairs, General Syarwan Hamid, and also Harmoko, the chairperson of GOLKAR, meanwhile openly accused the banned PRD of distributing the leaflets.[29]

The combative mood of the Mega-Bintang masses continued for several weeks after the elections and was provoked further by the announcement that GOLKAR had won more than 70 percent of the vote. Given the astounding mobilizations of anger against GOLKAR during the campaign, and combined with all the documented reports of cheating and manipulation submitted by journalists and the various election monitoring coalitions, the election results were widely seen as fraudulent. There were immediate further angry and large mobilizations against the results. These took place in several towns throughout the country. In some cases, again, police stations or government offices were burned down, occupied or ransacked.[30]

In Crisis

The 1997 election campaign was a major defeat for the New Order. The central tactic of the counter-revolution—the imposition of "floating mass" politics—collapsed. As the CSIS report on the elections noted, huge numbers of people, in a highly combative manner, had completely defied the security apparatus, the civilian government and the party leaderships.

Throughout the country, there were militant and large-scale mobilizations. The New Order was already in political crisis—long before the country was hit by the Asian economic crisis. The emergence of full-blooded mobilizational politics was at the heart of the crisis; however, the processes of the previous ten years had delivered defeats in other arenas. In particular, the regime had lost control of the management of the public political agenda.

When Ali Murtopo first set out his concept of "floating mass," he emphasized that the purpose was to "allow" the majority of the population—at that time based in the villages—to to be "wholly occupied with development efforts." Issues of political conflict were to be removed from the arena of concern of the population at large. During election campaigns, this was ensured by the regime's control of the party leaderships combined with regulations prohibiting criticism of government policy as well as of other parties. As a result of the accumulation of defiance and seepage into the public arena of issues of social justice and political repression over the previous decade, the regime had started to lose control in this arena as well. In a survey of the press coverage of the 1997 campaign, the CSIS report already cited listed the following issues frequently raised during electioneering:

- poverty and the prosperity of the "little people"
- access to education
- corruption, manipulation
- political renewal, democratization, the political laws
- equity in distribution of development
- human rights and rights of the *rakyat*
- labor and employment
- social justice and inequality
- national leadership and the role of the military
- clean government.[31]

The election results delivered a 70 percent result for GOLKAR but politically the New Order had suffered a major defeat and was in crisis. The regime continued its campaign against radicalism conducted in the form of a general propaganda attack against the PRD, but it was failing. Ed Aspinall sums up this failure well:

In a post-Cold War world, and with Indonesia's own conflicts of

1965 a distant memory, warnings of communist infiltration had lost their power to convince. They even seemed anachronistic to the more sophisticated urban population. Even immediately after the riots, newspapers printed readers' letters that openly questioned the official account. PRD leaders who remained at large gave press interviews, contemptuously dismissing government accusations. The National Human Rights Commission released findings on the affair, which contradicted the official version, stating that 23 persons remained missing, and that security forces were involved in the takeover of the PDI building. In one opinion poll of 500 urban dwellers, only 13 percent of respondents agreed that the PRD was behind the riots, a large majority blaming the security forces, Soerjadi or the government . . . The government's campaign was also hampered by considerable incompetence of execution, as when the family of PRD leader Budiman Sudjatmiko was accused of PKI links, it subsequently emerging that they were pious Muslims affiliated to Muhammadiyah.

Despite the repressive atmosphere, various opposition elements continued to seek ways to challenge the regime. Megawati's PDI focused on its series of legal challenges. The groups that had borne the brunt of the post-July repression, meanwhile, began to re-organize. Even the PRD, which had decisively made the transition to illegal opposition, began to re-build underground. Before the end of the year it was organizing demonstrations on several campuses using various "front" organizations. During a visit to Indonesia in late 1996 I was struck by the new optimism of many in NGO, student and other activist circles, even those in hiding. There was a growing feeling that the regime was turning in on itself and approaching terminal crisis: *pembusukan* (decay) was a term widely used to describe this process.[32]

Most significantly, protest action increased dramatically in the coming months, even apart from the unrest that developed after the economic crisis started to impact on Indonesian society after November 1997. The YIP list shows 110 protest actions between the May elections and the end of 1997. More actions were listed for these seven months than for any previous full year. The list, this time using seven papers only, gives demonstrations—again concentrating only on student demonstrations—in Jakarta as well as in Yogyakarta, Semarang, Solo, Wonosobo, Kendari, Purwokerto, and Malang in Java; Bandung, Tasikmalaya and Bogor in Sunda, Ujung Pandang in Sulawesi, Palembang, Peekanbaru, Medan and Bandarlampung in Sumatra; and Mataram and Selong in the Nusantenggara islands province. In the YIP list, the single largest number was from the student city of Yogyakarta. The YIP list describes actions with numbers of participants ranging between ten or a few hundred to thousands. Protests were against military violence, violence by GOLKAR gangs or other pro-regime gangs, the political laws, the dual function of the armed forces, corruption, the ineffectiveness of the legislatures, the existence of extra-constitutional security bodies, the refusal of officials to meet demonstrators, authoritarian behavior by university vice-chancellors, statements by regime officials that "spilling the blood of rioters is permissible," the 1997 election results, the new repressive labor laws, corruption in the cooperatives bureaucracy, the undertaking of mega-commercial projects, school and library fee increases, sexual harassment on campus, violation of farmer rights to subsidies, the corporatization of campuses, official involvement in illegal gambling, hunger in West Papua, price rises of basic commodities, demolition of homes for road widening, corruption of forestry licensing, official involvement and cover-up of the assassination of a journalist, as well as the US blockade on Iraq and the Israeli policy against Palestine.

What was later to be called the *reformasi* agenda was already present in political life and discourse in 1997 before the Asian economic crisis. The economic crisis hit Thailand in July 1997 but it was not until October and November that Indonesia began to feel the socio-economic impact, in terms of price rises and spreading fears of food shortages and loss of bank savings. By early October, it was also clear that the regime had no answer to the crisis when it sought assistance from the International Monetary Fund.[33] By the end of October, student demonstrations began to demand that the government halt the rises in prices of basic commodities. At the end of December, students organized big end of year demonstrations at the two prestige campuses of the University of Indonesia in Jakarta and the Gajah Mada University in Yogyakarta.

Over the next four months protest actions exploded but this time there was a clear political focus for all protests: the ousting of Suharto. For the period beginning January 1998 up until the fall of Suharto at the end of May, the YIP list reported 850 actions, about eight times more than had occurred in any full year during the previous decade. The list covered twenty cities only: Ujung Pandang (Sulawesi) 173 demonstrations, Bandung (Sunda) 130, Jakarta 127, Yogyakarta (Java) 108, Surabaya (Java) 69, Semarang (Java) 52, Medan (Sumatra) 36, Banjarmasin (Kalimantan) 44, Purwokerto (Java) 27, Jember (Java) 19, Denpasar (Bali) 18, Kupang (West Timor) 14, Bogor (Sunda) 14, Salatiga (Java) 13, Mataram (Lombok) 13, Depok (Jakarta outskirts) 11 and Bandarlampung (Sumatra) 10. But these demonstrations were taking place in almost every other major town, and many smaller towns. In the descriptions of the demonstrations on the YIP list the word *ribuan* (thousands) appears more and more frequently, as does *bentrok* (street fighting). The first demonstration listed as involving "thousands" was on the island of Bima in eastern Indonesia on 7 February and then in Solo on 11 February, in Majalengka, West Java, on 12 February and at the University of Indonesia on 25 February.

Mobilizations escalated after March when a stage-managed People's Consultative Assembly re-elected Suharto as president and he then proceeded to install a cabinet which included his closest cronies and his daughter. Based just on the listings by the YIP, it can be calculated that there were at least thirty to forty demonstrations across the country every day during the March–May period. Tens of thousands of people were involved every week and from all sectors of society: the semi-proletariat, referred to as the urban poor, including the tens of thousands of recently dismissed factory workers, as well as white-collar workers, bank tellers, doctors, teachers and farmers. One manifestation of the spread of *aksi* to all sectors of society was the mushrooming of women's groups involved in actions. These ranged from specific mobilizations of women university students through to *kampung* housewives and more middle- and upper-class women, who also initiated their own groups and activities.

Students were at the forefront of the mobilizations. Key student demonstrations were those that took place in Solo, Central Java on 17 March when fighting broke out between students and the military as students forced their way out of the campus. On 2 and 3 April, the same happened when thousands of students forced their way through army lines to march out of the Gajah Mada University campus. This was repeated on 13 April when the military occupied the campus for about eight hours. On 24 April, similar clashes occurred at the University of North Sumatra in

Medan, where students also used Molotov cocktails against soldiers. The campus had to be closed for several days.[34]

As *aksi* gripped the country, demanding that Suharto go, the regime itself seemed determined to cling to the counter-revolution's long-term central tactic: the masses must return to their previous passive state. The regime did not immediately recognize, or was not willing to admit to itself, that they had already lost this battle. Instead, they launched a campaign that was more suitable as pre-emptive action, namely, a campaign to capture and crush the force that they saw as the conscious agent promoting *aksi*, namely the PRD. PRD members were kidnapped, along with other activists whom the authorities had thought were PRD members. Most PRD members were underground but at least thirty were hunted down and captured. Most of those caught were tortured; at least fourteen were murdered, including the PRD's prominent poet, Wiji Thukul. Among those caught and tortured was the chairperson of the PRD Central Leadership Council, Andi Arief, as well as one of the PRD's international spokespersons, Mugyanto.

The effort by the regime was doomed to failure on two levels. First, the underground organization of the PRD was effective and key central personalities whom the regime was after were well protected. Second, and more fundamentally, the whole movement had grown beyond the PRD as had indeed the momentum for mobilization. On Saturday 2 May, demonstrations, each involving thousands of students, took place in almost every city in the country. The YIP report lists Jakarta, Yogyakarta and Bandung, where several separate demonstrations took place, as well as Denpasar, Malang, Medan, Solo, Surabaya, Ujung Pandang, Purwokerto, Semarang, Kupang, Palembang and Banjarmasin. Actions also took place as far away as Banda Aceh in Aceh and Jayapura in West Papua.[35]

When the regime announced increases in the price of electricity and fuel on 4 May, some of the biggest demonstrations took place, overflowing into clashes with the military, and often drawing in people living in the *kampung* around the locations of the clashes. Finally, the regime resorted to direct terrorization of the mobilized students themselves as distinct from seeking out the underground proponents of *aksi*. On 12 May, students returning to the University of Trisakti campus were fired upon by soldiers. Four were shot dead. Over 13 and 14 May, rioting broke out in Jakarta again, resulting in the greatest loss of life and damage to property that Jakarta had suffered from such rioting.

Demonstrations, drawing in every sector of society, multiplied even more dramatically. Between 7 and 20 May, the day before Suharto resigned, there are 310 demonstrations listed in the YIP list. Violent clashes with the police or military were almost inevitable, with the police or soldiers often firing rubber bullets. There were marches. Students and *kampung* dwellers (that is, workers and semi-proletarians) took over streets and held open forums. Local parliamentary buildings, governor's offices and other official buildings were occupied. In some cities, students took over the state radio stations and made their own broadcasts. They even attacked military outposts. In a column in *Kompas* newspaper on 14 May, Professor Sarlito Wirawan Sarwono, the Dean of the Faculty of Psychology at the University of Indonesia, expressed his fears of the student movement and mass anger uniting because of the regime's slowness to reform. He opened his column with words which summed up the whole of the elite's fears:

> Lately the student aksi in several cities and towns in Indonesia have changed to become mass actions. In Yogya, Solo, Surabaya and then also in Jakarta, pushing and shoving between students and officials has turned into fighting, throwing things (from stones to tear gas) and finally to shooting (although still using rubber bullets).[36]

On 19 May tens of thousands of students occupied the parliamentary grounds, stating they would stay there until there was a sitting of the MPR which would dismiss Suharto. On 20 May demonstrations with the same demands followed in every other major city. Using newspaper reports and YIP lists: Bandung—hundreds of thousands; Ujung Pandang—hundreds of thousands; Yogyakarta—more than 500,000; and others all in the tens of thousands or thousands. Many people in Yogyakarta claim that 1 million students and *rakyat* gathered in the main square on 20 May in a rally that was also supported by the Sultan of Yogyakarta.[37] Interestingly, where the rallies were largest and involved non-students, there was no significant rioting.

From 20 May, for the first time, the numbers involved were in the hundreds of thousands, which meant they no longer comprised just students. *Aksi* had become mass *aksi*. The trends had been very visible since at least the beginning of May and, little by little, elements of the New Order elite—starting from the outer fringes but moving ever closer to Suharto—started to abandon him. By 20 May, almost everybody had openly abandoned him, including his cabinet ministers and GOLKAR chiefs. Less openly, his military chiefs were also suggesting resignation. On 21 May, he resigned and Vice-President Habibie was sworn in as president.

Aksi and *Reformasi*

The political elite, including those close to the center of power, had dropped Suharto as part of their strategy to prevent the further escalation of mass mobilization and any political radicalization accompanying it. Already, the propaganda by the PRD and other radical student groups calling for the formation of a "People's Committee" as an alternative source of power to the formal structures was spreading and generating other more moderate but equally threatening scenarios. However the momentum of mass action did not stop after the resignation of Suharto. The mobilizations were being driven by more than just a desire to get rid of Suharto. A new agenda had been developing in the public mind, especially among students and workers—including the white-collar and professional workforce—as well as farmers and villagers, since the time of the student movements of the 1970s and Rendra. This process had intensified during the 1990s, the decade of *aksi*. The fall of Suharto would not satisfy the expectations around the new agenda—*reformasi*.

In June, General Wiranto as commander-in-chief of the armed forces complained that *reformasi aksi* were everywhere (*marak*). He declared they "were tending to challenge anything and everything." He was not exaggerating. The fall of Suharto was like the collapse of a dam. Mobilizations spread everywhere. The list of actions that the Yayasan Insan Politik documented also changes after the fall of Suharto. Although still entitled a "chronology of student actions," it includes more protests by workers and villagers.

The "challenge to anything and everything" had merged with a more formally defined, broader agenda. During the January–March period, and afterwards, this agenda was given the name *reformasi*—reformation. The *reformasi* agenda encapsulated all of the ideas and demands that had accumulated during the previous decade or more and was concentrated around the two central political demands that had been popularized by the PRD in its propaganda—repeal the political laws and end the dual function of the military—and the broader more collectively formulated demand to end collusion, corruption and nepotism, known as KKN.

Demonstrations after the fall of Suharto articulated demands ranging from rejecting the new president, Habibie, through to calling for the dismissal of village heads. It is impossible to know the exact number, but mini rebellions occurred in hundreds of villages throughout the country.[38] Villagers mobilized in their own *aksi* and demanded the resignation of village heads they accused of corruption. In some cases, the village heads were chased out of the village after having their offices or homes attacked. At least one village head died when he had a heart attack when confronted with the *aksi*. This kind of action later spread to campaigns demanding the resignation of district and regional heads. These mass campaigns set a precedent which still had power in 2004. One of the biggest mass campaigns, involving tens of thousands of people, occurred in 2004 in the regency of Kampas, in South Sumatra, when high school students and teachers carried out repeated strikes and rallies demanding the resignation of the regent for refusing to allocate sufficient funds for education. That campaign also succeeded. In 1998, demonstrations also took up issues of economic and social welfare, especially relating to price rises in the aftermath of the economic crisis. It was during this period that demonstrations also further popularized the use of the term KKN—*Kolusi, Korupsi, Nepotisme*—as one of the main enemies of *reformasi*.

The kidnapping of students, the shootings at Trisakti University and reports that mass rapes of Chinese Indonesian women during the rioting in May were organized by military agents also fueled a rise in demonstrations against the army. In the weeks immediately after the fall of Suharto, there were demonstrations outside local army commands in scores of towns throughout Indonesia. Student groups, directly or indirectly connected to the PRD, also played a spearheading role in these demonstrations but they spread beyond the PRD core.

Wiranto was absolutely correct—everything was being questioned. The YIP list gives more than 900 cases of *aksi* in the seven months after Suharto fell. But by this time the possibilities of adequately documenting the protests through news clippings and other documents had completely disappeared. Everything was *aksi*. There were demonstrations demanding the repeal of every repressive law on the books, whether they were legacies of the colonial period, the pre-1965 period or the New Order. There were also demonstrations trying to march into the street where Suharto lived, and there were several clashes with the military guarding the street. Moreover, mass actions also began to multiply in areas where repression had been the most intense: in East Timor, Papua and Aceh. In these three regions, where there had been an armed resistance to the New Order of one kind or another, Suharto had militarized the whole governmental operations. Control had been tight with military counter-insurgency operations deploying the usual methods of murder, torture, arbitrary detention and terror. With Suharto fallen, his elite and his military in disarray, the space opened for mass *aksi* in these areas also. Student groups in the three regions pioneered the *aksi* and they soon became frequent.[39]

During the first months of 1998, the momentum of the mobilizations had increasingly focused on the issue of power: out with Suharto! It was the question of power again that was both to refocus the whole spectrum of the *reformasi aksi* movement and to propel it onto a new scale of mobilization and level of combativeness. It was this question too that was to confront it with its most difficult problem.

7

Power

The "challenge to anything and everything" was known by the name *reformasi*—reformation or *reformasi total*. The *reformasi* agenda encapsulated all of the ideas and demands that had accumulated during the previous decade or more. This agenda was concentrated around the two central political demands that had been popularized by the PRD in its propaganda—repeal the political laws and end the dual function of the military—alongside the broader, more collectively formulated demand to end collusion, corruption and nepotism, KKN. *Reformasi aksi* continued to confront the government, the military, local authorities, companies and enterprises at all levels while a new momentum started to develop, focusing on the plans for an Extraordinary Session of the People's Consultative Assembly (MPR) announced for November 1998. Perspectives developing within the mass movement on the issue of power propelled this momentum.

Once Suharto had been ousted, the concept of *reformasi* and the broader agenda for political change took on greater importance as the next goal. President Habibie, supported by a circle of intellectuals and former activists, embarked on a rapid series of policy reforms meant to meet *reformasi* expectations. He affirmed that there would be elections as soon as possible and that there would be an Extraordinary Session of the People's Consultative Assembly to formally confirm these plans. He also ratified international agreements on labor rights, which had the effect of immediately relaxing, though by no means ending, state repression in this sector. New legislation was foreshadowed in a range of areas clearly meant to respond to the *reformasi* agenda, including legislation that would effectively repeal the repressive political laws that had been used to restrict most political parties and NGOs in their activities.

However, these moves clearly did not go far enough to meet *reformasi* expectations. First, there were ongoing cases of violent repression of protest actions taking place around the country, including in Jakarta. Second, there were no signs that any concrete action would be taken against members of the New Order inner elite accused of corruption or violation of human rights. Habibie, although advised by political actors relatively distant from the core New Order rulers, was still a part of the New Order coalition and could not act decisively against it, and probably did not want to do so either. Habibie's *reformasi* moves during the May–November period therefore fell short on a fundamental expectation among wide sections of the public: the removal of the New Order political elite altogether.

People's Committees and Presidiums

Within the broad *reformasi* effervescence, people were confronted with the issue of a replacement for the New Order political elite. Two general strands of thinking developed and were manifest in political discourse during this period.

The first of these was generated at the radical end of the spectrum by the PRD. They started to add to their printed propaganda and to include in their speeches at public forums and *aksi* the call for the establishment of People's Committees (Komite Rakyat) or People's Councils (Dewan Rakyat). This was a call aimed at making permanent what had so far been temporary. The concept of the People's Committee or People's Council was based on the idea that the various temporary, ad hoc committees and groups established to organize various *aksi* should coalesce to form more permanent formations, whether based in neighborhoods, villages or in workplaces. A form of such a shift from temporary to permanent was taking place as industrially active workers began to form new trade unions after Habibie's liberalization of the Suharto era labor laws. This particular manifestation of the trend from temporary to permanent has expanded even further since 2000.[1] The PRD assessment at the time was, however, that there was likely to be a further escalation of mass mobilization across the country in the lead-up to the November 1999 MPR sitting which would provide the mobilizing process with possibilities for more immediate and combative organization.

In August 1998, activists from the Sumatran city of Lampung announced the formation of the first People's Committee. Lampung is the closest Sumatran city to Jakarta, on the island of Java. It is possible to travel from Jakarta to Lampung by car in half a day, crossing the narrow strait between Java and Sumatra by ferry. Activist politics in Lampung was in constant contact with Jakarta. There had been large and militant mobilizations in Lampung since 1996. Most famous was the transport workers' strike and student mobilizations that had paralyzed the city for three days in December 1996, and had played a major role in restarting the momentum leading to the May 1997 election mobilizations. There had been very combative demonstrations on Lampung campuses, including the smaller private campuses, where students had even taken security personnel hostage. A statement issued by the Lampung People's Committee listed fifty-six member organizations, of which twenty-eight were various kinds of often village-based *posko* or local popular coordination centers.[2] The list also included political parties, trade unions, the main environmental and legal aid NGOs, student groups and some broad activist coalitions.

The statement also set out a comprehensive platform of goals and demands in the political, economic and cultural spheres. The political platform included "the setting up of *reformasi posko*," the formation of people's councils at all levels, the repeal of the dual function of the armed forces, new democratic political laws, the bringing to justice of violators of human rights and perpetrators of mass killings such as had occurred in Aceh, East Timor, Lampung and Jakarta, the freeing of all political prisoners and the holding of the earliest possible elections. The political platform also demanded that Suharto and his agents be put on trial and Habibie be rejected as a product of the New Order.

The statement emphasized in several places the importance of *aksi massa* which had been the main purpose for which the village *posko* had been established. On 2 September, a delegation of about 2,000 to 3,000 people representing sixty village *posko* demonstrated outside the governor's office. According to a statement issued by the Lampung Legal Aid Office, people arrived using forty trucks, four buses and scores of smaller vehicles. The People's Council successfully forced the local government to sign an agreement to establish a joint commission to deal with numerous cases of land disputes between villagers in sixty-three villages and nearby plantations.

Activists, in particular from the PRD, have told me of other such initiatives in Java. The People's Committee movement did not, in the end, take off during this period, affected by the fate of the huge mobilizations that took place in November 1998. However, agitation around this call was taking place all through the period June–October 1998. During this period, it was not yet clear whether the momentum would be there to propel the formation of such committees or other forms of organization.

The PRD was proposing an essentially revolutionary solution to the issue of a replacement power to the New Order elite: that power should be built up from below out of the mobilization process. Within the rest of the student movement, a more mixed concept developed. Among a broad range of students there was also a call for a People's Committee or similar bodies, such as a presidium of elite figures or community leaders. The interpretation of the concept outside of the PRD varied along a spectrum of different assessments or visions of who might make up an alternative governing coalition to the New Order. Some included student and activist groups, others tended more and more to concentrate on political figures from the broad political elite who had been able to escape being labeled New Order: in particular, Rais, Wahid and Megawati. All of these perspectives, which were continually in flux within a very fluid network of rising and falling student and activist coalitions, were bound by a basic proposition. This was that the Habibie government, as a product of the New Order, was illegitimate and that therefore it was legitimate for it be replaced outside of constitutional processes.[3]

This perspective was held widely outside the student sector also. On 12 November, one day after the demonstrations started, a group of prominent dissident politicians, former officials and a former general, known as the National Front (Barisan Nasional), called for the formation of a presidium as a provisional government to comprise "national and community figures, from the campuses and among students, from mass organizations and new parties." This presidium would replace the Habibie government and would, among other things, organize elections.[4] The idea of a presidium was discussed widely in the opinion pages of the press.

It was this perspective, this expectation of immediate regime change, that provided the basis for the next wave of mass mobilization that occurred at the time of the special sitting of the 1998 MPR session.

Almost all the student groups that had been active before May announced that they would mobilize for the MPR session to reject the legitimacy of the Habibie government and the MPR itself. On 28 October and then again on 9 November, students, activists and other political groups combined to organize large protest actions as kinds of warm-up events. The demonstration on 28 October was organized by a coalition that brought together almost every student group in Jakarta behind the demand of ending the dual function of the military. They mobilized between 20,000 and 30,000 people, mainly students, near the parliament building.

Then, as the November MPR session approached, the armed forces mobilized large numbers of troops in Jakarta. They also mobilized the Pam Swakarsa (Volunteer Security) militia who were armed with sharpened bamboo spears and knives. The military took the position that the MPR session itself was under threat and that students were intending to mobilize huge numbers to occupy the MPR and demand the resignation of Habibie. The events of 11–14 November indicated that the military's assessment was correct.

The mobilizations of 12–14 November in Jakarta, which were reflected in mobilizations around the country, brought hundreds of thousands, perhaps millions, of people onto the street and manifested a level of combativeness greater even than that of May 1997. In May, no non-student masses were mobilized in Jakarta until after Suharto had resigned. In fact, the majority faction in the student leadership kept the non-student masses out of the parliamentary compound in May. This time, from around 9 November, the *kampung* population of Jakarta became increasingly engaged in a confrontation with the military and the Pam Swakarsa militia it had formed. Van Dijk describes the combative attitude of the Jakarta proletariat and semi-proletariat towards the Pam Swakarsa militia as follows:

> . . . it became clear that some of the problems were being caused by Pam Swakarsa, who had armed themselves with bamboo runcing, bamboo spears, clubs, sickles, and rocks, and some even carrying kelawang, sabres and swords . . . Ordinary citizens, in particular school pupils and other young people, taking offence at the overwhelming and provocative presence of Pam Swakarsa in the streets of Jakarta and their own neighbourhoods, gave vent to this indignation by chasing and beating up Pam Swakarsa members, hurling stones at them. They turned against the security forces as well.[5]

The mood among the masses had been generated out of frustrated expectations. This included an expectation flowing from the call for the end of the dual function of the military: that military methods in dealing with social unrest would decrease. The *kampung* population was agitated by the brazen presence of the Pam Swakarsa and the military, mobilized clearly in defense of the regime and the MPR—still made up mostly of Suharto appointees.

In addition, there had been systematic mass leafleting by the PRD in key poor urban areas—using leaflets similar to those of May 1997. The leafleting had been targeted on urban poor *kampung* along some of the routes that students planned to use when they marched to the parliament buildings on 12 November. This tactic worked extremely effectively with almost all the non-student mass mobilizations where *kampung* people joined the marches occurring along these routes.[6] This tactic was also a direct response to the reality of the de-organized state of the people. One analysis by a PRD leader after the event emphasized:

> The choice of the best routes for the march in order to draw in the masses was crucial. Why is this so important? Because even up until now the people are not organized and the organized forces of resistance are very weak. The correct choice of routes on 12 and 13 November meant that a million people or more could be drawn into the actions.[7]

From the evening of 12 November until the evening of 13 November, Jakarta was in a general state of *aksi*. There was a planned build-up to the MPR sitting, which started on 12 November. On 9 November, thousands of students from a broad coalition of student groups marched from the Legal Aid Foundation offices in Central Jakarta towards the University of Indonesia campus in Salemba Street, also in Central Java. The groups involved ranged from the PRD-linked group, KOMRAD (which also included workers and urban poor), to the University of Indonesia Big Family (KBUI), a broad gathering of academics and students from that university. Student groups connected to liberal Islamic groups also participated. This action began the stream of actions that followed. Later in the day, thousands of students from the FORKOT coalition tried to march to the parliament building.[8] They carried banners demanding the formation of a People's Committee and rejected the special sitting of the MPR as illegitimate. Police and soldiers blocked the march. On 10 November, a new coalition called AKRAB, involving the groups who had mobilized on 9 November, organized a rally of thousands of students and ordinary people at the Proclamation Foundation in Central Jakarta. They also rejected the legitimacy of the MPR sitting and called for preparations to establish a People's Assembly. FORKOT, also mobilizing thousands of students, again tried to march to the MPR but was again blocked. On 11 November, the AKRAB coalition organized another rally billed as a People's Assembly. Tens of thousands of people mobilized. They tried to march from the Proclamation Monument to the roundabout in Jakarta's main street, but were blocked by the police and military. One University of Indonesia student used a car to smash through the army barricades, injuring a soldier from the Army Strategic Command, before he was beaten.

On 12 November, thousands of students attempted to march from the Catholic University of Atmajaya, also in Central Jakarta, to the parliament buildings. They were stopped again, and street clashes with soldiers broke out twice. Thousands of students and *kampung* dwellers were on the streets conducting rallies, giving speeches and singing political songs all around the area of Semanggi. Semanggi was one of the areas where the PRD had also concentrated its mass leafleting and agitation during previous days. In the evening, more clashes between students and *kampung* people with the army occurred when news spread that a high school student had been killed. More than 100 people were killed. Clashes and street rallies continued all night.

On 13 and 14 November, the mobilizations continued, fueled by popular anger over the killings at Semanggi. The AKRAB coalition organized a march on the MPR, still raising the demand that it disband and a new coalition government be formed by a presidium of non-New Order figures, who were to organize a speedy election. The mobilizations in Jakarta, and those occurring simultaneously around the country, were to provide the mandate for establishment of such a presidium. The Barnas group of dissident former officials, generals and student leaders had issued its call for a presidium on 11 November.

By the afternoon of 14 November, clashes with military units broke out in at least three areas in Jakarta and continued late in the evening. Hundreds of students and others were shot at Atmajaya University, where student protestors from the previous days had tried to march again. Nine were shot dead. Hundreds of thousands proceeding from other directions were still able to break through barricades to make it to the MPR by the evening.

Some of the student marches were organized to proceed along the major thoroughfares that cut their way through the densely populated *kampung*, where mass leafleting had been occurring during previous days. Along these routes, hundreds of thousands of people flowed out of the *kampung* lanes to swell the student marches to the MPR. Reinhardt Sirait, a student involved in this part of the mobilization, described the experience.

The important experience of the November 98 upsurge was that it succeeded in "awakening" and "drawing in" the urban masses. The anger stimulated by the students' resistance in May 98 found its moment in the Extraordinary Session of the MPR. This is how it began:

Tuesday, November 10, thousands of students were concentrated in Diponegoro St., and were blocked by Marines in front of Megaria [cinema]. Some committees moved in the direction of the Proclamation Monument, the place of the People's Assembly and the starting point for the next day's activities. The area was under the control of the Pam Swakarsa, but the people chased them out.

Wednesday, November 11, in the early afternoon, the People's Assembly was held by a number of *aksi* committees: Famred, Komrad, Front Jakarta, Megawati Support Committee, Workers Committee, and so on. In the late afternoon, tens of thousands of people moved off towards the parliament via Diponegoro St and Imam Bonjol. In the evening, there were blockades everywhere. A small clash occurred between a student driving his car and the military, injuring some soldiers. Two people were arrested.

Thursday, November 12, early in the day, Komrad and KBUI distributed tens of thousands of leaflets calling on the people to join the action to reject the MPR Extraordinary Session. They were distributed all along the Salemba-Matraman-Kampung Melayu-Cawang route. These routes were chosen based on the experience of July 96 and the 97 Mega-Star elections. In the early afternoon, thousands of students moved along Salemba towards Kampung

Melayu. Thousands of urban poor who were waiting along Salemba-Matraman-Kampung Melayu and Cawang joined. Hundreds had become thousands, which had become tens of thousands. Children, mothers, the supporting masses, all shouting slogans and clapping their hands. The students were stressed, always worried about provocateurs and whether they would be able to control the masses. Then they started to be confident that they could lead such an open resistance. Twice, military blockades could be ignored.

Towards evening, the long columns of student-people masses were blockaded in Gatot Subroto Street, directly in front of the Jakarta Metrpolitan Police headquarters. The columns were forced back. This was possible because the movement wasn't prepared and the military used guns. But now with experience in attack and defense, the student-people returned to the starting point in Salemba to consolidate and to prepare for the next day's actions. This was a valuable experience.

Friday, November 13, in the morning, the *kampung* were bombarded with more "People Unite" leaflets. The route changed: Salemba-Matraman-Kampung Melayu-Casablana-Semanggi. As predicted, tens of thousands of people were waiting to join the action. The day before, the Casablanca area had been "enlightened" by a long march by Famred. The students were now confident that they could lead. In Jatinegara the infrastructure [marshals, megaphones] for leading the masses was not adequate, so there was some rioting. Thousands of urban poor waiting in Cawang were moved off towards Kampung Melayu. Because there was not enough infrastructure, the masses became split into two groups. One went via Rasuna Said (Kuningan) and another through Karet heading for Semanggi. There were reports that some students and people had died, been injured. The sound of exploding tear gas and rifle fire had resulted in people coming out of their homes, out of the lanes and the street stalls to make barricades to slow down the military's movements. They attacked them with rocks and Molotov cocktails, defending the students.

November 14: Salemba, Senen, Matraman were in revolt. Without any instructions or plans, the people had gathered and were waiting. There were clashes. The Central Jakarta Police Station was

encircled by the people. A KODAM military vehicle was burned.
Angry over the Semanggi incident . . . they attacked any symbol of
tyranny. Around Semanggi, the people stopped all passing cars
looking for military. In Slip there were clashes between residents
and the military. Hundreds of thousands of people surrounded the
parliament building.[9]

Kees van Dijk, drawing on Indonesian press reports, also captures the
situation:

On November 13: During the afternoon and in the evening, parts of
Jakarta were to turn into what the Jakarta Post described as a "virtual
battlefield . . . pitting students, supported by the masses, against
heavily armed police and soldiers" (November *Jakarta Post*, 14–11–
1998). Another journalist wrote that watching TV was like watching
a war movie. Security units employed light tanks, armoured cars, and
water cannons. Soldiers could be seen taking up firing positions.
Protesters fought back with stones, Molotov cocktails, and any other
missiles which came to hand.[10]

On November 14: On the day following Semanggi, people held in
Jakarta what was described as razzia militer, checking cars and public
transport in search of soldiers and policemen, beating up such
persons when they could lay their hands on them . . . Sporadic
looting took place in various parts of the city, carried out by people
shouting that they were hungry and yelling "Long live the students."
No traffic was possible between the airport and the town. . . . On 14
November, marines had to warn members of the army that it was
dangerous to drive alone in the streets and that their military vehicles
might be set on fire by enraged citizens.[11]

The MPR compound was more or less occupied by the student mass
assembly by the evening of 14 November. The occupation came at the end
of three days of *aksi* takeover of the Jakarta political arena. Furthermore,
this had been part of a national-scale mobilization. Between 9 and 14
November, demonstrations took place in almost every major city in the
country as well as in many small towns and even villages. In Jakarta and
throughout the country, the same demands were being raised and the same

forms of struggle were being used. On 14 November, Jakarta, especially the Central Jakarta *kampung* areas, had been in a state of uprising, with the *kampung* population defying the security apparatus at virtually every point. The students had mobilized huge numbers to the MPR, had broken through the military barricades, and assembled at the MPR. However, despite the size and militancy of the Jakarta mobilizations and the national spread of the supporting mobilizations, the occupation of the parliamentary compound could not be sustained for more than a few hours. It was not disbanded by force, however; there were too many people and the army was already overstretched by the city-wide mobilizations and the collapse of the Pam Swakarsa in the face of mass hostility. The students dispersed the occupation themselves. In a self-critical report on the student consciousness, one analysis argued:

On November 14 (on the day after the killings of *mahasiswa* and *rakyat* at Semanggi and Gatot Subroto) the regime was indeed in a squeeze. The *rakyat* were angry. The mahasiswa and rakyat had gone into action and had reached the parliament building which had been the goal also the day before [but which they had not reached]. The regime had to let the mahasiswa and rakyat reach the parliament to avoid even bigger clashes.

But then what did the vanguard [that is, the students] do?

The vanguard did not have the consciousness that this was the moment to begin a new phase to launch a higher offensive at a moment when the regime was in a tight fix and was not capable of acting. The hundreds of thousands of rakyat and mahasiswa who had reached the parliament did not now want to defend the area that they controlled! Even though all the things needed to do this had come into being spontaneously: support from the mass media, especially electronic media; logistics, and support from other political groups. Their lack of consciousness that it was time to shift the focus of the struggle to defending their positions in the parliament compound meant that they reverted to past tactics namely to return to their respective bases and to let the people go home.[12]

At the the time, the student leaders who led the dispersal were also being affected by many rumors: that the army would launch an all-out attack, that thousands of Pam Swakarsa were massing. Neither was true. There was a more fundamental problem of consciousness. *Aksi*, in the form it had assumed up until that time, was not able to take the movement further. It confronted the question of power.

Elite Politics and the "People's Committee"

The development of the mass action form of politics was a challenge not just to the dictatorship but to all the edifices of the counter-revolution itself. Gradually, the whole of the political elite mobilized to try to save the system. The crisis of the regime that had become so exposed in 1997 was not a crisis of the regime alone or of Suharto's personal rule but of the system as a whole. Among the first to realize this were those politicians at arm's length from the center of power, not immersed in the machinations of suppressing the mobilizations, and who had some analytical capacity. The two most important of these were Abdurrahman Wahid and Amien Rais.

Abdurrahman Wahid, also known as Gus Dur, was (and is) a highly contradictory politician. Intellectually, he stands above almost all other politicians in the political elite that emerged under the New Order in the 1970s and 1980s. Ideologically, he stands closest to the social democratic tradition of the Indonesian Socialist Party (PSI), although he has never exhibited the same open hostility to the communist party as did the PSI leaders of the 1950s and 1960s—but then there has been no communist party as a rival after 1965. He is probably the only national politician who, before 1998, advocated reconciliation with the ex-members of the PKI and acknowledged that the massacres of 1965 were wrong. His main political vehicle for direct response to the democratization issue was his chairperson-ship of FODEM, a small, moderate pro-democracy grouping, with ex-student leaders who were closely aligned with PSI elders. At the same time, he had assumed the chairpersonship of the Nahdlatul Ulama in the 1980s, following in the footsteps of his father and grandfather, an organization based on a huge but loose network of traditional village Islamic leaders and the villagers under their influence. This network potentially reached millions of villagers, specially in East Java.

Wahid saw the danger to the system as early as July 1996. He was highly critical of the decision by the Megawati PDI, PRD and others to confront the regime by refusing to vacate the PDI headquarters in July 1996. He opposed the escalation of mobilizational politics, often articulating this opposition as a fear of the masses running amok.[13] After the round of larger mobilizations and riots in June–July 1996, he had a sudden reconciliation with Suharto and appeared to embark on an attempt to convince Suharto to leave the presidency so as to allow a reorganization of Indonesian politics that could better head off an impending clash with the *aksi* process. He attempted to reassure Suharto of his family's future by offering his support for a major role for Suharto's daughter, Tutut, in a post-Suharto scenario. He campaigned for GOLKAR in the 1997 elections, traveling around the country with Suharto's daughter.

Amien Rais was also following a change from within style tactic. He had joined and was active in an organization called the Indonesian Moslem Intellectuals Association (ICMI), whose titular head was Suharto and whose active head was B.J. Habibie, a minister in the Suharto cabinet for several years. A large number of intellectuals had identified Habibie as a figure who was prepared in the longer term to consider reorganizing the political format away from dictatorship. Rais was also a leading figure, and soon chairperson of another large Islamic organization, based more in the cities and towns, called Muhammidiyah. Muhammidiyah had not mobilized its memberships in politics for more than three decades and it had become passive and fractured, with some of its members aligning with the officially blessed PPP party of Islam and others seeking independent political channels. His position in Muhammidiyah gave him a high national profile. As criticism of the government strengthened even in the early 1990s, Rais engaged with some issues such as corruption. He also spoke out on the issue of succession, but did not campaign on it. When leaders of the churches advocated a boycott of the 1997 elections, he was also pressured to do so but declined. He, like Wahid, stood outside the massive May 1997 mobilizations. But, involving as they did the urban constituency that the Muhammidiyah had appealed to in the past and so connected with the PPP, he could not ignore the militant opposition of the May 1997 mobilizations. He began a campaign of increasingly sharp criticism of Suharto and started also to demand that Suharto resign. When the student movement surged forward after December 1997, he tried to position himself as a spokesperson for their sentiments. Between January and March 1998, no other figure from the political elite aligned themselves to the mass opposition as did Rais—neither Wahid nor Megawati.

Crucial to all the actions of all members of the political elite between February and May 1998—and indeed in the following several months—was pre-empting any further escalation of the mass mobilizations and of any qualitative leaps forward in terms of the emergence of new forms of organization. By March 1998, the central demand of the whole movement was the resignation of Suharto. Wahid tried to engineer an agreement for Suharto to resign without any confrontation, helping to convince Suharto to announce that he would reshuffle his cabinet and announce new elections in which he would not stand. However, this maneuver had no impact and the mobilizations continued to grow.

Having aligned himself with the mobilizations, Rais' pre-emptive role was targeted at preventing an escalation of mass mobilization in Jakarta, and in particular in preventing the mobilizations expanding to draw in the Jakarta proletarian and semi-proletarian masses. At the beginning of May, Rais had threatened to call a demonstration of millions in Jakarta. But it soon became clear, as demonstrations became more combative, large and frequent around the country, that such a mobilization might only further deepen politicization. Further, Rais had no real control over the process. Precisely because there was no permanent organization and the dynamic was fundamentally of an unfolding process rather than the maneuvering of stable, organized forces, the risks were too great. He soon backed off and even requested television time to tell people that there would be no such popular mobilization.

Rais gave an explanation for his retreat stating that he had been told that the army was prepared to carry out a Tiananmen Square style massacre. There has been no documentation of what decisions or deliberations were taking place in army headquarters and there may well have been officers expressing that kind of intention. However, the army had long lost the initiative in dealing with the protest movement. A Tiananmen Square style massacre would have been required not just in Jakarta but throughout the country. Even in Jakarta, May 1997 had shown that virtually the whole city could mobilize, either in organized defiance of barricades and authority, or in riots. It would have provoked more demonstrations and massive rioting, even possibly some kind of urban rebellion. Such upheaval would have further rocked the collapsing economy. The military, throughout these events, was an ineffective player in the political struggles underway.

A struggle also broke out within the Jakarta student movement leadership on the question of whether to call the masses onto the streets. Such a call, in order to have real authority, needed to be made by one or more of the broader student coalitions that had emerged out of the sudden explosion in campus activity and which had won popular recognition. The most important of these was Forum Kota, which brought together student activists from at least fourteen campuses. On 14 May, the students debated the call, with PRD-affiliated students and other radicals arguing for such mass participation, and those who were increasingly looking to figures like Amien opposing it. After hours of debate, the radicals lost the vote by a narrow margin.

This meant that Jakarta's demonstrations on 19 and 20 May did not achieve the scale and popular character of those in Bandung, Yogyakarta or Ujung Pandang, or of the mass and militant character of many of the demonstrations of other cities. However, the maneuvers by Rais and the caution of the more moderate students still did not prevent the Jakarta proletarian and semi-proletarian masses coming out to demonstrate. They did—except they did not join the student demonstration. They rioted. Their anger and rejection of the elite was still manifest and was to show itself again in the spread of actions throughout the country, with *aksi* even spreading to the villages and corrupt village heads chased out of office. The threat to the elite was not yet over, especially as ideas of "people's committees," "people's assemblies" and mass movement-mandated presidiums started to be propagated by the same forces and using the same methods which had successfully disseminated the call for the repeal of political laws and of the military's role in politics and for the ousting of Suharto.

It was Amien Rais who took the lead in campaigning against the call to establish people's committees. By mid-September, he was warning that the idea of a "people's committee" was "leftish," warning people that there were efforts afoot to revive ideas from the era of NASAKOM. He also stated publicly that the idea of "people's committees" was being borrowed from the Russian Bolshevik idea of soviets. Although those calling for people's committees were also calling for urgent elections, Rais directly counterposed the idea of these "people's committees" with the holding of

elections, stating: "This is very dangerous, because people are being told
not to believe in the process of democracy, elections are belittled, and then
parties will not be needed and people will just rely on mass strength, on
muscle."[14]

Rais, Wahid and Megawati were finally confronted directly with this
issue during the November uprising. The expectation among the majority
of student leaders was that these three figures needed to take the initiative
in demanding that Habibie step aside and make way for a presidium style
government. Some student leaders, mostly those associated with the less
ideological groupings around faculty student councils, began pressuring for
Wahid, Rais and Megawati to meet. Initially, there was no enthusiasm for
such a meeting; each of these three figures had their own ambitions. In one
attempt to arrange such a meeting, students had picked up Rais at Jakarta
airport and forcibly took him to the house of Wahid. The meeting still did
not take place and had to wait another day. Finally, the three of them,
together with the Sultan of Yogyakarta, met at Wahid's house on 10
November. The sultan was actually a member of GOLKAR and had been
governor of Yogyakarta for much of the New Order. He had won some
acceptance among some students when he supported the pre-May mobilizations and actually supported a call for non-students to join the 500,000-
strong or more 20 May rally in Yogyakarta. Many other dissident elite
figures, including those from Barnas, also assembled at Wahid's house in
the Jakarta suburb of Ciganjur, but were kept outside.

Rais, Megawati and Wahid remained consistent in their long-term
trajectory. They did not wish to legitimize or strengthen *aksi* politics. While
making the necessary statements in support of reform, action against
corruption and the demobilization of the Pam Swakarsa, they refused the
students' demands and issued a statement affirming that they trusted Habibie
to organize the elections, which would remain the major mechanism for all
aspects of the political transition. They were also unwilling to take a clear-cut
stand on the mass movement's demand to immediately end any military role
in politics. The key elements of the Ciganjur Declaration, as it became
known, responding to the demands of the mass movement read:

That general elections would be a democratic way to terminate the
transitional government of President B.J. Habibie; it also would be
the best way of establishing a new legitimate government. . . .

That ABRI's dual functions should be abolished gradually and the
last phase of it should take place no later than six years from the date
on which this statement is revealed to the public, paving the way for
the growth of a civil society. . . .

Everyone should return home and stop complicating the situation.

The failure of these figures to fully align with mobilized popular sentiment was
already known to both students and masses as they rallied and marched on 13
November. Amien Rais had appeared in a TV interview and angrily charged
that the mobilizations were being managed by radical groups with their own
agendas.[15] The mass anger at the violence used against the people as early as 9
November, then again on 12 November and during the day on 13 November
helped keep the mobilization momentum going. There were also hopes that a
large and militant demonstration and actual occupation of the MPR might
change Rais', Wahid's and Megwati's attitude. However, on the evening of 13
November, there were no signs of such a change.

Consciousnesss and Organization

The Suharto dictatorship was defeated by *aksi*. This was also the essence of
the New Order's political crisis: its inability to govern on the basis of the
"floating mass" policy, of enforced passivity. The story of the victory of
mass mobilization is on one level the story of the conscious decision and
persistent commitment of a small group of people to revive mass action as a
form of political struggle during the 1990s. In this sense, Suharto did not
just fall from power, he was pushed. The extent and depth of the spirit of
aksi and its political power has been powerfully captured in a brief aside by
Daniel Dhakidae in his mammoth scholarly work, *Cendikiawan dan
Kekuasaan Dalam Negara Orde Baru* ("Intellectuals and Power Under
the New Order State").[16] Dhakidae himself had been a student activist in
the 1970s and one of the editors of *Sendi* magazine. He later studied at
Cornell University in the USA and went on to head the research department at Jakarta's largest newspaper organization, *Kompas*, in Jakarta. In his
opening chapter in this work, he refers to something which "frightened the
New Order with all its armed forces."

He was referring to a few words about one line: in fact, a line from a
poem by Wiji Thukul, the poet of *aksi*. He had been a trishaw driver and

carpenter as well as a poet. He was a leader of the PRD and helped establish its cultural organization. He disappeared in 1998, probably kidnapped and murdered by agents of the military. Dhakidae quotes one of his poems, written in 1986, that became extraordinarily popular. Its last line, says Dhakidae, became so popular during the New Order that an equivalent can only be found in "Karl Marx's super-slogan *Workers of the World Unite* or the super slogan of the Indonesian revolution *Freedom or Death.*"[17]

> Warning
> if the people leave
> while the rulers deliver their speeches
> we must be vigilant
> perhaps they have lost hope
> if the people hide away
> and whisper
> when discussing their problems
> then rulers should beware and learn to listen
> if the people don't dare complain
> then things are dangerous
> and if what the rulers say
> may not be rejected
> truth must surely be under threat
> and if suggestions are refused without consideration
> voices silenced, criticisms banned without reason
> accused of subversion and of disturbing security
> then there is only one word: fight!

This last line—"there is only one word: fight!"—was indeed "a force uniting the activists who wanted to overthrow the New Order."[18] The Indonesian word *lawan,* fight or perhaps also translatable as resist, is a powerful word in the language, reverberating with a total rejection of compromise. In terms of political consciousness, that other key word of the national revolution, *rakyat,* gained a new and again combative content as *aksi* and *lawan* became its partners in opposing "floating mass," *massa mengambang.*

The spread and grip of this particular form of struggle—*aksi*—in Indonesian society, especially as it gradually became a mass phenomenon, as Aspinall put it, "presaged a head-on confrontation between state and society."[19] But *aksi*, of course, did not develop this power simply as some kind of metaphysical manifestation of the will of the radicals who began the movement back in the 1980s. At one level, *aksi* was a form of political action: protest mobilization in the form of strikes, land occupations, hunger strikes, rallies, marches and sit-ins. But as an intervention into other already existing social, cultural, political and economic processes, it became more than just a form of action.

A decade is long enough to delete the memory of specific historical facts: the memory of who did what and why. A decade is not long enough, however, to delete a social class's memory of the quality of an experience. Mass mobilization had been the essence of the *pergerakan* of the 1920s and 1930s, the period of the political and guerrilla struggle against the return of the Dutch colonial forces between 1945 and 1949, and the period of nation building which transformed into the movement for "Socialism ala Indonesia" in the 1950s and 1960s. The horrific terror and slaughter of 1965 did drive those who were most central to that experience—the millions of workers, peasants and students on the left—into a kind of dark silence, where the survivors of the mass murder could only whisper their memory of past organizational activity, if they were not themselves traumatized by torture or witnessing murder. But there was a more general experience of the mobilized *rakyat* that was entrenched in symbols less easy to completely eliminate. The most potent of these symbols was Soekarno, Bung Karno himself. Even twenty-five years later, simply bearing his name could provide the capital to propel an otherwise nondescript personality into a position of national stature.

The regime's campaign of terror in 1965 and 1966 was implemented on a scale and using such unrelenting horror—decapitation, disembowelment, mass execution, rape—that it did intimidate the memory of the past empowerment of mobilization into quiescence. The murders and imprisonments of the most articulate and courageous of the leadership of the socialist movement also strengthened this effect. But the tactical requirement to allow post-1965 students to use political mobilization, even if without the participation of non-student *rakyat*, meant that echoes of *gerakan* remained, and, in the big student protests of 1973, 1974 and 1978, these echoes were strengthened. *Mahasiswa* (student) became a word that belonged to the people and later *aksi, lawan* and *rakyat* went naturally side by side with *mahasiswa*.

The *mahasiswa* chink in the counter-revolution's "floating mass" strategy meant that there was really only the period between 1978 and 1988 where "floating mass" was being enforced consistently upon all sectors of society. This was not long enough to completely wipe out the form of political consciousness that had developed during the course of sixty years of the national revolution and in which an active role for the *rakyat* was a central part. Within just a few years of actions reintroducing the *aksi* method, a new momentum was launched. Furthermore, the new political consciousness as it developed during that decade took on an especially combative quality.

The consciousness of mobilization that developed during the 1990s was a consciousness that reflected a process of defiance, of wresting back something that had been taken away. It was more angry, combative and militant and was consistent with the necessity of confrontation on the streets. Before 1965, it was only among peasants that confrontation with the police and landowners occurred. While Soekarno remained relatively isolated within the state apparatus and the political elite, as head of state he lent an aspect of official authority to the mass mobilizations of the 1962–5 era. Even the chairperson of the PKI would appear at mass rallies wearing a ministerial uniform (even though as a minister he wielded no authority over any actual ministry). Many mass mobilizations were not experienced as acts of defiance against the state because of President Soekarno's support. After Soekarno was sidelined within the state structures after 30 September 1965, the full force of the state was brought down on all those who had mobilized.

This ambiguity has been absent from the *aksi* activities since 1989: all have been openly in defiance of the state and have faced state violence, mainly exercised through the military, throughout the period of the New Order. This has declined since the fall of Suharto, but has not disappeared. The state apparatus, in particular the police and military, are still used against workers, students and farmers. In 2004, in Ujung Pandang police raided and shot dead students on a major campus; demonstrators outside a mining company in Kalimantan were shot and killed; peasant activists were arrested and beaten. In Aceh, *aksi* reached its peak after the fall of Suharto in a 2 million strong demonstration (in a population of 5 million) demanding a referendum in November 1999. In 2003, the military was deployed in full-scale repression under military emergency rule.

As *aksi* mobilizations spread, zigzagging their way through a decade of political developments, this process also had facilitated the beginnings of a reorganization of the de-organized popular classes. The escalating and very combative opposition that the New Order faced during the 1990s was increasingly organizing more and more segments of society. Action committees, discussion groups, campaign coalitions and new advocacy groups mushroomed. Furthermore, this was a national-scale phenomenon, occurring from Aceh to Java to Papua. However, the most important phenomenon to grasp is that the *aksi* form itself became a form of organization. The structure of organization was always present in the *aksi* and in many cases documented in the *aksi* chronology. There was a division of labor, precise roles for the "membership" during an action and a conscious collective stand towards the state apparatus as well as other groups. Both as an activity that directly involved people and as something which people observed as an example or model, the *aksi* was a reorganizing mechanism.

It is not surprising that shortly after *aksi* activity restarted around 1989, the first attempts were made to establish trade unions and peasant unions. The rapid recruitment of people into Megawati's PDI in the mid-1990s, drawing on the humble social layers and networks that Aspinall described, was also a manifestation of this reorganizing process. The expansion of the PDI membership also brought with it an organizational innovation which was also a perfect manifestation of the widespread but temporary character of reorganization, namely, the *posko*—literally *pos commando* (command post). These were first established in 1997 as part of the campaign to defend the Megawati PDI against Suharto's moves to suppress it. *Posko* were grassroots coordination centers set up at neighborhood level. They usually comprised a small stall or hut marked with much PDI paraphernalia—banners, flags and so on. People gathered there to discuss, plan recruitment and organize actions. When there were major mobilizations under the PDI banner, the *posko* were absolutely crucial to the mobilization. There is no way to tell how many of these *posko* were set up, but there would have been thousands of them in the major and medium-size cities, organizing tens of thousands of people. As this method became more popular with PDI members, it also spread with many other organizations setting up similar public, well advertised coordinating centers for people to gather at.

There can be a tendency to underestimate the level of organization that was developing and therefore the political challenge that it threatened because of one fundamental characteristic of this organization that is peculiar to Indonesia's historical development after 1965. With *aksi* itself as the essential mechanism of organization, it was in a constant state of flux. Everything, or almost everything, was temporary. The proportion of politically mobilizing people involved in a permanent or stable political or mobilizing organization was small, even while almost the whole society was organizing through a myriad of temporary forms. Action committees rose and fell as the situation changed. Coalitions between NGOs, political groups, student groups and others rose and fell. Even where some remained stable, the membership came and went rapidly, often giving an organization dramatically different characteristics at different times. In 1997, the election monitoring organization, KIPP—established on the initiative of the most radical activists, including the PRD—was an organization that initiated *aksi* of all kinds. KIPP became permanent, existing even in 2003, but its composition changed and its activities changed radically as well, dropping *aksi*. In other words, the regime was not being challenged by the so-called archetypical "well-organized mass opposition movement" but rather by a process, by something coming into being.

Aksi and Power

Between 1996 and 1998, the broad political elite had divided into two camps. One camp, around Suharto, the armed forces and GOLKAR, comprised those who remained committed to continuing to enforce a "floating mass" regime, with murder and torture if necessary. On 18 April 1998—just one month before he was forced to resign—Suharto was still espousing a "floating mass" style view on politics on campus. Echoing Ali Murtopo's old insistence that everybody remain "wholly occupied" in their respective development functions, Suharto declared that the campus's true function must be protected. Through the military commander over the armed forcers in Central Java, Major General Tyasno Sudarto, Suharto declared:

> President Soeharto said that the campuses were built and functioned
> to educate and prepare the nation's future leaders. The occurrence of

protests on the campuses of course was disturbing the implementation of the educational process. The President has requested that the
function of the campus to educate future leaders falls into error and
that therefore they cannot carry out their function properly because
of these disturbances.[20]

A second camp comprised those desperate to prevent the reorganization
and repoliticization process revived by *aksi* from developing to a level that
might threaten the system as a whole. The "transition to democracy" in
Indonesia that was formalized in 1998 was, in fact, a transition from one
tactic to preserve the political and business elite—enforced "floating
mass"—to another new tactic: co-option of social and popular unrest
through new electoral and parliamentary processes. *Aksi* did not stop after
13 November. Indeed, for several weeks afterwards, there were waves of
demonstrations calling for the dismissal of the armed forces chief of staff,
Wiranto, and sharper demands for the ending of the military's role in
politics. There were more demonstrations outside military posts and offices
in many cities throughout the country—in most cases organized by groups
connected with the PRD. Many of these mobilized thousands of students.
But the overall political momentum, a momentum focusing the myriad
aksi on a specific political goal, diminished.

Aksi had defeated Suharto and won a major victory, the first victory,
against the counter-revolution. Neither the armed forces nor the civilian
state apparatus had been able to save Suharto or the policy of "floating
mass." The elite's new tactic was forced to concede the right to political
parties to organize at all levels and for trade unions to be free to establish
themselves, at least as free as in most liberal parliamentary systems. The
PRD, for example, was able to operate openly again. State censorship over
the press ended. And street protest and mass mobilization—*aksi*—was
acknowledged as an integral and legitimate part of the political culture. The
law was changed to end a ban on street demonstrations, requiring only that
the police be informed before actions. The military increasingly withdrew
from intervention to suppress *aksi*. "Dual function" lost its ideological
authority and the military had to seek other justifications for a role in
politics.

But in the form it had taken during the 1990s, *aksi* had not been able to
replace the New Order state, the political elite as a whole, with a popular

government. *Aksi* succeeded, but *komite rakyat* did not. A new mode of politics had been conceded: electoral politics, reflecting a new balance of power between the elite and the masses. However, it was the same elite. The only changes were that power and position had been rearranged among them. Suharto and his cronies were marginalized; the military elite had been pushed back; the GOLKAR bosses were now players on the same level as Megawati and her PDIP. Retired generals, former GOLKAR bosses and businessmen also flocked to join the PDIP. The elite was reconfiguring itself. At the same time there were many other more junior players. Power and position had also been redistributed downwards to the provincial, regency level and district levels of the party machines of these elite figures. In the Ciganjur statement, Rais, Wahid, Megawati and the Sultan had included a commitment to decentralization. This demand had not been important in the movement prior to this. It was a concession to their party machines and a signal of how their new tactics of co-option rather than repression would develop.

The failure of *aksi* in 1998 to bring about a people's committee style government was, in effect, a failure of the social and political reorganization process to go beyond temporary forms to achieve more extensive permanent forms of organization. The movement had won authority for and developed skills in a powerful new form of political action. It had developed a body of policy critiques and ideas stretching across the liberal democratic to socialist spectrum that provided the basis for the emergence of the *reformasi* agenda which the reconfigured post-New Order elite could not ignore. But it had not produced any mass-scale permanent organization held together by shared ideological orientation.

The campaign to build a political movement against the New Order based on mass action really only began in the early 1990s. *Aksi* had about seven years, compared to the New Order's twenty-five years, to develop before the two moments of confrontation in 1998: with Suharto in May 1998 and with the broader elite in November 1998. It is not surprising that the transition from temporary to permanent forms of organization were not achieved in such a short period. The *aksi* movement for political change had completely rolled back and destroyed the whole edifice of "floating mass," which had been enforced through the most violent and horrendous terror. This was its amazing achievement. However, it was also most likely that this first experiment with mass action would only be an opening phase in the process of the reorganization of Indonesian society and its de-organized popular classes. The movement had had a lot to overcome. The de-organization of Indonesian society by Suharto's counter-revolution had been severe and deep. It had used terror to suppress independent genuine self-organization among the popular classes. It had deprived the whole of society of a shared historical memory of the struggle for its own creation.

8

Aksi (and Politics after Suharto)

The forced resignation of Suharto in May 1998 opened the way for a rapid and massive spread of *aksi* among the general population. The mobilizations leading up to the march on the MPR in November 1998 was the most dramatic example of this, containing as it did the potential for a qualitative deepening of the radicalization. This mobilizational process collapsed when Megawati Soekarnoputri, Amien Rais and Abdurrahman Wahid (also known as Gus Dur) declared that they would support a process of political transition through elections to be organized under the Habibie government. They decided against an extra-constitutional transition enabled by the mobilization of the student-led parliament of the streets.

The November mobilizations in Jakarta involved hundreds of thousands of urban poor—workers and semi-proletarians—and students. The political conditions that enabled such an escalation of street mobilization were primarily created by the success of the movement in forcing Suharto to resign and in forcing a break in the cohesion of the political elite formed during the Suharto period. There was a massive boost in confidence at the mass level and *aksi* of various kinds around a variety of issues took place around the country.

In a book published in 2005, the Indonesian analyst Munafrizal Manan described the situation like this:

The era of transition, followed by political liberalization, changed Indonesian society very drastically. This society, where for thirty years freedom and political participation had been blocked, changed to a society free and with the courage to articulate its political participation. The great fear of articulating the demands that existed under Suharto, disappeared completely as soon as the transition began.

Since the beginning of mid-1998, the daring of society increased in a very impressive manner. Voices of protest and demands that would have seemed absurd to imagine occurring openly before became a part of the reality of contemporary Indonesian political life. Protests, demonstrations, rallies, and mass actions of different kinds, became normal political activities. Even before the year [1998] had ended there had been almost 3,000 demonstrations carried out by almost every social layer.[1]

Most of these *aksi*, of one kind or another, have not been documented systematically but it is still possible to identify the main trends and limitations. Probably the most immediate and dramatic wave of *aksi* after the resignation of Suharto were at the village and *kabupaten* level to force the resignation of village heads or *bupati*, and even governors, who were considered by large sections of the local population to be either corrupt or oppressive. Manan, in his book, notes the forced resignation of the *bupati* of Langkat in North Sumatra, the Lampung Regional Secretary in South Sumatra, the Banten *bupati*, the *bupati* of Maros in South Sulawesi as well as the *bupati* of Banyuwangi as examples.[2] There were many more such cases, including at the village level. There are estimates that more than 300 government officials, mostly village heads, were forced to leave their posts during the May–July period in 1998. In some cases, they were physically chased out of the village or their offices attacked, stoned or burned. The magazine *Pembebasan*, for example, reported that the inhabitants of forty-one villages in the Central Javanese *kabupaten* of Klaten mobilized in a coordinated fashion to remove all forty-one of their village heads. In Tuban, East Java, hundreds of villagers forced the local district head (*camat*) to resign and smashed up his office. In a village near Palembang in South Sumatra a village head considered corrupt was attacked and an acid used in rubber production was doused over him.[3]

These village *aksi* were not confined to protests demanding the resignation of officials. There were also many occupations of production sites, such as coffee, cacao, palm oil and sugar plantations as well as prawn farms. Such actions occurred in Jember, Tuban and Gresik, for example, in East Java as well as in Tangerang, Tapos, and Indramayu in West Java. In fact, there were examples of this all throughout the country. Land also became a major issue, with increasing examples of land occupations by farmers reclaiming their land from private developers or local government projects. As one study put it:

> . . . with the fall of Soeharto, occupations of land controlled by the state—and to a lesser extent corporations—exploded all over Indonesia. The Director General of the Department of Forestry and Plantations estimated that as of September 2000, some 118,830 hectares of national estate land had been seized, along with 48,051 hectares of private estate lands (as quoted in Fauzi, 2003). These occupations are enormously significant in light of the combined dispossession and repression of the Soeharto era. According to preliminary estimates made in early 2003 in Garut, Tasikmalaya and Ciamis districts some 14,000 families have occupied nearly 9,000 hectares of land in 41 locations that all have units of SPP. Even though this is not a large percentage of the extensive territory of the districts, the occupation and cultivation of this land has been significant for the plantation and forest managers.[4]

Manan in his book also cites several cases taken from reports in the daily newspaper, *Kompas*, between May 1998 and November 2001. It is worth summarizing some of these:

- 120 hectares of national housing company land occupied by 500 people who suspect (incorrectly) that the land is owned by the Suharto family.
- People occupy 2,165 hectares of land in Bogor, West Java owned by Suharto's son, Bambang Trihatmojo. The people fence off this rubber plantation land, which Bambang was planning to turn into a self-contained town development.
- Hundreds of garden vegetable farmers occupy and plant crops on the Cimacan golf course, which they claim had been vegetable growing land previously. Near Surabaya, in the district of Laka-santri another golf course was occupied. It was said to be village land sold without consultation with the village inhabitants.
- Hundreds of villagers from the village of Cibedug, in the district of

Ciawi, West Java occupied land on the Tapos cattle ranch, owned by the Suharto family. They divided up the land which they had previously claimed as land they had been farming.

- People from Muara Pahu and Jempang in Kutai, East Kalimantan occupied the base camp of the Lonsum Sumatra Company, which had 16,500 hectares of land that the villagers claimed the company had not obtained permission to log.
- Villagers from Suci and Pati in Jember, East Java occupy coffee plantation land managed by a local provincial government company. The police attempt dispersal and ten people are injured.
- Thousands of people from north Barito district in Central Kalimantan storm and occupy a gold mining area, angered by the gold mining company's arbitrary attitude to traditional land ownership.
- Between 200 and 300 farmers occupy 100 hectares of clove plantation in Blitar, East Java and cut down all the trees planted by the plantation company, stating the land was theirs. The police forcibly removed the farmers with two killed and sixteen injured.

Manan also documents four blockades organized by people in 2000, as further examples of this trend, In April 2000, in Kutai Barat, East Kalimantan, people blocked the road into the Kelian Equatorial Mining Company because of a land compensation dispute. On 15 May, villagers from Kayu Batu village near Jayapura, Papua, blockaded the Telkom offices in Jayaura also over land compensation issues. Also in May 2000, villagers from four villages in Muara Batang Gadis in North Sumatra blockaded the offices of the Kerang Neam forest company protesting their twenty-five years of forest clearing of people's lands. In June 2000, local people blockaded the Newmont Minahasa Raya mining company in North Sulawesi also over land compensation issues.[5]

These kinds of protest actions, and many others, have continued at a sustained pace since 1998. There has been no let up. *Pembebasan* monthly magazine, published by the People's Democratic Party, regularly reports a smattering of these protests in each issue. Each issue has reported at least twenty and up to 200 cases of various forms of protest involving almost every social sector: students, workers, farmers, neighborhood residents, teachers, doctors, nurses, electricity company employees, bank employees, the state airplane factory employees, victims of Suharto period injustice, squatters, public transport drivers, taxi drivers, journalists, street traders, fishermen, women demonstrating against sexism of various kinds; and so the list could go on.

Even the lower ranks of the police and army have mobilized. The August–September issue of *Pembebasan* reported that on 20 May 2002 more than 300 policemen demonstrated to protest what they said was the unilateral stopping of promotions by the West Java police chief. These 300 corporals were representing 2,000 of their colleagues. Then on 26 June, 325 soldiers demonstrated to press for information as to what was happening regarding non-appearing housing credit from an army-owned bank after they had already paid the bank their deposits.

The resilience of this phenomenon is reflected, for example, in the reportage of the July 2005 issue of *Pembebasan*. In its regular section entitled "The People Fight Back," covering the previous four weeks, it includes anti-corruption protests in North Sumatra; in Semarang, Central Java; in Sleman, Central Java; in Makassar, South Sulawesi; in Boyolali, East Java; in Bulukumba; protests against the budget in Jakarta; by teachers' assistants and casual teachers in Cianjur, West Java; students and street traders demonstrating against the arrest of students after a joint demonstration; university students in Aceh protesting fees; students and townspeople protesting unfair actions by a local election commission in Makassar; thousands of civil servants protest on the streets in Temanggung against the alleged arbitrary transfer of seventy-eight civil servants by the *bupati*; students protest the development of a new mall in the education quarter in Malang, East Java; in Yogyakarta hundreds of farmers protest the new water privatization bill; in Jakarta hundreds of people demonstrate against the privatization of the Pasar Rebo hospital; over 1,000 farmers and others demonstrate in Central Jakarta against a new regulation giving the government the right to seize land without compensation; a week later there is another demonstration against this; thousands of farmers are reported to demonstrate again in Semarang against the same regulation; more than 200 street peddlers demonstrate outside the Jakarta provincial parliament against being forcibly moved along; students at the premier Gajah Mada state university in Yogyakarta demonstrate against the doubling of some fees; farmers demonstrate in Lampung, South Sumatra on the issue of forcible removal from their lands; fishermen and workers in West Nusatenggara protest, demanding the sacking of a Labor Department official they accuse of corruption.

Pembebasan is a lively monthly tabloid which also publishes a range of analytical articles on domestic and international affairs. Being published by the PRD, which is a small party with minimal resources, it can only report a small selection of the *aksi* taking place. The fact is that since 1998, almost every section of the popular classes of society has been involved or touched by this spread of *aksi*.

A fundamental characteristic of these *aksi* is that they have not transformed into any kind of national political movement or movements. *Aksi* has remained a form of protest usually located at the site of grievance, only rarely reaching beyond that location. Student protest has, of course, not been so restricted to the site of grievance. While there have been regular protests and occupations of official buildings on campuses over campus issues, most student demonstrations have been carried out by politically affiliated student groups taking their protests off campus: to parliament, Suharto's house or a government office. However, these too have not transformed into a larger cross-sectoral political movement.

It is the fragmented and site-located nature of this endemic protest that forces the commentator to rely on gathering anecdotes and using the selected reports from *Kompas* (as did Manan) or the reportage in a magazine like *Pembebasan*. Unconsolidated into any political movements (and in the absence of any well-resourced systematic research or even a systematic scouring of all the national and local media), this socially endemic protest can easily be underestimated both in its extent and its significance. Such an underestimation provides the basis of conclusions that the popular classes are relatively absent from the political processes as significant political actors. When analysis looks to identify the existence of a large-scale and coherently organized social movement, it cannot find one. Similarly, if one looks for a growth in, for example, large and powerful trade unions or peasant unions, it cannot be found.

The Student Movement

Students, mobilized in cross campus activist committee alliances, had provided the vanguard platoons of activists leading the long march protests out of the campus throughout the whole country from late 1997 through

to May 1998 and on to November 1998. The organized student movement, except for the most ideological elements, also proved to be organized
on a temporary basis. Within a few years after November 1998, most of the
action committees, including the most active Jakarta groups such as
FORKOT, had shrunk or even disappeared. The period of their politicization and radicalization had been too short to ensure depth of radicalization
or permanence of organization. They had won their main demands, the
resignation of Suharto and the end of dictatorship, very quickly after they
began to mobilize. As the military retreated from involvement in political
repression after Suharto's fall, another radicalizing issue also quickly
disappeared.

Since 2000, the organized student movement has continued to weaken.
There remain two main legacies of its militant period. First, is that while
organized student politics has shrivelled for the time being, the experience of
the mobilization left a widespread democratic and critical sentiment among
the student population, many of whom have now graduated. The critical
tone of journalism; the flourishing, though fragmented, book publishing; the
experimentation in literature, theater and the arts are just a few of the many
manifestations of this sentiment. No conservative party or force, including
religious, has been able to win and sustain any support from this milieu. The
massive popularity of political satire on television, with shows like "All you
can do is dream republic," is another manifestation.

The second legacy is the perseverance of the more ideologically committed
political groups or networks, usually still quite small but very active, who
came out of this process. At the core of these groups, however, are activists
whose politicization was not concentrated just over the last several months of
Suharto's dictatorship, but extended back until at least the beginning of the
1990s. The most resilient of these remains the People's Democratic Party
(PRD). There are a range of non-party groupings—networks, associations,
advocacy offices and others—that have also sustained themselves, often with
a sectoral orientation, such as women, urban poor, laborers and others. Many
of these are staffed by former student activists.

During 1998 through to around 2002, the student organization associated with the modernist fundamentalist Islamic party, the Justice Party
(later renamed the Justice and Prosperity Party—PKS), was also very active.
Like the PRD, many of the key activists of the Indonesian Islamic Students
Action Front (KAMMI) had been politicized for a long period under

Suharto. They were also ideological, hardened, with an established cadreization process. However, as their mentor party, the PKS, has become more integrated into traditional elite politics, integrating also some of the student leaders, their activism has diminished, demoralized by reports of their elders wheeling and dealing. They have been much less of a presence on the campuses since 2005 or 2006.

However, a clearly defined social movement, large-scale unions or student movement organizations are not the only possible forms of organization. *Aksi* itself is a form of organization. During the period 1996–8, for example, it was the urban poor, that is, full time and casual workers, who mobilized sometimes in their hundreds of thousands and provided the momentum and the force that made the country increasingly ungovernable for Suharto and the political elite around him. Their form of organization was not trade unions or easily named or sustained social movements, but *aksi*. Their unorganized form of action was chaotic. After Suharto *aksi* have continued, and out of the student movement, intellectual ferment, as atomized as the *aksi*, has also been sustained.

Aksi and Constraining the Elite

Furthermore, it is not impossible that even in the early stages of a process of socio-political reorganization these *aksi* could have significant political impacts and manifestations. At the end of 2000, for example, a major controversy developed in the sphere of labor over a new regulation making it more difficult for employers to dismiss workers. This was Labor Ministerial Regulation 150/2000 on Resolution of Dismissal and Redundancy Payments, Payments for Longevity of Service, and Compensation which were issued on 20 June 2000.[6] This regulation imposed a number of obligations on employers not only making it more difficult to dismiss workers, including striking workers, but also introducing a range of financial obligations on employers to their workers. On 15 December, the Indonesian Textile Industry Association, Indonesian Footwear Industry Association, Indonesian Garment Manufacturers' Association and the Indonesian Toy Manufacturers' Association issued a joint letter explaining their objections to the regulation. The Ministry of Labor issued a revision of the regulation, No. 78/2001, removing or watering down all the sections that were objectionable to the employers.[7] The employers' position was also strongly supported by the Minister of Finance. The employers also directly lobbied Vice-President Megawati Soekarnoputri who was in the middle of a maneuver to try to oust President Abdurrahman Wahid.

This action was rejected strongly by almost all the trade union and worker organizations. The government moved again and moderated one provision in favor of workers' rights. However, this was a relatively minor amendment and the resistance from trade unions and groups advocating for workers' rights continued. Manan gives one description of the reaction:

> In several places in Indonesia demonstrations and strikes took place demanding the repeal of these two regulations. In Jakarta, thousands of workers organised by the All Indonesia Federation of Worker Unions (FPSI) demonstrated before the front of the Presidential Palace. At the same time hundreds from the Indonesian Prosperous Worker Union (SBSI), demonstrated in front of the Vice-President's Palace. In Medan, 5,000 workers from a range of organizations demonstrated to demand the same thing. Demonstrations also took place in Bandung (West Java), Sidoarjo (East Java), Makassar (South Sulawesi) and several other areas.[8]

The largest demonstration was that which occurred in Bandung on 13–15 June 2001.

> In this area, clashes took place between workers and security apparatus which then evolved into chaos. The West Java parliament was virtually destroyed as a result of being attacked by a hail of stones and other destructive acts by the masses. Several pieces of equipment were also destroyed or burned. Eighteen cars and 10 motorbikes were destroyed, 20 cars and 12 other motorbikes damaged. Bandung was paralyzed during the workers' demonstrations. The security apparatus had acted repressively toward the demonstration which transformed into chaos. Eighty people were arrested, almost all of them having been severely beaten.
>
> The governor of West Java decided to postpone the implementation of the new law and ordered the implementation of the original law which contained less provision detrimental to workers. The governors of Jakarta, East Java, Central Java, Lampung, Kota Batam

and several other areas followed suit, and, in the end, the government reinstituted the Labor Regulation No. 150/2000 and formed a new tripartite forum. This was done after holding a meeting with representatives of the government, employers and 30 leaders of trade union organizations.[9]

This was a major defeat for the government and employers, although they were able to retake what they had lost later in the year when a new, very restrictive law on labor disputes was introduced. The employers' defeat in June, however, was a reflection of the power of mass mobilization. The potential for mobilizations, both demonstrations and strikes, was under-scored by the extent of the strikes. Over a two-week period strikes and protests had taken place in every industrial zone in the country. Labor activists counted ninety-nine towns where there had been actions. In many cases, community or human rights organizations as well as students supported workers organized in local enterprise unions. This had been facilitated by the formation of broad-based committees in many cities earlier in the year to organize May Day actions.

The combativeness of those who had mobilized in their thousands in several cities also showed that workers were able to take on a directly political focus. In Bandung, workers had marched on both the Bandung *kabupaten* and town parliaments and had occupied and trashed them. In other towns also workers had protested outside regional parliaments. Furthermore, the strikes and protests then merged into a supplementary wave of strikes and protests around the country aimed at another more general government policy: the decision to reduce the price subsidies of various fuel products. Protests and demonstrations began against these policies around 15 June and also spread throughout the country. President Wahid had tried to delay the reductions until October, however, pressure from his economics ministers—no doubt pressured by the International Monetary Fund office in Jakarta—meant that they happened in June. This second wave was also characterized in many cities and towns by public transport strikes as drivers of buses as well as smaller commuter transport vehicles protested against both the fuel price in-creases and the consequent increases in fares, which threatened to reduce consumer patronage.

For the repressive wing of the state apparatus, this pattern was recognizable: the combination of organized, militant and politically focused *aksi* developing alongside explosions of *rusuh* (rioting). This had been exactly the pattern that had developed during the 1990s. The police revived the 1996 ploy of accusing the PRD of being behind the protests and riots. The PRD, and the union closely associated with it, the FNPBI, was involved in protests in Bandung, Jakarta, Surabaya and other cities. They were, however, a part of wider coalitions. In Jakarta, the police accused the PRD and the student activist grouping FORKOT, as well as eight other unnamed non-government organizations. In Bandung, the police raided the PRD offices, seizing computers, books and documents and arresting the younger sister of a local PRD leader. According to Brigadier General Sudirman Ail, the West Java police commander, several PRD members were arrested handing out leaflets inciting workers to strike.

Persistent mobilizations by students and transport workers over price rises in fuel (petrol and kerosene) have permanently constrained successive governments since June 2001. The threat of protests and demonstrations has not stopped the steady reduction in fuel price subsidies and the consequent price increases but it has slowed it. Furthermore, the government has had to restrict the extent of these price rises by retaining higher subsidies for kerosene, which is used by the urban and rural poor for cooking and boiling water on small kerosene stoves. Kerosene was originally included in this policy, required by the IMF, but was excluded after the second wave of demonstrations against price rises in January–February 2002. The latest rise in August 2005 was also introduced very hesitatingly and only with great propaganda support.

Beyond Constraint: *Aksi* and Political Challenge

The protests over labor law and fuel price rises have shown the power of *aksi* mobilization to constrain the government in its policy making. This is the case despite the fact that the discontent organized through *aksi* has not transformed into a political movement or sustained social protest movement. There are no large political parties based upon mobilized discontented elements from the popular classes. While trade unions have increased in number, they still only cover a tiny fraction of the population and are not politically influential organizations in and of themselves. One crucial question to be answered is why is this so? Why has such discontent, despite being militant and active (not passive) not produced any large-scale permanent political organization?

One way to gain insights into the issues involved here is through an examination of the single major case after May 1998—so far at least—of mobilized discontent intervening on the question of who should rule, who should govern. Large-scale mobilizations took place through the first six months of 2001—the same time as the fuel price rises and labor protests—demanding the dissolution of the GOLKAR party as a step to prevent the reconsolidation of political power of a reconstituted New Order elite. These mobilizations peaked with mass rallies and marches of almost a million people in Surabaya in February 2001.

Background

The massive November 1998 mobilizations collapsed when Abdurrahman Wahid, Megawati Soekarnoputri and Amien Rais refused to go down the extra-parliamentary path in confronting the Habibie government. The demobilization of the mass protests denied a national platform from which to speak to all of the political groups and individuals at the core of these mobilizations. Student groups and leaders, human rights groups, dissident politicians and radical parties, such as the PRD, were all suddenly deprived of the vehicle through which they acted and the platform from which they spoke. These groups were deprived of the main energy and infrastructure that allowed them to act on a national scale: that is, national waves of focused mass actions. This was a major obstacle for them in participating in the first post-Suharto general elections held in 1999. Most of the forces at the core of the mobilizations either did not participate in the elections or found themselves participating as a small organization no longer connected to the national-scale energies and infrastructure of the *reformasi* mass movement.[10]

This meant that the electoral process was dominated by the political organizations associated with the three "opposition" figures who had opted for the electoral method of transition and the two Suharto-era parties they had effectively compromised with, GOLKAR and the United Development ment Party (PPP). Megawati's Indonesian Democratic Party of Struggle (PDIP), Abdurrahman Wahid's National Awakening Party (PKB) and Amien Rais' National Mandate Party (PAN) dominated the election campaign alongside GOLKAR and PPP. The *reformasi* parties, such as the PRD and other new smaller parties, were marginalized in this process as a result of the November 1998 demobilization. An alliance of GOLKAR, PKB, PAN, PPP and several other smaller parties in the new People's Consultative Assembly, MPR, elected Abdurrahman Wahid as president, against Megawati, even though his party, the PKB, was one of the smallest in the parliament. Megawati Soekarnoputri, whose PDIP was the largest party with 35 percent of the seats, was elected vice-president.

This was an anomalous result reflecting an opportunist alliance between conservative Moslem parties and GOLKAR. The first group was opposed to a woman president while GOLKAR saw the PDIP as their main rival in the new era. The anomaly was that the new president, Abdurrahman Wahid, did not ideologically represent the majority coalition in the MPR that elected him. Wahid himself was somewhat of an anomaly in Indonesian politics, and was a figure of extremely contradictory political orientations and background. On the one hand, he was chairperson of the Nahdlatul Ulama (NU), a Moslem religious organization claiming millions of members. Formally, the NU is an association of religious clerics and scholars, called *ulama* or *kyai*. Wahid is also an *ulama* able to use the full title Kyai Haji Abdurrahman Wahid. He is the grandson of the founding *kyai* of NU. The NU is based in the more rural areas of Indonesia, especially East and some parts of Central Java. It has traditionally been a very conservative organization on religious and social doctrine as well as politically. Its youth militia, the Banser, played a significant role in the massacres of leftist farmers and workers in 1965. At the core of its structure and religious schools are the *pesantren*, who are often major landowners in their regions, making many *ulama* the backbone of the local rural landed elite. Kyai Haji Abdurrahman Wahid had a massive and very loyal following among the NU constituency since he took over the chairmanship in the 1980s.

Ideologically, however, Wahid was closer to the secular intellectuals of the social democratic Socialist Party of Indonesia. He had been educated in Egypt and Jordan and had adopted a modernist and secular-oriented interpretation of Islamic teachings. Parallel with this, he articulated political views that could be described as social democratic or liberal democratic. As well as being chairperson of the NU, in the 1980s he became chairperson of a small but high-profile group called the Forum

Demokrasi. His main collaborators in this organization were intellectuals usually considered close to the PSI current. As head of NU, he advocated a separation of religion and state, of winning "Islamic values" through cultural change rather than through enforcement by the state and even of adopting secular forms of greetings between Indonesian citizens rather than religious ones. As chairperson of Forum Demokrasi during the Suharto period, he argued for political liberalization, although in an extremely cautious and non-confrontational way. He was the first national political figure to criticize the massacres of leftists in 1965 and to apologize for the role of NU organizations in those events.

He had survived under the New Order by accommodating to the mode of politics imposed by Suharto. He often stated his support for Suharto's candidacy for president at election times and in 1997 even helped campaign for GOLKAR, while still advocating political liberalization. He was opposed to confrontation with Suharto and to mass mobilization politics, often equating calls for mass mobilization with provocations to mass violence.

He shared the political elite's aversion to mass participation in politics, but he did not share their other fundamental ideological outlooks. When he assumed the presidency, he advocated lifting the ban on communism and reconciliation with the pre-1965 left. This alone provoked opposition from Moslem and military elements who had been a part of the coalition in the MPR that had elected him. While Wahid's first cabinet included figures from all the parties which had supported him, at the core of his government was an alliance of figures drawn from a liberal democrat and Christian network of intellectuals and political figures. The shadowy Indonesian Anti-Communist Society (MAKI), though often making some bizarre accusations, did accurately list these individuals in one of its publications, naming, for example, Rizal Ramli (Minister for Economics and Finance), Wimar Witoelar (presidential spokesperson), Marsilam Simanjuntak, Bondan Gunawan and Lieutenant General Agus Wirahadi-kusuma. Simanjuntak had been Wahid's main collaborator in Forum Demokrasi. General Wirahadikusuma had emerged as a savage critic of corruption and abuse of power from within the armed forces, making many enemies of fellow officers. MAKI accused Wahid and his allies of con-spiring to attack the interests of GOLKAR, the army and Islam. They depicted this as a communist conspiracy and so classified all these people as being pro-communist and therefore also supporters of the PRD, which was depicted as a reborn PKI.[11]

Wahid's election as president immediately put at center stage contradictions that were to introduce deep volatility into the political situation. First, there was a quickly deepening contradiction that developed between Wahid and the majority in the parliament that had supported him and, of course, he had already earned the hostility of his vice-president, Megawati, and her party, the PDIP, when he took the presidency from her. His ideological perspective was too much for them, especially his support for legalizing communism and his promotion of General Wirahadikusuma to commander of the crucial Strategic Army Command (KOSTRAD). This was aggravated by the emergence of his governing network which was tending to sideline the established political forces from the Suharto period. Key figures from GOLKAR, PPP, PDIP and the TNI (armed forces) were dismissed by Wahid or forced from the cabinet between late November 1999 and April 2000.

The forces opposed to Wahid comprised an alliance between GOLKAR, the armed forces, some of the old Suharto-era smaller parties (such as the PPP), PAN, led by Amien Rais, and the PDIP, who were maneuvering for closer ties with the TNI. This was driven essentially by a GOLKAR-PPP-PAN-TNI alliance; that is, an alliance dominated by the parties of Suharto's New Order.[12] They were the parties that had put Wahid into the presidency. The PDIP was also a part of this alliance, but Megawati's tactic was to let GOLKAR take the lead against Wahid in parliament. She remained relatively silent on the issues that GOLKAR, TNI and others dug up to use against Wahid. The anti-Wahid alliance was very powerful. Wahid was not only isolated in the parliament but also inside the state apparatus, both at national and provincial level. More than 60 percent of provincial governors were members of GOLKAR, a legacy of the Suharto period. Most high state officials had similar links. Wahid, as president, was increasingly forced to rely on extra-bureaucratic techniques to try to get things done. Wahid's officials then approached the National Logistics Body (BULOG), an institution that organized the distribution of rice and other goods throughout the country, to obtain "tactical funds" which would enable him to circumvent some of this bureaucratic hostility. This attempt to get around the normal way funds are allocated became the main issue which the GOLKAR-TNI-PPP-PDIP majority in the parliament used against him—although the use of "tactical funds" from BULOG and other state enterprises had been common practice for the previous three decades. The majority in parliament set in motion impeachment processes that were to succeed in ousting Wahid from the presidency in July 2001.

This conflict set in motion a second but no less important contradiction that centered on the question of the revival of politically focused mass *aksi*. The issue was: from whence could Wahid draw support? He had the support of a majority section of the grassroots of the NU, although only a part of the rest of the leadership of the NU and the PKB, the electoral wing of the NU. He did have the support of the majority of the *reformasi* constituency, although this was usually qualified and critical support. The same groups which supported Wahid in the conflict with the GOLKAR-TNI-PPP-PDIP parliamentary majority and supported his perspectives on political liberalization and reform of the army were often on the streets opposed to the economic policies he was implementing, which flowed from the Indonesian government's agreements with the IMF. The protests against the labor laws and fuel price rises discussed above occurred during Wahid's presidency. Moreover, the primary organizational form of this constituency, the mass *aksi*, had been demobilized and the constituency had fragmented into its myriad of component parts and spontaneous processes. It was made up of smaller parties—the PRD, PUDI, PBSD and others—as well as human rights and community organizations, individual political figures, artists and intellectuals and ad hoc spontaneous action groups and committees. This constituency had no significant representation in parliament. When the conflict operated as one between a Wahid-NU and PKB *reformasi* constituency alliance and a GOLKAR-TNI-PPP-PDIP alliance, the issue of the necessity and the possibility of reviving *aksi* on a mass scale was immediately posed. From where else could come serious political force to counterpose to the majority in the parliament? The contradiction here was that Wahid as well as the PKB and NU leaderships were not supporters of mass *aksi* as a form of struggle. And among the *reformasi* groups, not all were in favor of being drawn into the conflict.

Towards *Aksi* on a Mass Scale

The conflict between Wahid and the GOLKAR-TNI-PPP-PDIP alliance began very quickly and was clearly visible by the beginning of 2000. The initial battles were manifest in the struggle over cabinet and other positions.

In November, the main leader of the PPP, Hamzah Haz, resigned from the cabinet. In February, after a series of tense face-to-face meetings, Wahid also dismissed as Minister in charge of Politics and Security the former armed forces chief, General Wiranto, who was seen as the main representative of the TNI's interests inside the government. In April Wahid dismissed the prominent PDIP figure, Laksamana Sukardi, as Minister in charge of State Enterprises. This was followed with the dismissal of GOLKAR business-man, Yusuf Kalla (who became vice-president in 2005 under President Yudhoyono and is also chairperson of GOLKAR). More PDIP and GOLKAR ministers were dismissed in August 2000 and some of Wahid's liberal democrat associates moved into cabinet positions. Then in August the GOLKAR-PPP-TNI-PDIP majority in parliament formally moved towards an impeachment process by starting a parliamentary investigation into the approaches to BULOG and into the way in which Wahid tried to circumvent the bureaucracy with monies donated by the Sultan of Brunei.[13]

At stake in this conflict was the status of the old forces of the New Order in the post-New Order political format. For those in the *reformasi* constituency, the opposition to Wahid from these forces, led by GOLKAR, was seen as resistance by the New Order to Wahid's support for political liberalization and his bringing into government of political liberals. The opposition was seen as an attempt at a New Order comeback. Throughout 2000, student groups and radical political groups, in particular the PRD, began organizing protest actions raising the demand of "Disband GOLK-AR!" as part of a campaign to fight off the attempt by GOLKAR and the TNI to reassert their former power. However, this began to escalate after the GOLKAR-TNI-PPP-PDIP majority in parliament began the impeach-ment processes in August. Alliances of student, worker and human rights activists began forming throughout the country in many cities. These alliances grouped the most radical activists behind the general slogan of "destroy the remnants of the New Order," "put GOLKAR on trial" or "disband GOLKAR." The campaign materials of these organizations reiterated the crimes of the New Order and pointed out the signs that the New Order political forces were still strong. In an article in *Pembebasan*, March 2001 issue, some of these arguments were summarized. Evidence of the rising up again of the remnants of the New Order included, stated the article:

1. the fact that none of them, for example Suharto and his cronies, have been taken to court for their crimes against humanity or corruption;
2. the laws being passed all legitimise their continuing existence in the political system, such as the laws guaranteeing representation of the TNI and police in parliament;
3. the success of GOLKAR in re-marketing itself to the public while neither having really changed nor having been brought to account for its past deeds;
4. GOLKAR has been able to maintain control of key state institutions, putting its people in government departments, and having its candidate the front-runner for heading the Supreme Court;
5. GOLKAR has ability to use the parliament as its platform, such as in the impeachment processes against Wahid;
6. GOLKAR still has 60 percent of governor and *bupati* positions outside Java and 40 percent in Java.

Demonstrations were fairly steady and of a moderate size during the October–December 2000 period, although usually very militant. There were frequent clashes with the military and police. However, even during this period there were signs of the possibility of the demonstrations escalating to a mass scale. These signs were connected to the possibility of cooperation in organizing mobilizations between this militant student sector, organized in a variety of ad hoc alliances in different cities, and Wahid's organizations, the National Awakening Party (PKB), Nahdlatul Ulama and other organizations connected to the NU, such as the Indonesian Islamic University Students Association (PMII). Wahid's weak position in the parliament with support from only the PKB, which had only a small contingent there, and another smaller Christian-oriented party, meant that he needed support from outside parliament.

The PRD took the initiative to begin communications with PKB and NU leaders about joint demonstrations in support of the demand either to put GOLKAR on trial for crimes committed during the New Order period or to disband GOLKAR. This was a complicated process because the PRD was also involved in other alliances with student and worker groups organizing protests against the Wahid government's policies to reduce the subsidies on fuel prices, a policy being pushed by the IMF and some cabinet ministers close to the IMF and the World Bank. There were debates inside the PRD and among student activists about cooperation with Wahid, who was categorized in both PRD and other activist analysis as a part of the grouping of "fake democrats," which also included Megawati Soekarnoputri and Amien Rais. However, the talks with the NU leaders revealed that they were willing to support demonstrations in favor of the demands put forward by the PRD, including the demand for a 100 percent rise in wages, as well as the demands for action against GOLKAR. The PKB and NU leaders made no attempt to steer things into a more moderate direction, for example, concentrating purely on a "defend Wahid" direction.

The PRD faced minimal problems with the PKB and NU leaders on the issue of demands and slogans for the demonstrations. But they soon found big problems as to whether the PKB and NU leaders would actually deliver on promises of joint actions or even deliver on promises to let PRD leaders speak at actions organized by the Wahid forces. The nervousness of the Wahid forces was not on the issue of the campaign against "the remnants of the New Order" but on the question of the method of struggle, the form of action or mass *aksi*. On numerous occasions, promised contingents coming from the Wahid forces simply did not arrive on site. However, the Wahid forces were caught in a bind. They had to show they had significant support outside parliament, given that it was becoming clearer and clearer that they were isolated inside parliament. Wahid himself began to openly threaten that he would call on his traditional support base to mobilize. From among this support base, groups emerged calling themselves the "Prepared to Die Squads." Wahid indicated that he might ask his supporters from East Java to mobilize to Jakarta. In January 2001, PKB officials warned ominously that they could not stop their mass base from NU coming to Jakarta: "All that we can do is to persuade them not to be easily provoked by anti-Gus Dur groups. We have no power to ban them," PKB Secretary General Muhaimin Iskandar told the press in Jakarta on 7 January.[14] It was also announced that 200,000 NU members were to arrive in Jakarta by 15 January. But this mobilization never happened.

By January 2001, the anti-Wahid forces had also begun their own *aksi* mobilizations. There were two prongs to this attack. Student groups associated with the Islamic parties in the parliament that were opposing Wahid organized regular demonstrations calling for his ousting. These were mostly peaceful and often quite large mobilizations. In Jakarta, they were often organized through the Student Executive Boards (BEM). These were a kind of student representative council operating at faculty level in some universities. Islamic student groups, associated with the Justice Party (PK), had been concentrating a lot of their efforts on winning control of these BEMs and were now using them to mobilize their constituency on campuses against Wahid. They were very effective in indicating that a significant and active section of the student body was opposed to Wahid. They concentrated on the issues of Wahid's attempt to raise "tactical funds" through BULOG and donations from the Sultan of Brunei.

A second prong of the attack was to mobilize other groups, sometimes students, sometimes paramilitary groups, against the PRD or other symbols of leftism. There were attacks on PRD offices in several places in late 2000 and early 2001. Later in May 2001, an international seminar organized by a research institution associated with the PRD was attacked by a para-military group associated with the PPP, after police detained the international participants. Anti-communist groups also declared that they would raid bookshops and confiscate and burn left-wing books. There were attacks on the PRD and the more militant student groups which were emerging as the key allies of Wahid against the GOLKAR-led alliance as well as a confrontation with Wahid's stated position of wanting to lift the ban on communism.

Even in this climate talks continued between the PKB and PRD about collaborating in organizing mass mobilizations. On 24 January, the press reported an agreement between the PRD and the NU. One of the English-language newspapers published the following news item:

PRD, NU to hold joint rally

Jakarta—The left-wing Peoples Democratic Party (PRD) and the nation's biggest Muslim organization Nahdlatul Ulama (NU) are to hold a joint rally against forces opposed to democracy.

PRD leader Budiman Sudjatmiko yesterday met with NU Chairman Hasyim Muzadi to discuss the agenda of the rally.

Budiman said there are clear indications that the old power and its anti-democracy groups may attempt to oust the democratically elected government. He said Muzadi is keen for NU and the PRD to join forces for the sake of upholding democracy.

The PRD and NU are to hold a joint massive rally. It will accommodate the non-governmental organizations, students and pro-democracy activists. It will aim to consolidate pro-democracy powers.

No date was given for the event. Budiman said he invited NU to join the rally, because Muzadi had recently declared 2001 to be the year of strictness. That means the pro-democracy groups have to take a strong stance against the old forces, which want to regain power.

Muzadi said that in some ways the PRD's ideas are similar to those of NU. We also want to find a way to thwart the attempts by the old power groups that want to eliminate the democracy process in Indonesia, he said.

Muzadi denied that he and Budiman had discussed the national leadership issue, saying the PRD and NU were more focused on the national interest, rather than the president.[15]

This was a clear statement of defiance of the military elements inside the government. On 10 January, General Yudhoyono,[16] then Minister for Politics and Security (now President), had told a delegation of student leaders: "Political disputes cannot be solved by mobilizing the masses. Let the political elite sit down together and find the best solution for our country."[17]

By the end of January tensions had deepened. On 24 January Wahid had been summoned before a parliamentary committee to answer questions on the BULOG and Brunei funds. He had walked out of the session before the questioning had finished.

The first real exhibition of the potential of an alliance between the Wahid forces and the more militant wing of the *reformasi* constituency occurred not in a joint PRD-NU mobilization in Jakarta but in Surabaya on 5 February 2001. An alliance had been established late in 2000 called the Front Reformasi Total (FRT). This alliance comprised youth organizations associated with the NU alongside the PRD and associated groups as well as a range of other student organizations and the local chapter of the high-profile environmental organization, WAHLI. The NU-associated groups included IPPNU (urban youth and students), East Java PMII (university students) and GP ANSOR (rural youth).[18] The FRT called for NU members to march on the East Javanese capital, Surabaya, from the surrounding areas. The official call of the FRT was for GOLKAR to be put on trial for its crimes during the New Order and if found guilty, disbanded and for the government to be purged of figures who held positions in the New Order regime.

According to the Central Javanese daily, *Berita Nasional*, hundreds of thousands of people massed into Surabaya on 5 February to demonstrate at the provincial parliament building. The paper reports thousands of trucks and cars filling the streets bringing people in from surrounding areas. Sit-downs of thousands of demonstrators blocked different parts of the city. Smaller towns on the outskirts of Surabaya also witnessed large-scale demonstrations. Workers also staged strikes in some of the industrial satellite towns. Student activists assessed the total mobilization at around 1 million in Indonesia's second biggest city, a major port and industrial center. *Pembebasan* also reported the total as 1 million. It was a huge and militant mobilization and showed the potential of the mass action form of struggle.[19]

The mobilization also saw the action flow over from a march or motorcade in surrounding towns and a peaceful demonstration outside the parliament to a march on the East Java GOLKAR offices. A section of the rally occupied the GOLKAR offices, trashed them and then set them on fire. The anger of the masses on the street and the attack on the GOLKAR offices quickly frightened the NU leadership. They all imme-diately moved to distance themselves not only from the arson at the GOLKAR offices but from the mobilization as a whole while still trying to squeeze some political mileage out of the event. One of the leaders of the East Java NU branch, Mas Subadar, told *Bernas* that the NU was not the "motor force" behind the 5 February mobilizations. But, he added, "That this was a result of the behaviour of the political elite in Jakarta, like Amien Rais (Chairperson of the MPR) and Akbar (Chairperson of the house of representatives) . . . The people of East Java cannot be held back any more."[20]

Later, the chairperson of the NU, Muzadi, made a clear statement that the NU did not support the action. This was followed by a similar statement by Mahfud, the secretary general of the PKB. This, in turn, was followed by a statement by Wahid himself that the violence at the GOLKAR offices was instituted by an outside party. Akbar Tanjung, chairperson of GOLKAR, immediately blamed the PRD and the student groups FAMRED and FORKOT for the violence and called for the banning of the PRD, echoing the policy of the Suharto government in 1996.[21] There was an increase in violent attacks—stone throwings and fire bombings—on PRD offices during the rest of February. Other student and radical groups were also attacked, for example the activist artists' group, Taring Padi, in Yogyakarta on 20 February.[22]

Television and newspaper reports on the massive mobilizations in Surabaya and the controversy generated by the arson at the GOLKAR offices focused national attention on the protests. As a result, more such demonstrations occurred, first around East Java, the NU heartland, and then all around the country. *Kompas* on 9 February reported demonstrations in Medan, Yogyakarta, Kudus and Makassar. These were mainly student and worker demonstrations, targeting GOLKAR offices. In Makassar there were physical clashes with the police.

While the moves against Wahid in the parliament continued throughout February, March, April and May, so did the demonstrations. Even in smaller towns in NU areas, militant actions occurred. In the town of Purwokerto, Central Java, for example, pro-Wahid demonstrators occupied the local state radio station and issued their own pro-Wahid broadcasts. However, the attempt to build the mass mobilizations foundered. Wahid raised the prospect of more mobilizations a few times but then would dampen expectations down. The focus was on whether a major mobilization could be organized in Jakarta behind specific demands that would obstruct the maneuvers in parliament by GOLKAR. Finally, in May, a series of demonstrations took place outside the presidential palace which combined the forces of the student radicals, including the PRD, and Wahid supporters. However, these demonstrations did not grow beyond a few thousand.

By May, the stakes had been raised as the impeachment process was leading to a session of the People's Consultative Assembly where, it became clear, the majority would vote Wahid out of the presidency and make Vice-President Megawati the president. In this context, what anti-GOLKAR mobilizations were taking place were now not only demanding that GOLKAR be held accountable for crimes under the New Order period but were also urging Wahid to issue a decree to dissolve parliament and call new elections. There was no constitutional provision for Wahid to do this. Any attempt to dissolve parliament would receive no support from the armed forces who were backing the GOLKAR-TNI-PDIP-PPP majority in the parliament. The only force that could possibly legitimize a direct move by Wahid to dissolve parliament and call new elections would be a massive show of mobilized public support.

On 31 May, the chairperson of the MPR, Amien Rais, a leading figure in the anti-Wahid coalition, announced that it would hold a Special Session on 1 August where there would be, one way or another, a vote on Wahid's presidency. As it became clearer that Wahid was indeed about to be removed as president and replaced by Megawati by the GOLKAR-led coalition almost all of the *reformasi* constituency united to call on Wahid to dissolve the parliament, dissolve GOLKAR and hold new elections. Activists from almost every democratic community, human rights, environmental, student, women's rights and trade union organizations were in and out of the presidential palace throughout June and July. There were more student demonstrations in many cities but the NU forces were never mobilized seriously.

On 22 July, one week before the MPR was scheduled to meet, Wahid finally issued a decree which (1) suspended parliament, both the MPR and the DPR; (2) stated there would be an early election to be held no later than within one year; and (3) dissolved GOLKAR. But with parliament and the armed forces defiant and having built no sustained show of mobilized public support, the decree was ignored by the MPR and DPR. The MPR instead moved forward its Special Session and on 23 July installed Megawati as president.

From January through to June the extent of popular mobilization was the greatest since 1998. The huge February mobilization in Surabaya and the wave of other actions provoked throughout the country was reminiscent of 1996, 1997 and 1998. Moreover, these mobilizations aimed against GOLKAR and all the other surviving forces from the New Order were taking place among a non-stop stream of protests, occupations and strikes around other issues. Apart from the strikes and demonstrations over the new labor laws and several waves of protests against fuel price rises, the myriad of other protests and strikes did not let up throughout this period. Nowhere throughout this period did Wahid provide a clear platform which might have organized or galvanized this discontent. He had the worst of both worlds. His perspective on political liberalization, including the legalization of communism; his attempt to bring other liberals into the government from outside the established political parties; and his support for the most outspoken reformer inside the armed forces set him against all parties that had supported his election as president. But neither did he put forward a platform that could galvanize popular support. His economic policies, involving imposition of IMF-prescribed austerity policies, was a barrier to winning popular support. Most crucially, he consistently pulled back from using mass mobilization as a means of organizing and demonstrating public support for his presidency.

There is considerable commentary, both within Indonesia and from international commentators, that Wahid's major failing was erratic behavior and bad management. Wahid is certainly a very complex personality, embodying very sharp and deep contradictions. He is head of one of the most tradition-oriented Islamic organizations in the country, whose basis is thousands of Islamic clerics educated primarily in Islamic jurisprudence as well as mysticism. At the same time, he has been the most consistent advocate of modernizing and secularizing Islamic political and social outlooks, advocating a significant separation between religion and state. He has been chairperson of Forum Demokrasi, while supporting Suharto at election time. He supported Suharto, who organized the counter-revolutionary massacres of communists in 1965, while calling for the legalization of communism. It is not surprising that such a contradictory personality might also make contradictory remarks.

However, the crucial factor in Wahid's "erratic behavior" has never been his personality, but rather the fundamental contradiction of his situation. He was a political liberal whose only possible power base was the very angry and discontented urban and rural poor. However, Wahid always eschewed such mobilization. This meant that his only recourse in any struggle with those opposed to democratic liberalization was political maneuver. He has been in a constant state of political maneuver against and among other political forces since the 1980s. This was intensified during the tense struggles during his presidency. Switching alliances with individuals, sacking and appointing people, switching public stances and throwing out unsubstantiated criticisms were the only weapons open to him while he rejected building alliances aimed at mobilizing public support in the extra-parliamentary arena.

The failure of the Wahid presidency was directly related to another wave of politicized mass mobilization. In many respects this wave was caused by very similar factors to those which caused the demobilizations in November 1998. At that time, the student and popular mobilizations were relying on Amien Rais, Wahid and Megawati to agree to the idea of forcing Habibie to resign and hand over power to a presidium. When they opted for transition by elections under Habibie, the movement had nowhere to go—or, at least, that's what the majority of the student leadership thought. Insofar as the mobilizations were oriented towards the question of governmental power, they were relying on the willingness of figures from within the political elite to support a "people's power" uprising as a means of forcing an incumbent out and then legitimizing coming to power by extra-constitutional means. This was again the situation in 2001. Neither the student movement nor organizations like the PRD had the size or authority to mobilize hundreds of thousands of people by themselves. They were dependent on Wahid and the NU leadership agreeing to and fully supporting a mass mobilization strategy—at least for a long enough period for a self-sustaining momentum to get under way, as had occurred in 1997–8. For brief periods when they had supported such a method of struggle, in February 2001, for example, it was possible to glimpse the potential scale and militancy of any future mobilizations based on a similar alliance.

The defeat of Wahid in 2001, however, seriously weakened the position of the last remaining national political figure from within the elite who was a potential ally or figurehead for any mass movement that might be mobilized for political liberalization. The individual liberal political figures and intellectuals who had been brought into government under Wahid were exiled to the political margins. Wahid himself remains an outspoken figure but he was gradually marginalized in his former bastion of the NU as the rest of the leadership tried to get back on good terms with the rest of the elite. The head of the NU, Muzadi, who had replaced Wahid when he became president, even stood as vice-presidential candidate to Megawati in 2005. The potential for Wahid to relaunch himself as a major figure representing a liberal opposition had been seriously damaged, if not completely eliminated.

In the first two years after the fall of Wahid, during the beginning of the Megawati presidency, there were attempts to recreate similar alliances that might wield the same authority among significant sections of the population. These efforts involved two dissident political figures who had a place on the national political stage, even if with considerably less profile and authority than Wahid. These two figures were Eros Djarot and

Rachmawati Soekarnoputri, one of Megawati's sisters. Djarot had joined the PDIP in the early 1990s as Megawati emerged as an alternative presidential figure to Suharto. He is credited with being an important advisor to her during this period. He broke with Megawati and left the PDIP in 2000 when differences emerged over the issue of alliances with elements from the old New Order power structure. Djarot opposed any kind of collaboration with GOLKAR, for example, while the leadership group around Megawati set off on a tactical collaboration with GOLKAR. This climaxed in the overthrow of Wahid.

After Djarot left the PDIP, he established a new party, the Partai Nasional Bung Karno (PNBK). Djarot's consistent opposition to the New Order during the 1990s and after 1998 gave him a certain authority among the *reformasi* constituency. In the same period, he had started up the political newsweekly tabloid, *Detik*, a lively publication which quickly soared to become one of the biggest circulation weekly publications in Jakarta and certainly the biggest circulation paper covering politics. Moreover, he had a separate national profile as a popular songwriter of some standing and as a film producer. He thus combined profile and authority from the arenas of both popular culture and opposition politics. Of course, his level of authority was not as great as Wahid's, for example, or Megawati's. He had stood for a senior position in the 2000 PDIP congress but had been defeated by that section of the party more willing to compromise with the old Suharto-era political forces.

Rachmawati Soekarnoputri had taken a different political path than Megawati having refused to participate in any political institutions established under the New Order. After the fall of Suharto, Rachmawati was a prolific columnist in the popular newspaper, *Rakyat Merdeka*, often attacking Megawati for subservience to the USA, both in the economic and foreign policy areas. Rachmawati has consistently framed these criticisms using a vocabulary borrowed from Soekarno's writings. She had also helped establish a party, of which she was chairperson, namely the Partai Pelopor (Vanguard Party).

Neither Djarot nor Rachmawati had been able to establish a level of authority to mobilize large numbers of masses around their program. However, in 2002 there seemed to be the prospect of a coalition emerging that might combine these two figures with a range of other *reformasi* groupings, including those with a record of successful *aksi* work, such as the PRD.

On 22 January 2003, more than 300 journalists and other observers crammed into a room in the Struggle Museum in Central Jakarta to hear representatives of several political and social movement organizations announce the formation of a new coalition, called the Koalisi Nasional (National Coalition—KN), which included both the PNBK and Partai Pelopor.

Key activist student groups which are members of KN include the Indonesian Islamic Students Movement, a large left-liberal Moslem student group; the National Democratic Front, an alliance of left-oriented activist groups; the National Students League for Democracy (LMND), the student organization led by members of the radical left People's Democratic Party (PRD). Labor organizations include the Indonesian Front for Labour Struggles (FNPBI) and the Indonesian Workers Prosperity Union (SBSI). Democratic rights and community groups include the Committee for Vigilance Against the New Order, the University of Indonesia Alumni Association and the National Small Business Association. The Social Democratic Labour Party (PSDB), which was established by labor movement figure Mochtar Pakpahan; and the People's Struggle Party (PPR), a small party made up of older people who were active in the pre-1965 left, were also members.

Other organizations based on more activist currents in the PDIP membership also joined the NK. These include the 27 July 1996 Youth Movement and the Nationalist Youth League. The official youth wing of the PDIP, the Democratic Youth (PD), was also affiliated to the NK. The previous PD congress had elected well-known activist and author of the recently banned book "I Am Proud to be a PKI Child", Dr Ribka Ciptaning, as its secretary general.

The KN issued a statement declaring that the Megawati government had failed and that there needed to be a struggle to replace it with a new government "based on the demands of the people's movement"—for the withdrawal of the planned price increases on petrol, electricity and telephone usage; an end to interference in the Indonesian economy by the IMF and the World Bank; rejection of privatization and defense of majority state ownership of all vital economic assets; and trial of all political and economic criminals and human rights violators during and since the New Order, both individuals and political institutions. The KN's political platform called for an end to the military hierarchy's interference in politics and demanded a complete purging from the state apparatus of individuals involved in repression or corruption during the New Order era. It also demanded the full political rehabilitation of the victims of political repression during and since the New Order. The KN's economic platform emphasized the need for a sovereign national economy and demanded the cancellation of all debts flowing from agreements between the New Order regime with the World Bank, IMF and Asian Development Bank.

The platform called for the development of a system of control over and access to all means of production, distribution and capital in all sectors of enterprise that impact on the dignity and livelihood of the majority of the people, and for an immediate 100 percent increase in wages for workers and civil servants, and the salaries of all officers, non-commissioned officers and the ranks of the armed forces and police. It also called for the reinstitution of subsidies for agriculture, especially to provide technology and capital to small farmers, as well as a rejection of trade liberalization in the food sector.

However, this alliance was short-lived. Its strength lay in bringing together groups with the skills and perspective to build mobilization-based campaigns, especially the PRD and student groups, and political parties whose leaders—Eros Djarot and Rachmawati Soekarnoputri—had a national profile and access to the media. The breadth of the alliance also may have had the potential to reinforce the authority and profile of Djarot and Rachmawati. The formation of the KN took place, however, in a context where there was a rival form of political activity to extra-parliamentary *aksi* looming on the horizon: national elections. In this context, the PNBK and the PPP decided to go it alone in their preparations for the 2005 elections and deprioritized the KN. Within a few weeks it had ceased to function as a serious organization. Both the PNBK and PPP failed to win seats in the elections.

The failure of the KN at the beginning of 2003 reinforced the pattern of site-of-grievance social protests characterized by an absence of any large-scale political mobilizations which has continued until today. There was no political leadership with the profile and authority to call such mobilizations, as there had been during the de facto alliances between the PRD and Megawati in 1996, the student movement-Megawati-Amien Rais-Wahid combination in 1998, and the PRD-*reformasi* NGOs-Wahid alliance in 2001.

In July 2003, another attempt at a coalition took place, this time without the participation of any high-profile dissident from within or at the margins of the elite. On 26–27 July 2003, 300 representatives of sixty organizations gathered in Jakarta to establish the first political party attempting to form a broader structure for this process. The 26–27 July congress formed the Party of United People's Opposition (Partai Persatuan Perlawanan Rakyat—POPOR). This party went on to seek electoral registration, meaning that it needed to prove it had branches in two-thirds of all provinces and in more than half of all districts in each province. It succeeded in gathering sufficient participation to pass through the initial stages of this process but was unable to consolidate it to pass the rigorous final stage which required face-to-face meetings between local party executives and electoral commission officials and a host of other administrative requirements.

Key among the initiating organizations was the PRD. But most of the other organizations were trade unions, peasant organizations, NGOs and action groups not formerly associated with any national network. The congress adopted policy platforms presenting alternatives to neoliberal economic policies and the continuing entrenchment of the privileges of the political elite inherited from the New Order. The formation of POPOR was an extremely significant development, despite its collapse in the lead-up to the 2004 election campaign. The initiative put the question of the national political organization of locally based class-oriented groups on the national political agenda in a clear way for the first time. At the same, its failure underscored the nature of the kind of alliance work that the site-of-grievance form of *aksi* politics required. Solid alliances could not be built at the national level; rather, in every town and region alliances had to be built among a myriad of ad hoc formations, all united by populist sentiment and pressing grievance related needs, but without any ideological glue. Before looking at the issue of ideology among the popular classes in this whole process, it is necessary to briefly paint a picture of the political economy of *aksi*, of the sociology of grievance underpinning its persistence.

9

The Political Economy of *Aksi*

The political campaigning launched in the late 1980s against Suharto and using *aksi* has reinstated mass action as a legitimate and indeed popular political method. The spread of mass mobilization methods has started a process of re-establishing the organization of the popular classes. While this organization remains mainly ad hoc, semi-spontaneous and mostly local or regional, it does represent the beginning of a reorganization process. There are examples of attempts to start provincial or national organizations which indicate that a new dynamic is working its way through political life, even if slowly and in a grueling way.

The situation with trade unions reflects this. On the one hand, the post-Suharto period has seen a mushrooming of enterprise or workplace unions, that is, site-of-grievance unionization. Some of these unions are continuations of workplace organization breaking away from the straitjacket of the single, permitted and government-controlled trade union, the SPSI from the Suharto period. Others are connected with some of the independent initiatives taken in defiance of the New Order during its last years. Some are totally new phenomena where workers have taken advantage of more relaxed labor laws and more political space to set up a new workplace union. Ministry of Labor statistics mention around 12,000 unions of different kinds, but there may be others not yet registered, or whose registration does not necessarily find its way from the provincial to the national ministry office. Workplace unions emerge and collapse also in response to the establishment of new factories or the closure of old ones. While the percentage of the workforce, including the stable proletariat, unionized remains quite tiny, the steady trend for these workplace unions is to expand. At the same time, there is also a trend to begin organizing national unions. There were sixty-seven registered national unions in 2003 and a persistent trend among the workplace unions to organize along industrial lines and form national structures.

More fundamentally, it is now possible to detect a nationwide pattern in the political streaming of trade union organization. Under the Suharto regime, only one trade union organization was recognized which was set up on the initiative of the regime and used as an instrument of control. Military personnel and personnel managers of businesses dominated the decision-making processes.[1] This union was first known as the All Indonesia Workers Federation and later the All Indonesia Workers Union (SPSI). In the early 1990s, as the new wave of opposition to the dictator-ship emerged, there were initiatives to form oppositional trade unions. There were two of these that were able to sustain themselves into the post-Suharto era. One was the Indonesian Prosperous Workers Union (SBSI), associated with the leadership of Mochtar Pakpahan, who was imprisoned by Suharto for a short period. The other was the Indonesian Centre for Labour Struggles (PPBI), which later became the Indonesian Front for Labour Struggles (FNPBI), an initiative by the same forces that established the PRD.

The period under Suharto was characterized by the enforced dominance of the SPSI and a range of oppositional initiatives of the SBSI and FNPBI, the former concentrating on lobbying, but with some strike activity, and the latter concentrating on mass actions.

As noted earlier, after the fall of Suharto, the situation has become more complex. First, the links between the SPSI and the state have become much weaker. This has resulted in some sections of the SPSI being able to break away and form independent bodies in their workplaces. Even where workplace units have remained with the SPSI, the union itself is no longer directly controlled by the state apparatus or government, although business managements often dominate so that it remains a very conservative union. It is the biggest union. Second, in addition to independent breakaway unions from the SPSI, there are now more independently formed work-place unions, established in the free political atmosphere. The SBSI and the FNPBI both remain active.

This complex terrain of thousands of workplace unions forming or reforming in the political semi-chaos of the immediate aftermath of the fall of a dictatorship and the economic semi-chaos of intensified neoliberal

policy implementation is gradually beginning to exhibit the early signs of
ideological differentiation, which overtakes local or sectoral consciousness.
Three ideological streams are emerging reflected in the continuing existence of SPSI as a conservative force, the SBSI as a pole of attraction for
moderate unionism and, since 2005, the emergence of an alliance of
radicalizing unions called the Alliance of Accusing Labour (ABM—Alliansi
Buruh Menggugat).

The ABM includes the FNPBI. The FNPBI is an officially registered union
with a small national membership of about 15,000 workers in branches on
Java, Sumatra, Kalimantan, Sulawesi, Bali and in eastern Indonesia. In
addition to the FNPBI there are several other unions of similar or smaller
size. They include the Congress of Indonesian Labour Union Alliances
(KASBI—Kongres Alliansi Seerikat Buruh Indonesia). KASBI held its first
congress in February 2003. It has branches in Jakarta, Java and North
Sumatra. KASBI has a connection with the left-oriented national network,
the Working People's Association (PRP—Perhimpunan Rakyat Pekerja).
Another is a split from the SBSI and another is a split from the SPSI. Their
branches are also spread around the country. There are also around thirty local
enterprise unions. These unions cover a range of different industrial sectors,
including garments, electronics, metal working, journalism, docks, food
processing and others. There appears the prospect that the ABM, now
operating as a semi-formal alliance, may move towards formalizing its
cooperation and establishing itself as a recognized union confederation.[2]
The ABM adopts positions going beyond demands for improvements to
wages and conditions; it also opposed the overall neoliberal policy prescriptions put forward by the IMF and adopted by one government after the next.
The ABM supports the demand for the nationalization of oil, gas and mineral
industries and the cancellation of the foreign debt. Most of the ABM unions
are not represented in state-initiated tripartite bodies, while unions from the
other ideological streams do participate.

This is not the total picture of patterns in trade union reorganization
with some unions also orienting to the PDIP. The political evolution of the
unions covering employees in the hundreds of state-owned enterprises and
in the civil service and teaching sectors is still at an early stage.

The same pattern exists with peasant farmers. Given the nature of
agriculture, with farmers' problems varying from region to region, there
have been significant steps forward in organizing on a regional level,

especially in West Java.[3] However, organizations such as Konsorsium Agraria and AGRA also reflect how ideological differentiation is creating national political streaming in this area as well. There are significant attempts to also establish national peasant unions such as the Federation of Indonesian Peasant Unions (FPSI—Federasi Serikat Petani Indonesia), which has branches in Sumatra, Java and eastern Indonesia. The National Peasants Union (STN—Serikat Tani Nasional), associated with the PRD, is smaller but also has branches on Sumatra, Java and Bali. Even some people living in areas where the traditional norms of subsistence life still survive to some extent—the *masyarakat adat* areas—have formed a national organization, Alliansi Masyarakat Adat Nasional (National Masyarakat Adat Alliance—AMAN.)

The process of re-establishing national organization among the popular classes—workers, peasants, urban poor, fishermen, traditional subsistence communities, for example—is a slow and uneven one, still primarily being driven, at this point in time, by factors of political economy. While ideological differentiation and the formation of national ideological streams within the reorganization process are visible, they are still at an early stage. The economic strategy adopted by governments after the economic collapse of 1997–8 and the first agreements with the International Monetary Fund have been setting the framework for the persistence of *aksi*. On almost every front, this strategy has increased the level of economic grievance throughout the popular classes.

Political Economy of *Aksi*

Royseptia Abimanyu, a writer on economics and activist, reviewed the Indonesian economy in 2003 in the magazine *Inside Indonesia*. He wrote:

After six years of crisis, there are no signs of recovery for Indonesia. Key economic infrastructure has continued to degrade. Parts of many cities, especially outside Java, are now experiencing regular electricity blackouts, as the power capacity drops due to lack of maintenance or to just bad, uncoordinated, planning. The railways have seen a 64 percent increase in accidents due to ageing tracks and facilities.

The budget for the fiscal year 2002 was literally suffocated; 25 percent (Rp 88.5 trillion) of it went into the payment of the interest on loans alone. As a result, spending on social infrastructure plummeted. Health and education spending, for example, goes nowhere near meeting the needs of a population suffering deteriorating social conditions. In the 2001 budget, the percentage allocation to education fell to the lowest it has been since Indonesia became independent in 1945. The government guaranteed that things would improve, but the current allocation for education is only Rp 13.6 trillion (A$ 1.56 billion)—just four percent of the total state budget, not the 24 percent promised.

The IMF-sponsored programs have been a particular blow to agriculture. The IMF insisted that effective tariffs and quotas on sugar, tobacco, soybeans and rice were abolished, and that these commodities no longer be sold centrally through a logistics board. The results have been devastating for national food production.

According to the National Sugar Council, the share of locally produced sugar fell from 95 percent of overall consumption in 1995 to just 55 percent in 2002. To make matters worse, liberalisation of the sugar market has encouraged speculation and politically-motivated profiteering in the sector. In March 2003, prices shot up in some regions and sugar disappeared from the market in others. Raids by sugar farmers on warehouses and trucks found huge stock of unreported sugar imports. No wonder that thousands of angry sugar farmers swarmed the imported sugar warehouses in Central Java and dumped imported goods into the streets and rivers.

Soybean farmers have also been unable to compete against cheap imports. In 2002, national soybean production was half that of 1996. Cheap imported rice also has resulted in a downturn of national rice production. Even natural water supply is being privatised. In August 2003, farmers protested a law allowing water springs to be owned by corporations.[4]

In a later issue of the same magazine, Bonnie Setiawan, from the Jakarta-based Global Justice Institute, further elaborated on the agricultural sector:

Through the Letter of Intent and the Memorandum of Economic and Financial Policies of 11 September 1998, the IMF demanded that tariffs on the importation of rice be completely abolished. This demand was extended to other food products such as corn, soybeans, flour and sugar. This was in accord with Indonesia's ratification of the Agreement on Agriculture of the World Trade Organisation, which aimed to eliminate or reduce tariffs and subsidies on agricultural products.

Further LoI price liberalisation regulations were passed for fertiliser and other inputs into rice production, effectively ending government subsidisation of the production of basic foods. Subsidies to farmers through the Farmers Credit scheme were also reduced. As a result, farmers faced rapidly increasing production costs and rapidly falling prices for their goods. Cheaper rice was imported from overseas, and local farmers could no longer compete with these imports.[5]

Abimanyu added further commentary on the plight of sectors outside agriculture:

Outside the 21 million peasant families, urban livelihoods are also under threat. The government and its privatisation schemes have faced resistance from the workers who fear the downsizing policies that often accompany privatisation. In 2003, the new board of directors of Semen Padang, a subsidiary of Semen Gresik (owned by Mexican Cemex) found out how angry workers could get. They were not able to enter their own offices because the factory was barricaded by its trade union. There has been similiar unrest in Indosat throughout 2002 and into 2003. In June 2003, maintenance workers at Garuda, the country's state owned airline, went on strike. They were protesting their transfer to a newly created subsidiary— usually a preparatory step for privatisation.[6]

The neoliberal economic strategy, applied on top of a devastated economy since 1997, generates issues of grievance in all sectors of society. Neoliberal policies—deregulation, privatization, austerity—create a grievance generation process which has become an embedded feature of social reality. Neoliberal policies institutionalize the absence of policies of amelioration, whether they were in the past policies of industry protection or price subsidization of commodities used by the mass of the population. The dismantling of these policies reduced the Indonesian government and, more seriously, masses of poor people to the level of using an amelioration policy of simple cash handouts.

This policy was announced in November 2005: a US$30 handout to people on an income of less than $25 per month as compensation for rises in fuel prices. Individuals would be given a three-monthly payment. According to the Central Bureau of Statistics (BPS), 10 million people—2.5 million families—dropped below the official poverty line in the course of one month. The previous poverty line had been Rp175,000 ($25) income per month, but with a 17 percent inflation rate in 2005 this rose to Rp 216,000 ($30). While Rp 216,000 was used as a measure of poverty, the minimum wage in Jakarta was about to be set at Rp 819,100 ($110). Seventy million people qualified in a population of 230 million. Since the scheme began in October 2006, the BPS says that 10.6 million people have registered for the handout.

On 15 November 2005 the *Kompas* daily newspaper carried an extensive report detailing how workers' wages can now be eaten up by transport costs. In Surabaya, the report detailed, 50 percent of wages could be taken up by transportation. The workers described how they now had to get off the bus or other public transport half way to work and walk the remaining kilometers on foot. The same article reported similar or even worse effects in other cities in Java, Sumatra and Kalimantan.

Waras Warsito, the West Java deputy chairman of the National Workers Union, told *Kompas* that there had been a flood of workers seeking to borrow money from the factory cooperatives just to buy daily necessities, which meant that on pay day they ended up with only half their salary.

Meanwhile, the BPS also announced that unemployment has grown steadily at 5.5 percent every year since 1996. Some 1.9 million people have come onto the labor market every year, unable to find real work. The National Development Planning Board estimates that unemployment has been growing at 9.5 percent annually.

The 15 November *Kompas* also reported that 4,400 workers were laid off in a plywood sawmill in East Kalimantan. The same day, the paper reported that 30,000 workers in an industrial estate in Medan, North Sumatra, were soon to lose their jobs as the factories announced they would have to close down due to the increase in fuel prices and the electricity shortage.

On 17 November, *Kompas* reported that another 20,000 workers were laid off in the fishing industry as 200 tuna fishing ships were stuck in port, their owners no longer able to pay for fuel. Meanwhile in Banten, West Java, the fisheries department reported that 19,000 of 26,000 fishers in their region could not afford to take their boats out. It cost Rp 200,000 ($27) for enough petrol for one trip out and they could only expect to make that amount in total per trip.

Farmers have also been hit. *Kompas* reported a case of farmers in Bekasi, just outside Jakarta, ripping out acres of spinach. *Kompas* reported piles of rotting spinach along the roads. The farmers reported that increases in the price of inputs since the fuel price rises have meant that it is no longer profitable to keep the spinach in the ground. Inputs increased drastically, while the price of spinach fell 75 percent, farmers told the newspaper.

In September 2006, the Indonesian Bureau of Statistics issued figures stating that 39.05 million people, out of a population of 220 million, were living on Rp 152,847 (US$16.80) per month. Approximately another 75 million were living on or just above this official poverty line, bringing the total living at this miserable level to almost 50 percent of the population.[7]

This disastrous socio-economic situation sits upon an economic structure which, despite twenty years of high levels of petrodollar income, remains fundamentally under-industrialized. In November 2000, the United Nations Industrial Development Organization (UNIDO) completed a detailed study of the Indonesian economy. It described a picture of very shallow industrialization.

> While the government assiduously promoted export-oriented industrialization since 1985, neither the government nor the private sector accompany this drive with the necessary measures to diversify export products and markets, to deepen and diversify the manufacturing base, and to enhance the competitiveness of Indonesian firms. The absence of these measures to compensate for known market failures in building up manufacturing capability such as inadequate information, high risks and long and expensive learning process . . . and the sheer rapidity of industrialization, led to a relatively shallow industrial structure, while the promised foreign exchange earnings failed to materialize.

A number of other structural problems emerged. The oil and gas sector generated only limited net revenues. Low productivity plagued the small and medium-scale industries, while significant market concentration by a few large firms prevailed in large segments of manufacturing. Manufacturing production remained concentrated in Java, and in Greater Jakarta in particular. The capacity to absorb, adapt and develop process and product technology as well as human resources remained weak.[8]

The UNIDO report analyzes the industrial depth of manufacturing and the nature of the technologies being deployed.

The pattern of Indonesian industrialization differed from that of other countries with similar degrees of industrialization. Between 1985 and 1997, the contribution of higher technology industries to manufacturing value-added did not increase, *while the production of low-technology industries expanded, mainly at the expense of medium-technology industries.* The increase in the share of low-technology industries was due to the rapid growth of labour-intensive industries such as textiles, garments and footwear, and to a lesser extent to the expansion of the resource-based food, paper and wood industries. In contrast to the decline of the share of medium-technology industries in Indonesia (including rubber and plastic industries, fertilizer, cement, basic metals and simple fabricated metal industry), virtually all countries in the region and elsewhere have maintained the share of medium-technology industries in their manufacturing output. Similarly, the contribution of physical-capital intensive products to total exports also declined during this period.[9]

There are flow-ons from this pattern of *"while the production of low-technology industries expanded, mainly at the expense of medium-technology industries"* for the nature of employment.

The medium and large-scale manufacturing establishments employed some 4 million workers or just 4% of the total work force of around [urban] 90 million. Starting in 1992, manufacturing wages began to rise by about 10% p.a. . . . The annual surveys of medium and large-scale manufacturing industries show that the value added-employment elasticity declined from 0.5 in 1989–93 to 0.3 in 1994–97 in the manufacturing sector as a whole, and from 0.4–0.3 to 0.1 in textiles and garments. . . . The low elasticities in these two relatively labour-intensive industries were the result of very small additions to the workforce, of the order of 1% versus 10%–15% p.a. in the previous period, while continuing to post healthy 10%–15% annual growth rates in output.[10]

Moreover, enterprises of 500 workers or more, employing a third of the workforce, produced 80 percent of manufacturing value added. A massive two-thirds of the workforce—60 million plus—employed in medium (twenty to ninety-nine workers), small-scale (five to nineteen workers) and household industries (one to four workers) accounted for only 5–6 percent of total manufacturing value added.[11]

In other words, the Indonesian urban workforce of about 90 million remained overwhelmingly comprised of a semi-proletariat with uncertain employment in a huge ocean of small enterprises, with miserably low productivity and with the concomitant low incomes. This was reinforced by figures in the World Bank's 1997 *World Development Indicators* (using the International Labour Organization's 1995 *Yearbook of Labor Statistics*). In 1993 "employees" (which includes bourgeois managerial personnel, highly paid middle-class professionals, as well as wage-workers) accounted for only 37.8 percent of Indonesia's economically active population, while "employers and own-account workers" (that is, capitalist employers and self-employed workers—which can include not just petty proprietors but also much of the urban and rural semi-proletariat) accounted for 39.4 percent of the labor force. A further 20.8 percent were classified as "unpaid family workers" (which leaves 2 percent not accounted for). The latter category are most likely family dependents of petty bourgeois peasants, small manufacturers and traders.[12]

This is the underlying condition that militates against trade unions becoming the major vehicle of worker mobilization. In these conditions *aksi* (and *rusuh*) become the two dominant forms of organization or action. The workplace can become a site of grievance and organization, but it is often temporary and ad hoc. The neighborhood or *kampung* can be the more usual basis for mobilization, or even the *gang* (the maze-like laneways

in the *kampung* along which people live in small crowded, small houses).
The semi-proletariat, or urban poor, as they are called in Indonesian
political discourse, develop a specific form of political culture in these
kampung. This is described well in an interview with a leader of the People's
Democratic Party in 1998.

> What we call the urban poor are made up of the unemployed, the
> lumpen proletariat (pickpockets, burglars, con men, sex workers,
> drug sellers, guys who jump up onto moving trucks and grab some of
> the load) as well as peddlers, government clerks and employees. In
> north Jakarta, they also include factory workers, shop assistants,
> supermarket and department store employees (mostly women),
> coolies, public transport drivers, street stall owners and so on. Most
> of these people live in squalid *kampung* [geographically delimited
> "villages" inside the city zone]. Rubbish is piled up everywhere, there
> is no water, the drains are blocked, mosquitoes abound, the rooms are
> tiny so that people pile up next to each other like sardines to sleep,
> and they wash and defecate in public toilets where they have to pay.
> Electricity is around 100 watts total per household (if you're a bit
> better off you can get up to 450 watts). It's rare for anyone to get a
> senior high school or university education. Incomes are around 100–
> 300 thousand rupiah (US$20–US$60) a month. Most families have
> two to five members. Children regularly suffer cholera, typhus,
> meningitis, dysentery, skin disorders, influenza, sinus and eye infec-
> tions and malnutrition.
>   At demonstrations, protest most often takes place around the
> demolition of their homes, the increase in public transport vehicles
> which cuts into the incomes of existing public transport drivers [paid
> by commission and not wages], the banning of street stalls and
> peddlers by local government, the closure of small kiosks without the
> operators being given somewhere else to operate or being forced to
> wait too long for a new place. The urban poor usually read papers like
> *Sentana, Swadesi, Pos Kota, Suara Karya* and *Inti Jaya*. In Surabaya
> [Indonesia's biggest metropolitan and industrial center after Jakarta]
> the public transport drivers read the middle class paper *Jawa Pos* and
> the sensationalist *Memorandum*, whose editorials are often very
> radical. (The military has instructed the paper that the editorial

writer may be published only twice a week!) Reading these papers means the urban poor have been able to learn from the protest actions by students and peasant farmers when protest delegations to the parliament and the National Human Rights Commission are common. They imitate these actions, using leaflets, posters, placards, press releases and even giving interviews to the media.

The urban poor also read the penny novels of Fredy S and the Chinese sword fighting stories of Wiro Sableng and Kho Ping Ho which teach of the holiness of pure love and that those who struggle for justice and truth are always victorious, always survive. Many of them are members of the PDI and use the sense of *kampung* solidarity to involve their neighbours in PDI actions. Many were supporters of the PPP during the May elections. Gossip about government officials, their wealth, scandals and corruption, is their daily staple. Many of these *kampung* have come to the same conclusion as the students as to the source of their problems. Many too, ever since they were teenagers in junior or perhaps senior high, have become accustomed to violence in the form of fights and mass brawls between students from different schools (often with knives and guns) or with the police trying to separate the warring students.[13]

Asked about the combative mentality of this urban poor compared to the factory workforce, he continued:

The urban poor are more aware of the contradictions around them [than some factory workers] because in their daily lives the rich pass back and forth before their very eyes. They experience all kinds of criminality, including the criminal actions of the government and the violence and arrogance of the military in the form of extortion, bribes and beatings. They live among people from all walks of life and they have time to discuss and debate things with their *kampung* friends. They also have greater access to different kinds of reading materials, so their culture is more urban, more liberal-radical and they are open to new ideas.

However, while the situation of two-thirds of the urban workforce located in this "urban poor" sector predisposes them to *aksi* or *rusuh*, it has other consequences. First, it strengthens their sense of being *rakyat*, starkly differentiated from the wealth of the middle classes and the high product-ivity sector of the economy that the prosperous layers relate to. This thus helps reinforce the hold of this ideological legacy of the national revolution. Second, it helps reinforce a sense of politics where the role of the individual leader, the personality, plays a predominant role. This is the kind of popular culture in which they participate—the world of the sword-fighter hero—and it is also the nature of the day to day socio-economic reality they experience. Life as a semi-proletarian, working in a variety of different small enterprises, means they are not dealing with anonymous corporate owners, but often with owners who are friends or relatives, as much as with totally unknown people. Whether their employers are ratbags or easy to get on with plays a big role in their experience. This experience can reinforce a psychology brought in from the village where patron-client relations exist. It is, therefore, not surprising that among big sections of this sector Megawati Soekarnoputri became a symbol of leadership that could mo-bilize millions of people. But there are contradictory trends embodied in the dynamics of this situation.

The existence of a huge low-productivity, semi-proletarian sector, where the large workplace is not a center for organization, sociologically under-pins the *aksi* form of organization as well as the predisposition for forms of action such as rioting. However, as more protests take place and a more extensive discussion develops of the causes of the socio-economic situation, the understanding also starts to spread that solutions to these situations require changes in national policy. For the most politicized sections of the working class and peasantry, this perception is manifested in their member-ship of organizations with a national outlook and connected to specific ideological currents.

The first of these initiatives taken within the framework of political organizations were those that emerged at the beginning of the 1990s opposition to Suharto and were able to develop and sustain an ideological orientation. There are few of these. All of them are still small, and only one has developed a significant political profile, namely the People's Demo-cratic Party (PRD).[14] Other such national networks include the Indonesian Youth Struggle Front (Front Perjuangan Pemuda Indonesia—FPPI), the National Students Front (Front Mahasiswa Nasional) and the Socialist Youth (Pemuda Sosialis).[15] The Agrarian Renewal Consortium (Konsorsium Pembaruan Agraria—KPA), the Agrarian Reform Movement Alliance (Alliansi Gerakan Reforma Agraria—AGRA) and the Indonesian Environmental Forum (Wahana Lingkungan Hidup—WAHLI), although looser and, excepting AGRA, with weaker ideological focus, are also significant national networks of reorganization.

The political economy and the socio-economic conditions are a constant source of grievance among the Indonesian poor. Since *aksi*, as a method of struggle, was legitimized through the processes of the anti-dictatorship struggle, this has become the common method of airing grievances and struggling for solutions. The fact that these grievances flow from the implementation of a specific set of economic policies—those embodied in the neoliberal prescriptions of the IMF and the World Bank—provides the basis for organizing around these grievances to begin to take a national form and to be based on specific ideological outlooks. At the same time, fragmentation remains the dominant feature of this terrain—at this point in time. A major part of the reason for this is that grappling with national policy issues takes place in a context of a suppressed ideological life and collective class memory of earlier struggles. The process of recovering the kinds of ideas that informed mass political activity and working-class and peasant-class consciousness up until 1965 is only just beginning.

10

Back to the Future: Memory, Class Consciousness, Ideology

At a public question and answer session held on the occasion of his eighty-first birthday at the Jakarta Arts Center in January 2006, Pramoedya Ananta Toer asked a very important question: Why has the youth, who succeeded in the amazing achievement of overthrowing the military-backed Suharto regime, not produced a political leadership with national authority? Pramoedya had been pointing out that it had been the youth who had repeatedly provided the leadership and energy for major change at all points in Indonesian history. But in the past, he noted, these youth leaders had also become national political leaders. Why not now? "Is there some sociological or psychological explanation?" he asked.

There is little doubt that the situation in 2006—sustained, widespread but small and site-of-grievance social protest—does indeed reflect a problem of generational leadership change. The national political stage remains dominated by figures and groups who trace their origins back to the New Order elite or, at the most, to the elite-based opposition of the 1990s. Some of the political parties based on these layers of the elite have successfully co-opted activist leaders from the grassroots *reformasi* sector, but this co-option has undermined their authority, rather than their new affiliation enhancing the authority of these parties.[1]

What can explain this leadership vacuum? *Reformasi* resonated so powerfully in 1998 and 1999.

The answer to this question relates to the stage which the process of relaunching the national revolution has reached. The state of Indonesian politics cannot be fully understood without grasping that the period of 1965–89 was one of counter-revolution against the national revolution, suppressing and winding back the gains made during the previous sixty years. The counter-revolution, designed by Ali Murtopo and implemented by Suharto, had several phenomena which it wished to eliminate. These were: (a) mass action, or mass mobilization politics; (b) national organization of the popular classes; and (c) the ideological life coming out of the national revolution.

Mass action as a legitimate political method was re-won during the struggle against the Suharto dictatorship. Driven by the need to respond to economic crisis and the consequent policy issues, national-scale reorganization among the popular classes has begun but remains difficult and slow. It is in the area of ideology where the process of winning back the gains made by the popular classes appears to be advancing the slowest. This rests on the massive suppression of the left in 1965, including the physical elimination of over a million people. It also rests on the systematic destruction of the collective memory of struggle that was implemented during most of the Suharto period. The *rakyat* sentiment remains and a connection with the Soekarno name, but little else.

In this arena, the struggle to re-win ideology has had to start almost from scratch, although not entirely. *Rakyat* is not only a sentiment, it is also an idea. It is worth elaborating on this a little more.

Class Consciousness and Its Ideological Content During the National Revolution

In trying to trace the course of changes in class consciousness among the popular classes in Indonesia, a crucial determining factor has been shared experience in political struggle on a national scale. There are studies of individual factories, villages and so on which attempt to describe the nature of class consciousness on the basis of a localized description of workers', peasants' and informal sector workers' daily experiences. In the field of peasant studies, there is quite an enormous body of literature along these lines, pioneered by people such as James Scott, with his *The Moral Economy of the Peasant.*[2]

However, studies such as this are totally inadequate for drawing any conclusions regarding the development of class consciousness. Consciousness flows out of social experience, which includes experience of collective political activity and struggle, not just shared experience at the location of production. In the case of Indonesia, participation in national-scale political struggle was a fundamental shared experience of all the exploited classes from the beginning of the twentieth century until 1965. This experience peaked in the early 1960s with at least half the adult population, and big sections of the youth population, mobilized. During the last part of 1965 through to 1968, another shared experience flowing from political activity was the brutal and murderous suppression of all such mobilization.

The dominant ideology among the mobilized popular classes, from at least the 1920s, was Soekarnoism. Soekarno held overwhelming ideological sway over all open political discourse that took place among the popular classes, with only small pockets quarantined from this who were under the influence of one or other Islamic ideological outlook. Soekarno wrote hundreds of articles and gave even more speeches during this whole period. After independence these speeches were often broadcast over the radio as well.

During this period there was a number of basic ideas that he popularized.

Unity of the Impoverished

First, there was the idea of the existence of a fundamental unity among the impoverished masses of Indonesia. In scores of speeches, he explained the existence of three basic social components among these impoverished masses. These were the proletariat, the peasants and other impoverished people (peddlers, other ekers out of a livelihood). In the 1920s, he also formulated the concept of the "Marhaen" (the name of a poor farmer he had spoken with). Originally, the Marhaen referred to that layer of people who owned some instrument of production (for example, a buffalo) and worked for themselves but were just as impoverished as the factory worker or plantation worker. Soekarno was identifying the reality of the existence of the country's huge semi-proletarian and pauperized petty bourgeoisie.

In the 1960s, the term "Marhaen" began to be used interchangeably to refer to the workers, proletarians and others combined, as well as to the specific Marhaen category.

Even though the PKI did not officially adopt Marhaenism, preferring to use a typology of classes taken from Mao's writings, the regular speeches by Soekarno in all avenues, including at PKI rallies, helped solidify this concept—which also emphasized unity of interest among these components.

But it was not just the incredibly effective techniques of explaining this idea by Soekarno that gave it power, but also the fact that on a daily basis political discussion and activity at the mass base took place among workers, semi-proletarians, poor peddlers, stall owners, mechanics and so on in a socio-cultural framework that was only minimally differentiated. First, the semi-proletarians and impoverished petty bourgeois were the overwhelming majority and their huge numbers provided the material base for the cultural life that developed. Second, in both town and country, all these components lived together in the same neighborhoods. Third, most of the stabilized proletariat was very new and young and had most of their family still in the village or surviving as part of the semi-proletariat. The economic basis of this and its socio-cultural consequences were discussed in the previous chapter. The period since 1965, with its shallow industrialization, has brought the Marhaen phenomena to the cities.

Another manifestation of this component of class consciousness during this whole period was the emergence of a very specific term and concept, that is, the *rakyat*. *Rakyat* literally means people. But the word cannot be used for "people" in every context. You could not use *rakyat*, for example, "There are many *rakyat* at the opera today." You could not even use *rakyat* in the sentence: "There are 500 people as members of parliament." Everybody knows that the members of parliament are not *rakyat*. The very word for "people" has been given class content. It refers only to that mass of Marhaen, workers and peasants, the impoverished, the "little people."[3]

Unity of Interest and Action

Both the speeches and writings of Soekarno and those of the PKI and other left leaders and activists also stressed that the immiseration of the *rakyat* or Marhaen has specific causes. Soekarno used the word *melarat*, which is worse than poor, it is to live in misery. But he would always repeat a formulation along the lines: "or more precisely these are masses made impoverished by capitalism, colonialism and imperialism." The misery was the result of a system, which had to be overthrown. Being victims of this system was a part of the very definition of "people."

One misunderstanding about Soekarno relates to his emphasis on unity.

He is seen as the archetypical Third World, non-bloc nationalist who valued national unity above all else. This is a very careless reading, indeed misreading, of Soekarnoism and carries with it the danger of not understanding fully the way class consciousness among the popular classes has developed.

To start with, there is the fact that must be noted of the very class character of the word for "people." *Rakyat* is an anti-unity word, when viewed in a national framework. Those who are not being impoverished, that is, exploited by capitalism, colonialism and imperialism, are not part of "the people"! This in itself points to a process of ideological formation that underscores contradiction in society, not unity, or a common national interest, throughout that society.

In addition, the whole history of Soekarno's political life also underscores his emphasis on drawing out contradictions. During the colonial period, he fought those Indonesians supporting cooperation with the Dutch, resulting in the ideological institutionalization of "non-co" and "co," and of "*sana*" (over there) and "*sini*" (here). After independence, the *rakyat* and Marhaen were not pitted against capitalism, colonialism and imperialism as "concepts" or systems in the abstract. Dutch and then British companies were nationalized. As a layer of corrupt bureaucratic managers developed, these were identified as *kabir* (bureaucratic capitalists) and there were campaigns to have them dismissed and for worker representation in management councils. Soekarno supported the campaign for land reform, taking land from large landowners. The political party most attached to domestic capital, the MASYUMI, was banned after it supported an armed rightist mutiny. The political party most aggressive in its support for economic cooperation with the West, the Indonesian Socialist Party (PSI), was banned after supporting the same rightist mutiny. The Indonesian National Party (PNI), which had heavy representation of business and landlord interests, came under heavy campaigning pressure to purge the party of these elements, which began to be implemented in 1964. Even internationally, Soekarno began to break from the non-aligned bloc, and its view of a world divided into three, and began advocating an analysis which saw only two blocs, which he popularized under the terms "old established forces" and "new emerging forces." The latter included both the socialist countries, growing socialist movements, anti-Western Third World governments as well as movements such as the civil rights movement in the USA and so on.

Soekarnoism thus contributed an ideological content to the collective political life of the popular classes which emphasized unity of interest and action among their component parts, and helped locate their identity in a specific contradiction with other classes in society, namely, capitalists, landlords and cooperators with colonialism and imperialism.

Personality and Class Consciousness

Probably the most fundamental contradiction in Soekarno's role was connected to how he related to this only weakly differentiated popular mass. The socio-cultural life of the urban and rural poor existed in an environment that had not undergone the kind of tumultuous overturning of feudal, rural society as happened in Europe. There had been no enclosures act and industrial revolution. The Dutch modernized the economy only insofar as it was necessary to get the exports from its colony that it needed. At the end of Dutch rule no more than 10 percent of the population had any kind of high school education. The country was still overwhelmingly rural, with only one city with a population of around 400,000 people. Religion had not been challenged by the cultural changes that flow from an indigenously grown scientific and formal educational establishment—this did not yet exist—or from the secular routine of industrial society. Most people who were in the towns worked for small enterprises where a feudal-style personal relationship often still existed.

People still lived in *kampung*, whether rural or urban, which—while more and more dominated by a money economy—still retained many elements from pre-industrial society. Patron-client relations, of one kind or another, were prevalent. Whether organized through a workplace, networks of debt within extended families, and other forms of debt through a mosque or religious network or through friendships, this was still the dominant form of social relationship, overarching the capitalist-worker relationship, for many people. In this environment, a popular culture developed where the role of the individual figure—leader—loomed larger than or equal to disciplined organization and division of labor. The "modernizing" impact of modern proletarian life was alleviated by this ongoing pattern of patron-client relations that permeated this social environment, dominated as it was by millions of semi-proletarians and pauperized petty bourgeois.

Furthermore, the continuing influence of religion and traditional beliefs stirred into the ideological pot all kinds of concepts linked to the pre-capitalist past. The pre-capitalist past across the archipelago had been very culturally diverse so that the cultural vocabulary of these masses of people was also diverse.

It was these conditions that provided the basis for somebody like Soekarno to play the role of popularizing the ideas of the modern revolutions: the bourgeois, proletarian and anti-colonial revolutions. He quoted from the political thinkers and leaders of all these revolutions, from Rousseau, Robespierre, Thomas Paine, Sun Yat Sen to Lenin. He sought out metaphors from the Indonesian people's own experience to try to explain these ideas. It is simply a fact that nobody else had the skills to do this. His personal role in the spread of these ideas was enormous. Given the psychology of patron-client culture, this tended to put Soekarno into a "patron" role. A major limitation in his politics was that rather than working to stop this happening, he agreed to policies that reinforced this role, such as the acceptance of various extravagant titles, for example, Great Leader of the Revolution. He did emphasize the need for the masses to organize themselves, which is why he supported the role of the left political parties and their mass organizations, but his tendency towards allowing a cult of personality to develop militated against this. He accepted the descriptive title "Extension of the Voice of the People." There is no doubt he did articulate the sentiments and thinking of tens of millions of Indonesians—indeed he helped form them. At the same time, his adoption of and emphasis on this role in his writings and speeches institutionalized a process of weakening the popular classes' own mechanisms of articulation.

It is very difficult to overestimate the weight of the presence of Soekarno in mass consciousness, especially in the years leading up to 1965. Soekarnoism did provide the ideological framework in which the class consciousness of tens of millions of people developed. It gave a class struggle, radicalizing and unifying content to that consciousness, which was reinforced by the mobilization in campaigns of these millions of people around demands such as land reform, nationalization of foreign companies, worker representation in management councils of state enterprises and free education.

At the same time, the overwhelmingly dominant role Soekarno played as articulator of the popular classes' consciousness meant that the development of their political consciousness was constrained: these mobilizations were suppressed before they developed to the stage of preparing the popular classes to organize for power. In the period 1960–5, when mass mobilizations increased in size and frequency, their role was primarily to bring public opinion behind Soekarno's attempts to remove the right-wing parties and military officers who dominated the government, and move in more politicians, officials and military officers sympathetic to the left. In this sense, the mass mobilizations were playing the role of back-up to maneuverings within the state apparatus. A great deal of hope was being invested in Soekarno being able to use his position as president to change the balance of forces within the state apparatus. This also coincided with the way his role was being emphasized to the people.

The Resilience of Some Ideas: Soekarnoism and *Rakyat*

This deep contradiction in Soekarnoism—its radical class content and sense of class struggle in contradiction with the popular classes' voice being monopolized by one man—helps explain both the resilience of some of Soekarnoism's ideas as well as the limited form in which they have survived suppression. It is worth returning again to the resilience despite the New Order's suppression of two "ideas": Soekarno and *rakyat*.

Soekarno

During the thirty years of the Suharto dictatorship, the ideological life of Indonesia had been subject to a real counter-revolution. Indonesian cultural life from the beginning of the twentieth century up until 1965 was a cultural life born, first and foremost, out of revolution, specifically national revolution, which then began to develop in the direction of social revolution. Its vocabulary drew from the immediate struggles of the peoples of Indonesia against colonialism, but also from all previous and concurrent revolutions, including the French Revolution, the American revolution, the Russian revolution and the first Chinese revolution. The vocabulary of processes which had aimed at overturning old, corrupt systems and unleashing new energies in the name of justice and equality, both individual and national equality, supplied the vocabulary also of the newly emerging Indonesian national culture. This while the cultural fabric, emerging over sixty years, was destroyed, and wiped away. School and university curricula were rewritten by the armed forces History Center. Feature films were produced to remove popular struggle from the popular memory of history, and replace it with a series of generals as heroes. This was a systematic and ruthless campaign carried out after the killing of a million people—so there were absolutely no alternatives raised during these thirty years. This was a kind of counter-revolutionary version of an ideological year zero.

Despite this both murderous and systematic suppression and ideological management, the appeal of Soekarno, however vaguely felt, could not be eradicated. There are a number of reasons for this. First, there could be no removal of the historical fact that it was Soekarno who had proclaimed Indonesian independence on 17 August 1945 and that he was able to do so because he was the most popular nationalist leader at the time. His photos and biographies remained available, even if most of the biographies avoided the 1960s. Second, much of the negative propaganda against him that continued after the first round of mass murders concentrated on allegations about his personal life, namely, that he had many lovers. There was never any propaganda against his ideas, as the government wanted no discussion of these, neither was there any negative propaganda against him as being corrupt, as there was no evidence of any corruption—he died poor. The negative propaganda did more to strengthen his popularity.

Third, major international historical events, such as the Asia-Africa Conference in Bandung, Indonesia in 1955, which is widely considered to have started the Non-Aligned Movement, has made it difficult to erase from the national psyche his standing as an international figure.

So the figure of Soekarno, the fighter against the Dutch, proclaimer of independence, Indonesia's most important international figure, endowed with a certain charisma and sex appeal, has not been erased, even if most of his ideas have been.

The continuing resonance of Soekarno as a symbol of closeness to the popular classes was so visibly manifest in the rapid rise in popularity of Megawati Soekarnoputri, chairperson of the Indonesian Democratic Party, between 1990 and 2000. By simply adopting the Soekarnoist policy of "non-cooperation" with the Suharto regime in the 1990s, and with no other policies or achievements to recommend her to the people, her name alone was enough to make her the pre-eminent symbol of opposition to the dictatorship in that period among the mass of urban and rural poor. This popularity declined dramatically when she was in power between 2001 and 2004, and was seen increasingly not to be a part of the *rakyat*.

Rakyat

Probably the most resilient component of the class consciousness that developed between 1910 and 1965 was the concept of the *rakyat*, the definition of the "people" as the exploited and oppressed, implying the existence of a "non-people" part of society. Other words with a class connotation, such as *buruh* (worker/laborer), were removed from use in the political sphere for at least twenty-five years. *Buruh*, for example, was replaced with *karyawan* (a class-neutral term for anybody who works, including a manager or capitalist).

But *rakyat* could not be eliminated. It was in the name of the parliament: Dewan Perwakilan Rakyat (Council of People's Representatives) and in the names of many other institutions.

Neither could *rakyat* easily be given another, less class-consciousness meaning. The reason for this was that the whole socio-economic strategy of the New Order was reinforcing a divide between rich and poor, between the rulers and the middle class and *rakyat*. The huge gap between rich and poor, people living in a high-productivity sector versus those in the massive low-productivity sector, has grown steadily, in fact in leaps and bounds, and has been institutionalized in a whole range of conspicuous items of material culture: for example, luxury malls, condominiums, luxury cars and international shopping. All these are depicted daily on national television. In the latter period of the New Order, the word *elit* entered the common day political vocabulary as the opposite of *rakyat*. The widespread use of the word *elit* or *elit politik* actually reflects a new, heightened ideological institutionalization of the class content of *rakyat*. While it had always had this specific exclusionary content, it was the New Order period that finally produced a word that labels those excluded from the *rakyat*.

Rakyat is as real today as a concept among the *rakyat* as it ever was.

Political actions and ad hoc organizations emerging out of the direct actions of workers, peasants and other elements of the popular classes, almost inevitably use this word in their propaganda materials or names of their organizations. They almost always speak in the name of the *rakyat* or in defense of the *rakyat*'s interests. Among the most conscious attempts to establish opposition or radical political groups, the word *rakyat* is used. The most stable of the radical parties, the People's Democratic Party, used *rakyat* in its name, and defines its ideology as "socio-demokrasi kerakyatan" (popular socio-democracy). Other groups do the same. Perhaps the most vivid expression of this was the huge sympathetic response to the hundreds of thousands of "Mega-Bintang-Rakyat" leaflets demanding an end to Suharto and the army's rule during the massive 1 million-strong mobilizations against Suharto during the May 1997 general elections. The urban poor mobilized in their hundreds and thousands, against the instructions of the government, the army, the police and their own leaders, carrying spontaneously created placards calling for an alliance between Megawati Soekarnoputri (Mega) and the Islamic opposition (Bintang, the star) against Suharto and GOLKAR. When leaflets appeared calling for a Mega-Bintang-Rakyat alliance, they were extremely popular and created great concern among the mainstream party leaders and government.

The anti-dictatorship movement produced one iconic song of struggle which also vividly captured the strength of the ideological hold of *rakyat*. This song became a virtual anthem of the *aksi* movement and was sung at many demonstrations, strikes and protests. Its lyrics are, in translation:

Blood of struggle
This is our country
Where rice is piled in abundance
Its oceans seething with wealth
Our land made fertile by God

In this jewel of a country
Millions upon millions of the people are covered with wounds
Hungry children unschooled
Village youth with no work

They have had their rights stolen from them
Thrown out of their homes and hungry
Mother bless us if our blood is spilled in struggle
To free the people

Their rights have been stolen
Thrown out of their homes and hungry
Mother bless us if our blood is spilled in struggle
We take a vow to you, mother.[4]

In fact, the unremitting reality of a cruelly oppressed class of poor was reflected equally vividly in the 1970s poetry of Rendra. Remember Rendra's classic poem quoted in Chapter 3 with its bitter verses alluding to this class and its oppression:

My people's faces are lined with pain.
They move like ghosts,
all day,
reaching out,
turning this way and that,
finding nothing.
By sunset, their bodies are pulp.
They lie down, exhausted,
and their souls turn to condors.

Thousands of condors,
millions of condors,
moving to the high mountains,
where they can rest in silence.
Only in silence
can they fully savor their pain and bitterness.

However, those who make up the *rakyat*—proletarians, semi-proletarians and pauperized petty bourgeoisie, including farmers—do not have access to the organization and ideas that gave the concept form and power before 1965.

Islam: An Alternative Source of Ideological Resistance?

Re-establishing continuity with the radical heritage of the national revolution is the primary ideological challenge necessary for the revolution to be resumed. But it is necessary to ask whether there are signs of any other ideological resources being taken up in the context of the restoration of the rights and standards of life of the *rakyat*: political Islam, for example? Since the fall of Suharto there have been a series of ideological controversies provoked by the assertiveness of political Islam in some areas. In some districts, for example, local parliaments have enacted decrees establishing some aspects of Islamic law. In the national parliament, there was an attempt to pass a law that would have begun to make compulsory conformity with conservative interpretations of Islamic law on women's dress. Those parts of the law were forced to be watered down substantially in 2006.

The prominence of Islam in this way highlights the issue of ideological vacuum. Organized political Islam is in fact weaker than it has ever been— in terms of unity, organized and mobilized membership, electoral impact, and ideological impact on actual social life and political life. In the 1950s, for example, modernist urban Islam was represented by a powerful single party, MASYUMI, led by political figures of national authority, some of whom served as prime ministers. During the New Order, this constituency was forced to channel all its political energies through one government-manipulated party, the United Development Party (PPP). After Suharto fell, and the PPP lost its state backing, it has shrunk to a miserable shadow of its former self. But it has not been replaced either by any equivalent of the old MASYUMI party. Instead, this urban Moslem constituency is represented by a plethora of splinter parties, usually at odds among themselves. Since 1998, these parties have tended to split into smaller groups each year. John Sidel describes well the picture that emerged in the wake of the first elections after Suharto fell:

> In the elections of June 1999, moreover, the fiction of a united Moslem population . . . dissipated in fragmentation and factionalism among a welter of Islamic parties, and dissolved in the face of strong electoral showings by non-Islamic parties, among Moslem and non-Moslem voters alike.[5]

Neither has any of them produced political figures with a national profile or following. Early contenders, such as Amien Rais, former head of the Muhammidiyah and a founder of one of these new parties, the National Mandate Party (PAN), was mooted as a possible presidential candidate for a while, but he had lost any significant following by 2005. This was despite Rais holding the position of Speaker of the People's Consultative Assembly (MPR), a platform from which he might have been expected to project himself. The same applies to the current Speaker of the MPR, Nur Hidayat, from the PKS, which won 7 percent of the votes in the 2004 elections (but did much better in Jakarta.)

This splintering reflects the change in the social composition of the urban Islamic constituency, with a greater class differentiation and other secularizing factors coming into play. Many of these children of former supporters of MASYUMI have entered the civil service, business or the professions after receiving a secular education and developing secular ambitions. Those that remain pious, and there are still many, tend to see their religion as a matter separated from state and politics and more related to family life.

Even the more stable constituency of traditionalist rural Islam, represented historically by the Nahdlatul Ulama, has been weakend by internal splits and struggles over leadership. Its most prominent leader, Abdurrahman Wahid, did become president for a short period. The ease with which he was later dumped by the rest of the political elite, through their representation in parliament, underlines this constituency's political weakness. After Wahid was dumped, other key NU leaders aligned themselves with Megawati Soekarnoputri, a major force behind the process to dump Wahid.

The social, rather than political weight of this constituency is reflected not just in the lack of major Islamic political figures but also in the fact that those Islamic figures who do have, or have had, national prominence have operated outside the political sphere in a kind of public "family" sphere. The most obvious example of this was A.A. Gym, a television preacher who sermonized about family values and moral character. He won enormous popularity in the late 1990s and is still popular—though much less so—today. There have been other similar figures. Like their American counterparts, they can easily fall from grace. A.A. Gym experienced a palpable loss of popularity in 2006 when he announced that he was taking a young, second wife in a polygamous arrangement. Women's rights activists, including Moslem women, attacked him on his own "family values." So did many other community and religious figures.

There is a contradiction in the fact that the social influence of Islamic groups is probably greater than their organized political weight. Their social weight tends to act as the social strength upon which Islamic religious leaders can speak out, taking advantage of the ideological vacuum. This can give a sense that organized political Islam is stronger than it actually is. However, there is another factor which further strengthens this perception. The ideological vacuum—the absence of the radical variant of Soekarnoism or socialist ideology—is legitimized formally. In 1967, a purged People's Consultative Assembly (MPR) passed a resolution banning the "spreading of Marxism-Leninism." During discussions in parliament after 2001, reviewing the Indonesian Constitution and some of the basic legal elements of the New Order, there was some discussion of rescinding or amending this ban. Repealing the ban was advocated by Wahid during his presidency. However, it was not repealed. There is thus a virtually unanimous support at the parliamentary level—the body formally representing the whole of society—for the banning of Marxist ideas, even if most of the parties in the parliament rarely agitate around this issue.

As a result, when some anti-communist groups, raising an Islamic banner, threaten to raid bookshops to remove left-wing literature, or invade public meetings and force them to close down, or attempt to forcibly disperse meetings of political parties that they label as communist, they can more easily claim that they are carrying out a legitimate activity. This makes it easier for the police to accede to their pressure and to move against the activist groups on the grounds that the seminar or party meeting is "provoking community restlessness." After all, the whole parliament has reaffirmed the ban on such activities, they could claim. Such acts have, in fact, been rare. Threats to sweep through and raid bookshops in 2002 and 2003 were never really carried out. However, in 2006 a seminar on Marxism hosted by a bookshop in the city of Bandung was successfully disrupted and the seminar organizers detained briefly—rather than the group forcibly invading the seminar. Also, in late 2006 and early 2007, a group calling itself the Indonesian Anti-Communist Front (FAKI) and the Islamic Defenders Front (FPI) tried to forcibly disperse the founding congress and some regional congresses of the United Party for National

Liberation (PAPERNAS). These small groups are able to act under the cloak of legitimacy flowing from the reaffirmed 1967 ban—the legal formalization of the ideological vacuum.

Perhaps the starkest depiction of this political weakness of Islam is in the answer to the question: What role did organized Islamic political forces play in the biggest political event of the recent period, the fall of Suharto? Did they play an important role in either trying to prop him up, or in forcing him to resign? While Islamic figures such as Abdurrahman Wahid, head of the NU, and Amien Rais, head of Muhammidiyah, and others, all joined in the maneuvers within the political elite at the time, none were able to mobilize significant forces under an Islamic banner either for or against Suharto. They were swept along, responding as events developed, driven by the student-led mass actions. There was some speculation in late 1998 that Islamic political forces might unite around the figure of President Habibie who had been head of the rather secular Indonesian Islamic Intellectuals Union (ICMI). But as Sidel noted, this was shown to be an illusion as the Islamic forces splintered during and since the 1999 elections.

At the same time, the decline of the political strength of these parties and the general secularization of urban life has produced a backlash from within the pious Islamic communities frustrated by this decline. The scattering of radical fundamentalist networks around the country is the main manifestation of this. Where these groups have ideologically intersected with similar sentiments in other parts of the world, such as Afghanistan and the Middle East, the result has been actions such as, after 2002, suicide bombings in Bali and in Jakarta. However, the groups at this end of the spectrum remain small and isolated.

Are there possibilities of one or other radicalizing streams—in whatever form—of the Islamic sector winning mass support as a response to the social, cultural and economic problems that are generating the thousands of grievances, the thousands of *aksi?* To date, the only Islamic party that has made any gains in this area is the PKS. A modernist fundamentalist party, led by many professionals and recruiting students at secular universities, it has combined presenting itself as modern, moral and free of corruption with being based on religion. It has also emphasized solidarity with Palestine and opposition to the US occupation of Iraq. It has used charitable works at the grassroots to win support. In the immediate years after the fall of Suharto, its student wing, KAMMI, was at the forefront of campaigns against corruption and government policies to increase prices of basic commodities. In recent years, KAMMI has become increasingly inactive, with young people disenchanted with the PKS's immersion in elite politics. There still may be scope for the PKS to grow beyond its current 7 percent of the vote, but its general support for the same socio-economic policies supported by all the other parties—the IMF recipe—ultimately will restrict its appeal among the mass base.

Outside of the party structures, especially among young people affected by the student politics of the 1980s and 1990s, elements of a "liberation theology" have made some impact. Abdurrahman Wahid himself has promoted discussion of these ideas, or at least guaranteed space for them, during his tenure as chairperson of NU. As president, his support for the lifting of the ban on communism and call for reconciliation with the pre-1965 left also helped open up that space. Wahid spoke at the 2002 launch of the PRD's tabloid newspaper, *Pembebasan*, and at the 2004 launch of Hasta Mitra's publication of the first Indonesian translation of Marx's *Capital.* The various joint activities of the NU and the PRD during Wahid's presidency also facilitated this kind of opening up to radical ideas. There is a range of youth-based Islamic organizations with these kinds of orientations, connected to the NU as well as the urban Moslem consti-tuency. Some, such as the Yogyakarta-based group, Syarikat, play an active role in building communication with the victims of the 1965 repression. Others are more oriented to grassroots advocacy work. Some, among intellectuals, are aimed at building support for pluralist and secular liberal democratic ideas, such as the Reform Institute and Jaringan Islam Liberal. Islamic-oriented universities, such as Paramida University in Jakarta or the Indonesian Islamic University in Yogyakarta, among others, are also developing as a basis for a critical political culture.

However, it is the Islamic parties in parliament that dominate popular perceptions at the moment. Most of these parties' ideological outlook, like all the other parties in the parliament, represents an ideological continuity with the New Order rather than with the legacy of the national revolution.

Ideological Continuity and Class Consciousness

The rise and fall (still so far, at least) of Megawati Soekarnoputri was not associated with any attempt to revive Soekarnoism as an ideology, but rather with an appeal to vaguer populist sentiment. The PDIP's use of Marhaen *posko*s (neighborhood command posts) appealed to the populist sentiment where there was a lingering connection between the Soekarno name and the *rakyat* concept. At almost all mobilizations of mass support through the PDIP structures or spontaneously, as in the 1997 elections, crowds carried photos, not only of Megawati but of Soekarno himself. The authorities under Suharto were aware of the potency of this connection when they banned crowds from carrying pictures of Soekarno. In the regulations governing the 2004 elections, no party was allowed to use the word "Soekarno" in the party's name.

There are other parties which also proclaim a continuity with the ideas of Soekarno. These are the Partai Pelopor, led by Rachmawati Soekarnoputri, PNI Marhaenisme led by Soekmawati Soekarnoputri, and the PNBK, led by Eros Djarot. While Megawati has lost much of her support, these three parties and their leaders have remained at the margins of politics. None of them were able to mobilize significant votes at the 2004 elections, although the three leading figures still have a certain access to the media.

During the post-Suharto period, a key feature of the political methods of the PDIP, Partai Pelopor, PNI Marhaenism and PNBK have been their general accommodation to the primarily parliamentary framework established during the Habibie period. During the last years of the Suharto period, the PDIP and its mass support were drawn into mobilizational politics. Since Suharto fell this has stopped and the *posko* structures have withered away. Some branches of the PNBK have mobilized the membership for street protests around specific issues, however, this has been rare. Neither Partai Pelopor nor PNI Marhaenisme has developed such a capacity.

A fundamental feature of Soekarnoist politics, and indeed a fundamental feature of class consciousness at the mass level during almost all of the sixty years of national revolution, was its emphasis on extra-parliamentary activity. Independence was not won by election. Although there was enormous participation in the 1955 general elections and the 1957 local elections, the struggle to implement changes that would further the national revolution was based on mass mobilization. This included struggles such as the repudiation of the foreign debt to Holland in 1956, nationalization of Dutch enterprises in 1956–7, campaigns for worker participation in state enterprise management, land reform, the nationalization of British firms, and the reincorporation of West Papua still under colonial rule—these were all achieved through mass mobilization, not as a result of an electoral struggle. By eschewing this fundamental aspect of Soekarnoist politics, what Soekarno called *actie massa* for the purpose of *machtsvorming*, these parties have not been able to re-establish real continuity with the politics of the national revolution nor have they been able to take the populist (*rakyat*) sentiment embodied in the proliferation of *aksi* to a higher level. While *aksi* have spread and become endemic, they stand apart from this process, alienated from the dynamic towards the restarting of the national revolution.

The political party most connected to the struggle to re-establish mass mobilization as a political method has been the PRD. In many respects the PRD came into being in the early 1990s as a party with a central aim of reintroducing mass action. Even after the fall of Suharto it restated this commitment. In its booklet, *Demokrasi Multipartai*, published in 1998 in the lead-up to the 1999 general elections, it concluded this presentation of its platform with a section entitled: "Conclusion: mass action is the key." In this section, it was emphasized:

> The struggle still demands a high level of militancy in organizing mass actions. Mass action is the only effective method of struggle, which represents real pressure, which can drive a stake into the heart of the Habibie ruling regime and the anti-people regimes that will follow. Political parties must be based upon the masses, if they want to become a real power. And a mass base can only be achieved through a combination of mass struggle and mass organizing. How many of the masses a party can mobilize is an indication of how much mass support there is for the program and strategies of any party.[6]

Alongside arguing for mass action as the fundamental strategy for over-throwing the Suharto dictatorship and establishing a more democratic order, the PRD has been prolific in its elaboration of a general program. They have called the ideological outlook that underpins their program *socio-demokrasi kerakyatan* (popular social democracy). The essential elements of their platform are set out in their 1994 manifesto, printed in this book at the end of Chapter 5.

Many of the ideas presented in these and other documents possess continuity with the program of *socialism a la Indonesia* as espoused in the 1960s by Soekarno and other forces on the left. This is especially so in relation to the PRD's critique of capitalism and the role of foreign capital and financial institutions. This program and this critique have been developed, however, as something new, beginning from scratch. The PRD has not attempted to build upon the theoretical work done by either Soekarno, the PKI or anybody else active prior to 1965.[7] It is not surprising that the PRD has started anew in formulating an ideological perspective, a world view that can contextualize their program and platform. The severity of the ideologicide of 1965–7 and the systematic wipe-out of memory that continued made this almost inevitable. When the activists who later went on to found the PRD began their ideological work, Soekarno and the PKI were no longer a real presence. The survivors of the Soekarnoist left had not been able to organize any kind of significant revival. Instead, the nearby example of the Philippines and books on left-wing political theory combined as the starting point. The Philippines model also helped strengthen an ideological framework that emphasized anti-dictatorship struggle, informed by traditional leftist class analysis.

There is another pressure that has reinforced the "starting from scratch" character of the PRD's ideological work. The international context is radically different from the 1950s and 1960s, which was a period of anti-colonial national revolution before socialist politics had suffered the defeats represented by the turn to capitalism by the People's Republic of China or the collapse of the Soviet Union. Ideas flowing from revolutionary processes still held considerable sway. This was even reflected in the heart of the imperialist world itself with the rise of the civil liberties movement in the USA, followed by the movement against the Vietnam war, which brought with it a period of social radicalism extending into the late 1970s. The ideas of revolution—both the radical enlightenment ideas of the great bourgeois revolutions as well as the socialist ideas of the nineteenth and twentieth centuries worker revolutions—still resonated strongly, especially among the peoples of nations who had been struggling for independence and had won it. Pramoedya Ananta Toer suggests that the very idea of "humanity" was introduced by Soekarno into national political discourse with direct reference to the ideas of these revolutions:

The concept of humanity only first appeared with the birth of the Panca Sila, coming from Bung Karno. And it is not surprising that Bung Karno said: humanity or internationalism. Because the origin of the concept came from developments among humankind internationally: 1. The Declaration of Independence, which liberated the American people from British colonialism; 2. The Communist Manifesto, which liberated the lower classes from structural oppression; 3. San Min Chui, written by Sun Yat Sen, that formulated the nationalist framework for the colonised peoples of Asia.[8]

In the 1990s and today, the resonance of, and even familiarity with, these ideas and documents, were much weaker. It was not the great wave of anti-colonial revolution and economic advance of the Soviet Union and China that framed ideological effort by the PRD (and other activist groups). The 1965 defeat of the left and thirty years of military-backed dictatorship in Indonesia and retreat by the left internationally was the new terrain.

This situation presents a contradiction, the resolution of which is not yet clear. Despite the ideologicide of 1965–6 and the counter-revolutionary suppression of class struggle memory since then, the historical legacy of a class consciousness developed out of collective national struggle, embodied in the resilience of the idea of *rakyat*, the charisma of Soekarno and the extraordinary rapidity of the re-emergence and spread of *aksi* political activity remains a fundamental feature of Indonesian politics. Without these factors, Suharto would not have fallen in the way he did—to the echoes of cries for *reformasi total*, legitimizing the sentiment for democratization and social justice. On the other hand, the political group most connected to this process as a conscious, planning agency, the PRD, developed an ideological framework in a political period where politics was severed from the radical ideological legacy of the national revolution. Those claiming such a continuity—the overtly Soekarnoist parties—have been severed from the actual praxis of mass action politics.

Pramoedya again sums up this problem:

This extraordinary movement of the students and youth now appears to have met a roadblock. What has been called *reformasi* has not given birth to a widely accepted national leadership. And the rising up of the peasants in the interior, something that could be fairly identified as the beginnings of a social revolution, has also not developed further, and has also not given birth to any national leaders.

Why? In the 1920s the movement was able to give birth to leaders that won wide acceptance, whether they were Javanists, Indonesianists, or ethnic leaders. Why in this second year of the 21st century has this not happened? At first I thought this was a result of some kind of psychological problem, that there was something not quite right, not quite fitting, off balance. I told this to many of the younger generation who came to visit me. After thinking about this more, I have come to another conclusion: that it is not a psychological issue.

The problem is that the starting point of the younger generation and students, and also the peasants in the interior has been *reformasi*: a movement only to restructure and give new content to the New Order. This not only involves avoiding but even negating our national history. We nationally have been born through the national revolution and we succeeded in defeating imperialism, we did that. The stage of the national revolution was followed in 1950 by the stage of the struggle to complete the revolution: now it has been extinguished completely. Forget about things like "nation and character building," instead now there has been more and more actions murdering the nation, including reviving the old colonial practice of sending Javanese soldiers to the regions to subdue the regions outside Java.

Why is all this continuing to happen? My conclusion is that the course of developments since the New Order has turned its back on history as a source of understanding the proper starting point, thereby losing direction, and therefore does not know its destination, in other words, has lost its way.[9]

The neoliberal economic offensive has deepened class divisions, multiplying socio-economic grievances, creating a huge population of workers, semi-proletarians and peasant farmers collectively suffering under this offensive. This has ensured that the sense of class consciousness among the popular classes, of being *rakyat*, has remained strong. This sense has found its way too into the political thinking and culture of all the waves of protest and struggle against the dictatorship. Among these classes, and among other layers, such as students and intellectuals, there are the beginnings of national-level organization and the development of radical critiques building on this class consciousness. There exist social forces that have the potential to be the agency of a process, a struggle, to restart the revolutionary process.

Pramoedya cried out for these processes to also encompass the struggle to regain history for the popular classes. This too had already begun under Suharto as part of the resistance to his dictatorship. Pramoedya's own works were a part of this. The work of the 1980s generation of intellectuals, such as the founders of the Jaringan Kerja Budaya, also began this. Now there is a flowering of historical writing of enormous proportions. There are scores of new books republishing the writings of Soekarno. New publications of the writings of the PKI leaders Aidit and Nyoto can be found in the bookshops. There is a continuing debate in the newspapers over the school history curriculum.

The first tentative steps towards meeting Pramoedya's cry for reconnection with "the struggle to complete the revolution" and to revive it following its years of extinction have well and truly been taken. Regaining *aksi* was the first great advance starting a new age of motion. Regaining history will be the next big advance, even as day-to-day political organization and campaigning and social struggle over the thousands of socio-economic grievances provide the terrain for this new endeavor. The struggle over that history and to regain the idea of revolution will be at the center of the next decade of Indonesian history.

Conclusion

Aksi, Nation, Revolution

The explosion of interest in history—a real history war—is a symptom of the pressure for a reconnection with the past among some sections of Indonesian society. Whether this pressure leads to a reconnection of *aksi* to the process of national revolution is, however, more a political matter than simply a question of more history books. We also need to look for signs of this reconnection within politics itself, and, in particular, within the realm of *aksi*, of social discontent and political mobilization. Fundamental to any reconnection with history, that is with the past, with the national revolution that was in progress before 1965, is the idea of the necessity for national liberation, that is, a sense of national oppression.

It was the anti-colonial struggle, as a struggle for national liberation, that set in motion the processes that started to create one of the key components of any nation: a shared psychological outlook, manifested in a national culture. As outlined in the bird's eye view history of Indonesia in Chapter 1, it was the anti-colonial struggle and then the struggle post-independence against neocolonialism that produced the literature and art, including the huge wealth of political writing and thought, as well as the mode of political life—mass mobilization—that constituted the foundations of a new national culture. Elements of pre-national traditional culture were drawn into this to the extent they buttressed the new culture. By the 1960s, cultural sovereignty was espoused by the most mobilized section of society as a conscious goal of this process.

The counter-revolution of 1965 overturned the politics of national liberation, opening up the economy and culture to foreign penetration. National culture was redefined away from the values and ideas produced by the revolutionary process and focused upon pre-national traditional ideas and values, often those originating from the feudal courts and embodied in things, such as traditional costume, dance and architecture. A concept of archipelagic culture was developed, rejecting interaction and renewal as the essence of the relationships within the archipelago and between the archipelago and the rest of the world. Instead, the archipelago was projected as a mosaic of traditions—of pre-modern and pre-national cultures.[1] The most visible and iconic representation of this was the huge theme park built on the initiative of President Suharto's wife, Tien Suharto, in the 1970s—the Beautiful Indonesia in Miniature. While this sprawling display of traditional architecture, costume, textiles and artifacts assumed a central place in symbolizing the national culture, the reading of modern Indonesian literature in the schools disappeared. Not only did all the left-wing writers, such as Pramoedya, disappear from libraries because they were banned, but even the major conservative writers who emerged during the first sixty years of the national revolution were no longer read.[2] National literature, the foundation of the new culture, was rendered esoteric. The opening up of the economy to international capital on terms formulated by the international financial institutions and major Western companies also fostered the development of powerful pockets of a highly cosmopolitanized, consumerist culture among the middle classes of the major urban centers. Projected through film and television soap operas, this cosmopolitan consumer culture became the second cultural mode, layered over and parallel to the traditionalism which dominated so much official cultural symbolism, promoted under the New Order.

This was a complete reversal of the values and ideas on culture that were coming to dominate in the 1960s. Despite the fact that the main forces that had been promoting a nationalist or anti-imperialist approach to economic and cultural development before 1965 had been suppressed, the first wave of opposition to the New Order government between 1973 and 1978 was still characterized by a critique of foreign economic and cultural domination very similar to that espoused by the left before 1965. Student councils took up the issue of foreign debt and of the sudden influx of foreign investment and the consequent disruption to the national economy. Indonesia's domestic capitalists in the textile sector campaigned against the establishment of Japanese textile mills. The student protests and urban riots of January 1974 took place as a protest against the visit of Japanese Prime Minister Tanaka. After the students were suppressed in January

1974, Rendra produced his 1975 hit play *The Struggle of the Naga Tribe*, which was a frontal critique of American, Japanese, European and (what he saw as) Chinese commercial domination of the Indonesian economy and the comprador and corrupt relationship between the military, acquiescent politicians and the foreign corporations and their governments. A second wave of student protests in 1978 also focused on the increasing foreign debt burden created by the government's policies.

Following the suppression of the 1974 and 1978 student movements, including the arrest and detention of Rendra for several months, this nationalist or anti-imperialist critique of regime policy and of Indonesian society almost disappeared as a major component of anti-regime campaigning. Even after the protest movement began to reorganize after 1989 and during the period of its escalation between 1989 and 1998, nationalist or anti-imperialist critique was not a major part of the armory of ideas of the anti-dictatorship movement. Even the overarching, radical cry that emerged in 1998 itself—*reformasi total*—did not reflect any nationalist critique. The call for reform, even total reform, revolved around the demand for an end to corruption, cronyism, nepotism, dictatorship and military rule. Fifteen years of New Order reality had diminished the sense of nation, or of national oppression.

Whatever the foreign economic and cultural incursions allowed under the New Order, the objective basis of an Indonesian nation was not completely undermined, even if its cultural vitality was weakened. The protest movement that emerged between 1989 and 1998, while not articulating a conscious critique of national oppression, did develop as a national phenomenon. *Aksi* did become a national phenomenon. All the forms of protest action and mobilization of this period occurred in almost every part of Indonesia, from one end of the country to the other, from Aceh to Papua. New political organizations, such as the PRD, the SBSI trade union and a range of critical human rights organizations and other NGOs with a national perspective emerged. The wave of student protests that exploded between October 1997 and May 1998 was characterized by a national scope, with a dialectic of mutual support between actions in the provinces and actions in Jakarta.

As an objective phenomenon, the movement was national even if there was little discussion of the relationship between the country, its problems and outside forces. A nationalist critique of the relationship with the

International Monetary Fund following the 1997 Asian economic crisis
and the Suharto government's first signed agreement with the IMF
imposing an intensification of neoliberal policies may have been delayed
due to the fact that it was Suharto who led the first attempt to resist the
IMF. Suharto, with assistance from renegade US economic advisors, tried
to devise a scheme to avoid floating the rupiah as demanded by the IMF.
This was mainly an attempt to protect the rupiah assets of the Suharto
family and other crony capitalists; coming from the dictator at the height of
popular resistance to him, it did not contribute to a widening critique of
neoliberal policy prescriptions being imposed by the IMF in return for
bailing out the Indonesian economy.

However, it would not be correct to say that there were no manifestations of a consciousness of the 1990s anti-dictatorship struggle as having
consequences for national self-determination. While there was minimal
critique of the foreign economic and cultural influences, there were a few
important signs that the movement for change could (and will) reach back
to the national revolution for connections that can help define the future.
Probably the most important of these was the widespread adoption,
starting in 1989, of the *Sumpah Mahasiswa* (Student's Oath). The oath
is formulated to mirror the 1928 *Sumpah Pemuda* (Youth Oath) which
formalized the beginning of the national struggle.[3] The words of the
Sumpah Pemuda were:

> One nation—the Indonesian nation
> One people—the Indonesian people
> One language—the Indonesian language

The words of the *Sumpah Mahasiswa* were:

> We the men and women students of Indonesia
> Affirm, we are one nation a nation without oppression

> We the men and women students of Indonesia
> Afiirm, we are one people, a people addicted to justice

> We the men and women students of Indonesia
> Affirm, we have but one language, the language of truth

In this oath, there is the element of continuity with the revolutionary past for which Pramoedya yearned.

However, the immediate aftermath of the fall of Suharto saw greater and greater surrender of policy sovereignty to the IMF on the one hand and a sudden, radical decentralization of policy and fiscal administration to the sub-province (*kabupaten*) level. This revealed that there was an inherent inability on the part of the country's business and political elite to understand the extent to which the country's problems were ones of loss of national sovereignty and national perspective.

Between 31 October 1997 and 10 December 2003, the Indonesian government signed twenty-four "Letters of Intent," "Memoranda of Economic and Financial Policies" and "Technical Memoranda of Understanding." According to the IMF, a Letter of Intent "describes the policies that Indonesia intends to implement in the context of its request for financial support from the IMF."[4] As each Letter of Intent was negotiated and signed, the range of areas in which the Indonesian government made policy commitments to implement IMF prescriptions expanded enormously. The impact of these prescriptions on socio-economic conditions is described in Chapter 9. Very few areas of economic management are not covered by these agreements. The Indonesian government has put up very little resistance and when that has occurred it has been more in relation to defending the immediate interests of bankrupted big business owners than to areas of macroeconomic management impacting on the economy as a whole. The dismantling of subsidies on the price of fuel and kerosene and on other basic commodities of mass consumption has symbolized for many people this surrender of policy sovereignty. Throughout this whole process, between 1997 and 2003, all the parties in the parliament, no matter who was president, supported all the most important of these measures.

In 2003, the program of post-1997 crisis assistance from the IMF ended. However, the twenty-four agreements remain in place and there is an intensive program of monitoring the implementation of the policy commitments made by the government.

Almost at the same time as this surrender of policy sovereignty to the IMF, there emerged a push for decentralization of some fiscal and policy administration from the central government to *kabupaten* level. The demand for this decentralization was not a part of the anti-dictatorship movement that forced Suharto to resign. It is not clear how the demand for this policy first arose. However, it reflected a severe weakening of the power of Jakarta business capital in the wake of the collapse of the mechanisms of dictatorship. Decentralization has been strongly supported by the IMF and the World Bank. Since 2000 the push for decentralization has been accompanied by attempts by many regions to elevate their adminstrative states from district to *kabupaten*, or from *kabupaten* to province. This happened not only outside Java but also on Java. It reflects a push by local business and political elites to enhance their access to financial resources. It reflects the strength of local business elites and the weakness of a national business class. It sets up a dynamic where regions rich in natural resources demand that a bigger share of the income generated from those resources stay in their region. This contradicts any sense of national solidarity with provinces which are poor in natural resources. This resource rivalry can even take place within a local ethnic group or even between neighboring *kabupaten*. In this atmosphere of resource grabbing and business elite rivalry, predatory economic activity increases, exacerbating the general austerity being imposed, as described in Chapter 9. The Indonesian scholar, Vedi Hadiz, sums up this outcome of decentralization:

> . . . the point to emphasise is that the decentralisation process in Indonesia has largely been hijacked by interests that have little to gain from local governance characterised by greater accountability to local communities, transparency, and the like. Although the design of decentralisation was faulty in the first place—being full of legal contradictions and ambiguities—this was not the main reason that the process has descended into an arena for predatory politics. It was the persistence, and indeed "victory," of predatory interests in contests over power that has had the most important implication for decentralisation (and local-level democratisation) in Indonesia. The key was that they were not swept away by the fall of Suharto, but managed to reinvent themselves in the new democracy.[5]

Much of the political discourse on decentralization counterposes it to authoritarian centralism. This counterposition—authoritarianism versus democracy is the same as centralism versus decentralization—has a fundamentally anti-national political character. It conceives of two counterposed entities—center and local region—rather than of a single integrated entity, the nation, with a national economy.

These two trends—surrender of economic policy sovereignty to foreign institutions and increased rivalry and parochialism in the administration of the economy—are the chief characteristics of the policies of post-Suharto governance. In the first five or six years after the fall of Suharto, it was these discourses—the alleged necessity for foreign help and for decentralization—that dominated much of the public discussion in the press and, as a result, in the general ideological realm. But by 2002, going into 2003, these directions, especially that relating to loss of national economic sovereignty, have started to come under challenge.

New Nationalisms

Critiques of the surrender of sovereignty over economic policy and the national economy emerged both from within and without the business and political elite. From within the elite, these emerged most clearly during the presidency of Megawati Soekarnoputri, from within her government. Her minister for development planning in charge of the Body for Development Planning (BAPPENAS) was banker Kwik Kan Gie.[6] Although as a cabinet minister he had led negotiations on some of the Letters of Intent, by 2002, he had become a critic of the IMF. His criticisms began with an emphasis on the IMF's interference in micromanagement of the economy but later extended to criticisms of its insistence that the government privatize all its state-owned companies. He soon appeared isolated in Megawati's cabinet, which continued its defense of the economic policies being prescribed by the IMF, but was never sacked.

Another manifestation of the emergence of a nationalist critique came from the group of thirty-five economists called "Indonesia Rise Up!" This grouping comprises both moderate and radical critics of the IMF prescription. It includes Ramli Rizal, a minister in the Abdurrahman Wahid government as well as the radical nationalist economist Revrisond Baswir, based at Gajah Mada University in Yogyakarta. In February 2004, the "Indonesia Rise Up!" group issued a declaration opposed to the further privatization of state-owned companies. The group also consistently opposed policies of reducing subsidies on petrol and fuel because of the burden it would pose on the majority of people. Their critique ranges across those policies impacting negatively on both state-owned and private business as well as the IMF-prescribed policies they see as impacting on mass welfare.

"Indonesia Rise Up!" has continued to be outspoken into 2006, opposing an agreement to give Exxonmobil a dominant role in managing a new oil field on Java. In this it was one of a wide range of voices taking up this case. There was also a demonstration of thousands of people in the area on Java, Cepu, where the field is located. This was probably the first major *aksi* demanding the nationalization of an oil venture.[7] In September 2006 the group launched a critique of a major speech by President Yudhoyono where he gave false figures on Indonesian poverty levels. He was forced to backdown and issue realistic poverty figures.

In June 2006, a new organization formed, the Indonesian Nationalist Alliance (Pernasindo—Perhimpunan Nasionalis Indonesia). Pernasindo's chairperson is Kwik Kian Gie and its secretary general, the academic commentator and writer, Sukardi Rinakit. *Kompas* newspaper reported Kwik as stating at the launch:

> The people are being kept ignorant, and this has entered right into the heart of public opinion. There is the constant effort to convince people that it is normal to base development on debt, while it is the debt that is causing suffering to the people. . . . The very large number of poor and the very poor face difficulties in getting across their concerns about the shambles that the country is in. They suffer malnutrition, there is even starvation, and not even minimal health services. It is the nation's elite that is to blame for selling independence, becoming cronies, and the comprador to nations that are exploiting the Indonesian nation.[8]

Outside of the elite, nationalist critiques of current economic policies have become entrenched in a range of non-governmental organizations. Some of these critiques are reflected in the passages quoted in Chapter 9. This trend is reflected in the critiques of debt and dependency articulated by the umbrella group covering most non-government development-oriented organizations, namely INFID. New organizations have developed such as the Anti-Debt Coalition, the Institute for Global Justice and a host of others.

In the political party sphere, however, the PRD remains the only party that has consistently taken up this kind of critique reflecting the fact that nationalist critiques have not been taken up by the politically organized sections of the elite, by the parties represented in the parliament. One recent political initiative of the PRD has been to launch a new expanded party formation, the United Party of National Liberation (PAPERNAS). It's platform includes the launch of a campaign demanding the repudiation of the foreign debt, the nationalization of the oil, gas and electricity sectors and the mobilization of funds via the state for a program of national industrialization.[9]

All these developments point to the seeds of a revival of a nationalist critique of Indonesia's place in the international political economy. They have the potential to be a bridge back to the national revolution which was a movement against colonial and neocolonial domination. At this early stage, the nationalist critiques of economic strategy and the debates over correcting falsifications of history are developing separately. There is as yet no real conscious struggle to regain an interest in the foundations of national culture, namely, literature.[10] In this period, where these arenas are not yet overlapping and thereby strengthening popular under-standing of the history of the struggle for the nation, and where traditionalist and consumerist cultural trends still dominate, other re-sponses to the loss of sovereignty and its socio-economic and cultural consequences emerge.

In the period of the national revolution, the rejection of the subordina-tion and inequality of the emergent Indonesian nation was most popularly expressed by Soekarno with the formulation that Indonesia refused to be "a nation of coolies, and coolie among nations." This was a popular formula-tion both under Dutch colonialism, but even in the 1950s and 1960s when the concern was to break out of the constraints that the world economy imposed upon a former colony. In the absence of this kind of anti-imperialist political culture, in fact in the absence of a strong sense of nation at all, for one sector of the population, the vacuum has been filled by the concept of religious community. A "coolie nation" (*bangsa kuli*) has been replaced by the idea of a "humiliated religious community" (*ummat terhina*), providing the basis for a deepening of the political commitment among a sector of the pious Moslem community to their political organiza-tions.[11] In this sector, there is less of a development of a critique of Indonesia's cultural and economic position and more of a politics of identity with a range of Islamist resistances to US policies in the Middle East.[12]

Aksi and the Nation

Among many sectors of the political public in 2006, there is a word that one hears more and more: *fragmentasi*. The fragmentation referred to here is not one that is feared to result in the Balkanization of the archipelago. It is a fragmentation that is more connected to a fear of country-wide dysfunctionality. The fragmentation is visible in many areas: the rivalry among regions, among religions. But perhaps its most evident manifestation is the widespread and continuing phenomenon of *aksi*. This endemic social protest, and the associated mobilizations that continue unabated across the country never wanes and yet it also never congeals or crystallizes into any kind of national political movement, even on a sectoral basis. New national political and sectoral organizations are forming, pointing to possible future directions. However, during the years since the fall of Suharto, they remain fragmented, a never-ending stream of protest mobilizations at the site of grievance. The fragmentation, while local, is not on a regional, ethnic or religious basis, but simply around the fact that the grievances appear different.

Nowhere else is the national question posed so sharply and clearly. The *aksi* are fragmented in the extreme. Ten thousand different grievances produce ten thousand different fragments of political action. But not only are the *aksi* fragmented in the extreme, both the *aksi* and their fragmentation are national phenomena. Indonesian nationalists used to describe the national struggle as extending from Sabang (an island off the tip of Aceh) to Merauke (at the extreme eastern edge of West Papua). *Aksi*, coming out of the history described in this book, are indeed phenomena spreading from Sabang to Merauke: they are national phenomena.

The method of struggle of the national revolution, mass political mobilization, has been regained. Political organization of the popular classes has begun, but remains at an early stage, held back by the counter-revolution's suppression of ideological life, of the people's memory of the national revolution that created Indonesia. The revival of the interest in history and the new nationalist critiques of economic strategy are signals that it is unlikely that the counter-revolution's success in this arena will last too much longer.

Epilogue 2008

Escaping the Conjuncture?

I am writing this epilogue in January 2008, so I cannot know for sure what will happen in 2008, a year which will mark the tenth anniversary of the fall of the dictator Suharto. I can, however, point out the tensions in the contradictions of Indonesian politics and society, tensions which are intensifying, and what processes they are starting to unleash. One of the theses of this book has been that there exists a tension between the political thinking and praxis of the most advanced activist forces that emerged during the 1990s and the analysis of the long-term dynamics of Indonesian history articulated by the most advanced political theorists who were activists prior to 1965 and then gaoled, especially Pramoedya Ananta Toer.

The terror, suppression of the left and the erasure of the collective memory of the intensely democratic processes of the national revolution created a deep rupture in the course of Indonesian history. Of course, there is no so-called natural course of history—everything depends on what people do within the terrain that they are presented with. However, there was an enormously creative process underway, shaping the country through the years 1900–65. Millions of people were being drawn into political and ideological life in an active and productive way. Newspaper and magazine circulation boomed; mass mobilizations increased steadily and then dramatically after 1960. Trade unions, peasant organizations, women's and cultural organizations grew and spread. It was a tumultuous, trial-and-error process, polarizing society, especially within the intelligentsia and between elite and masses. It deepened rapidly. At the end of the 1950s the word "socialism" was a rarity in the Indonesian media. By 1961–2 discussion of socialism dominated the media. The trial-and-error struggle lasted only six years before it was squashed violently and bloodily. And even during those six years, those proposing "socialism a la Indonesia," led by Soekarno, never really wielded full state power. The left was isolated in the cabinet; President Soekarno was a minority in his own cabinet. Then they were tortured and killed, or tortured and gaoled, and millions were silenced. Millions more have had their history stolen from them.

The struggle for democratic change that started to grow after 1989, and then more rapidly after 1994, laid the foundation for the mending of the great rupture of 1965 and the New Order. But it did not and has not mended the rupture itself. That there is a possibility of it being mended is well indicated by the frightened reaction of the most aware representatives of the generation of 1965–6, those who benefited most from the rupture. The specter of history free to be interpreted and studied, for example, still haunts them.

In March 2007, the Attorney General banned fourteen history textbooks. In 2006, writers and even education ministry officials had been summonsed as part of a criminal investigation initiated by the Attorney General's department. The historians' "crime" was that they no longer labeled the actions of the military officers who detained and later killed seven generals on 30 September 1965, as part of a plot by the Indonesian Communist Party (PKI). The military officers who led the action to arrest their seniors, whom they claimed were plotting to overthrow President Soekarno, called themselves the Thirtieth of September Movement (G30S). General Suharto, whose faction seized control of the army, started a campaign to describe the G30S as a PKI conspiracy, labeling it the G30S/PKI.

A new generation of historians wrote textbooks that referred to G30S without the "PKI" and, sometimes, provided alternative explanations of what happened in 1965. That they do not continue to blame the PKI is considered a criminal act by the Attorney General's department. On 28 March, several score members of the Anti-Communist Movement (GERAK—Gerakan Anti Komunis) protested at the Indonesian Academy of Sciences, calling on it to clean itself of communists and singling out historian Asvi Warman Adam, one of the most active writers and campaigners for an end to the falsification of history, particularly the events of 1965. Other groups demonstrated at the Attorney General's department supporting the ban on the history textbooks.

Through June–August 2007, despite protests and as a petition signed by scores of mainly younger intellectuals, the Attorney General's department working with the education department began raids on schools in several provinces, seizing the banned texts. In August, in several towns the local government offices involved carried out public burnings of literally thousands of books. The whole process of banning and burning these books was initiated by the government after a delegation of 66 Generation intellectuals met with MPs and complained about the books.

Freeing history from its Suharto period straitjacket is not a marginal academic issue in Indonesia: it threatens to open a Pandora's box that lets loose forces suppressed and cowed in 1965 but not removed from the country's reality. History, freed from this straitjacket, can start to give the populist sentiments symbolized by the words "rakyat" and "Soekarno" concrete content.

Even ten years after the fall of Suharto, organization and mobilization around ideas connected to the national democratic revolution provoke the same fear as an open approach to history. The same day that GERAK protested outside the Indonesian Academy of Sciences demanding the sacking of Asvi Warman Adam, other forces, under the banner of the Islamic Defenders Front (FPI), attacked a protest by PAPERNAS.

According to PAPERNAS chairperson Agus Jabo, on the morning of 29 March around 2,000 PAPERNAS supporters, many of them members of urban poor campaign groups, headed for Jakarta in buses. They had been saving for months, donating a few cents a day so they could hire the buses. As they arrived at the second of their protest destinations, the Shangri-La Hotel where a UN conference was taking place, they came under a surprise attack from around 100 members of the FPI and other groups wielding knives and canes. The attackers threw stones into the crowd and smashed at least twenty bus windows. The overwhelming majority of the PAPERNAS supporters were housewives, unarmed and many with young children. They were forced to disperse, heavy rain making the situation even more difficult. The PAPERNAS supporters later regrouped back in their base areas, but had to cancel their planned afternoon Jakarta People's Rally at the Independence Proclamation Park, where another 300 or so FPI members and others were also waiting.

At least ten people had to be taken to hospital. According to *Kompas*, the head police detective was also injured. Despite knowing of the threats, the police mobilized only a very small contingent to the event, which was totally ineffective in protecting the rally. The police only issued the paperwork making the rally and march legal at the very last minute, using the threats and possible violence as a reason for holding up the bureaucratic permission process.

Similar attacks had taken place in Surabaya and Yogyakarta earlier, and have since been repeated in Yogyakarta and in September 2007 in Lampung, South Sumatra where a pro-elite group, the Pemuda Panca Sila, occupied a building hired by PAPERNAS for a mass meeting and stopped PAPERNAS from using it.

While a range of NGOs and other political groups issued statements protesting the harassment of PAPERNAS by these groups and the acquiescence of the police in the harassment, the events remained marginal to "mainstream politics". Similarly, while there have been protests and petitions against the public book burnings of the history texts, these too have remained relatively marginal. The PAPERNAS and history initiatives remain fragments, albeit the most potentially explosive fragments, among thousands, or even tens of thousands, of other fragments of social protest, cultural dissent and political resistance. Street protest—still spontaneous, small and ad hoc—remains endemic. In September 2007, members of parliament said that in any redesign of parliament a special arena would be set aside for protests, so regular and frequent had such protests at the parliament become. But nothing was joining the fragments together. History and ideology (and the beginnings of ideology can be found in looking back at the history of popular struggle) could provide some glue— or glues, as more than one unity might be possible.

The central issue in trying to answer why no glue has been produced despite ten years of relative freedom of organization and ideas, of expanded room to organize and write, is essentially a question about agency. Who will or can do it? The book burnings and harassment of PAPERNAS do not allow us to explain the situation in terms of repression. The book burnings prove the fear that some have of history and tell us also that in the school textbooks history is still being falsified. But today the history is available. While still formally banned, the works of Pramoedya Ananta Toer can be bought in the bookshops. Even the works of the chairman of the PKI and other PKI leaders are available. All kinds of new books are now published by scores of small publishers. The history is there, available, even if flittering in and out of circulation, as the small publishers collapse, or the small print runs disappear from the bookshops. These thousands—yes, thousands—of publishing initiatives are also fragments, separated one from the other, through their ad hoc and fleeting character.

And there are equally radical and left-wing organizations active in Indonesia now as there were under Suharto. Apart from the PRD, and its PAPERNAS initiative, there is the Working People's Union (PRP—Perserikat Rakyat Pekerja) as well as the National Students Front. There are more left websites. There are more progressive and radical NGOs. But everything remains at the level of fragments, neither united under a single ideological banner nor growing as competing currents.

Beyond the Conjuncture

The dynamic of increasing mass mobilization that overthrew Suharto developed amazingly rapidly after 1989, and even faster after the PRD-initiated worker-student rallies of 1992–4. This reflected the correctness of the founders of the PRD in their emphasis on reviving mass mobilization of workers, semi-proletarians and peasants, as well as students, as the first priority of the anti-dictatorship movement. While not conscious of the relationship between this process of reinstating mass action as a method of struggle and the challenge of regaining all the heritage of the national revolution, they did see it as reviving something lost. Their emphasis was correct. Reinstating mass action as a method of struggle was a strategic victory—in the context of the movement to overthrow the dictatorship.

In the context of restarting and then completing the national revolution, and of deepening it into a social revolution of liberation, the reinstatement of mass action as a method of struggle was, however, primarily a tactical victory. In and of itself, apart from an implicit logic of mass empowerment, the method of struggle brought with it no strategic program beyond the overthrow of the dictatorship and the immediate democratic reforms: withdrawal of the army from politics (that is, from repressive activity) and repeal of the repressive political laws controlling political parties and organizations. This is not to say that more radical strategic ideas cannot be found in the writings of the PRD, for example. Rather, it is to emphasize that it was not on the basis of a deeper strategic outlook that the movement as a whole, and even the vanguard as a whole, was built.

The *reformasi* movement and all its organizations were very much productions of a specific political conjuncture, represented by the movement to oust Suharto. Of course, all political movements and organizations are products of their time, of their circumstances. However, in Indonesia's circumstances it was a conjuncture after a deep, conscious and institutionalized rupture with the past. It was a conjuncture without a history. The movement against Suharto was a movement without a history. Its organizations, including the PRD, were organizations without histories. Suharto had created Indonesia's own year zero. It was this disjuncture that Pramoedya lamented in his speeches after 1998. They don't know where they have come from, so they don't know where they should go! This was the spirit of his lament.

Rediscovery of a history of mass struggle, of leftist and radical ideas, of the national revolution itself will not answer all of the questions about the future. It helps pose a question: what has already been won and what is yet left to be won? What has already been done and what is to be done now and into the future? It means understanding that the causes of the socio-economic and cultural backwardness are not to be found in the facts of the conjuncture. It is not a result of neoliberalism or of the bankrupt policies of current governments. These are manifestations of the crisis, not the underlying cause of the crisis, which is to be found in the historically formed semi-colonial relationship between Indonesia and imperialist centers of the world and the economic, cultural and political structures imposed under colonialism and inherited by the Indonesian republic. Completing the revolution is a question of dismantling those structures and engaging in a struggle to ameliorate and eventually end the semi-colonial relationship.

What are the signs of a break out of the conjunctural straitjacket?

In terms of changes in the objective situation, in the broad underlying processes, there is no doubt that 2007 has already seen an increase in critiques of Western and Japanese economic policies towards Indonesia. The trends identified in this direction earlier in this book have strengthened. Ranging from very significant controversies over foreign access to the oil deposits in Cepu on Java to clashes with the European Union over the rights of Indonesian planes to fly to Europe, there has been a non-stop string of "nationalist" issues. Articles listing the string of Indonesian banks and other companies that have shifted into foreign hands are regular fare in the newspapers and the subjects for discussions at public forums.

On the streets, too, the increasing frustration at being a humiliated nation, as well as being a nation led by hopeless leaders, is palpable. Hariman Siregar, the student leader of 1974, was one of the few politicians who has worked with members of the New Order elite trying to win a platform for at least democratic forms, pre- and post-1998, but who never took a position in the New Order. While trying to work from within, he also maintained contact with the new forces that drove the processes during the 1990s. In January 2007, on the anniversary of the 15 January demonstrations in 1974 after he was arrested, he organized a protest action of his own attempting to respond to the sense of anger and hostility to the regime on the streets. His call was for the people to "withdraw their mandate" from the current President, Susilo Bambang Yudhoyono, elected in 2004.

Around 200 pick-up trucks and cars comprised the long snake of a protest caravan that made its way along Jakarta's main thoroughfare, Jalan Thamrin, after the rally outside the presidential palace. In the lead pick-up truck, Siregar was accompanied by Dita Sari, chairperson of the People's Democratic Party, and Eggy Sujana, a politician of Islamic background who was recently arrested for insulting the president. Sujana took his case to the courts, which ruled that the law against "insulting the head of state" was unconstitutional. Speakers on the platform outside the palace included poet and long-time critic of Suharto, W.S. Rendra.

At the press conference that announced the "withdraw the mandate" protest, Siregar argued that Indonesia's democracy was a formal, procedural democracy, without substance. "Current policies were aimed at strengthening institutions, but without any empowerment or strengthening of the people themselves. And in the end the politics of the institutions was based on money."

He criticized the political life of these institutions, arguing that in the parliament, for example, there is no significant focus being given to the major problems of the country. Instead the focus is on what he described as "celebrity issues." He was talking about recent scandals, such as the circulation of a short video, taken with a mobile phone, of a naked MP in a hotel room with a popular singer.

He replied to criticism coming from supporters of the government, or

rather the president, that the theme of the protest—withdraw the mandate—amounted to a call to rebellion and was outside the constitution, by
emphasizing that the people were not supposed to go to sleep after the
elections just because the government had won. He also emphasized that
people who were not members of a political party should continue to have
political rights to protest and raise their concerns.

Reflecting a criticism that is heard more and more widely in the press
and among the public, Siregar told me later that the government operated
only at the level of general perspective, with no real firm initiatives to
develop solutions. He pointed to the statistics that the protest was high-
lighting: 143 million people below the poverty line; 3.5 million unem-
ployed graduates; 12 million children under five malnourished; 2 million
children dropping out of school; 13 million illiterates; and 400,000 small
businesses bankrupt.

He also raised the issue of the extensive surrender to foreign control of
most of Indonesia's natural resources, as well as its banking and insurance
industries. He made a reference to the well-known, oft-repeated statement
by former President Soekarno that Indonesia refused to become "a nation
of coolies, and a coolie among nations." In an interview with a journalist
from the magazine *Gatra*, he stated that repayments of the foreign debt
should be stopped and the money used to provide education and health
services for the people.

But other proponents of this nationalist discourse can cover ulterior
motives. Aspiring Indonesian capital wants a better deal, a bigger slice of
the cake. Indonesian professionals want recognition and equal pay in the
international institutions and professional organizations. Nationalism
proclaims that all components of the nation have the same interests,
something which is denied by the experience of the last forty or more years.
It has been Indonesians who have sold off the country and accepted an
economic strategy proffered by US and other foreign capital, which has
condemned the majority of the population to low productivity, poverty,
misery and backwardness. That section of the Indonesian nation is not, in
fact, interested in national liberation.

The nationalism generated by the general frustration among all sectors of
society with the dead end of current development policies creates an
environment conducive to a discussion of the need for national liberation.
But not all those espousing nationalism will turn out to be part of the

agency that will lead the way in discovering the strategic approach to national liberation, reviving the national revolution, deepening it and taking it further.

Where, then, are the possible elements that will make up a vanguard for national liberation?

First, there are the signs of a broader struggle to liberate history, reflected in the flourishing of historical writing. There is little doubt, I think, that as a new agency of change crystallizes, we shall find some of the new generation of historians actively taking part in regaining all the legacy of the revolution and formulating strategic perspectives for the future.

Second, there is the beginning of an exciting ferment in the arts, literature and culture. Despite the fact that literature is not taught at all in schools, and therefore that Pramoedya Ananta Toer's books still reach only a tiny portion of the population, his standing and the number of those influenced by his thinking steadily increases. During 2007, a theatrical adaptation of his novel, *This Earth of Mankind*, was performed in at least seven regional cities to packed houses and extensive media coverage in Jakarta. The play, entitled *Nyai Ontosoroh*, was written around the character of a Sanikem alias Ontosoroh, a child concubine sold to a Dutch businessman in the colonial era, who fought for herself and her rights and gained freedom from her owner, becoming, in Pramoedya's fictional imagining of history, the teacher of one of the first great Indonesian democrats and writers, Tirto Adhisuryo. It was written and produced by activists from the women's liberation movement, including Faiza Mardzoeki who had also helped produce in 2002 an Indonesian adaptation of the novel, *Woman at Point Zero*, by the Egyptian feminist, Nawal El Sadawi. One of the regional theater groups involved, in Lampung, South Sumatra, is undertaking to produce plays based on the three other novels that are sequels to *This Earth of Mankind*. There is also a Pramoedya Institute, Pramoedya email lists and several new books about Pramoedya and his writings as well.

This is just one example of the progressive cultural ferment. Wiji Thukul is still celebrated and new books about him and his poetry have been published in 2007. The playwright Ratna Sarumpaet also used the stage to raise issues of the repression of workers, the violence in Aceh and even the terror of 1965—although more as laments than as deconstructions of the regime's propaganda. Rendra is still in demand among campuses for poetry readings and political poems are always on top of the agenda. More generally, everywhere young people are exploring and experimenting with the arts—in writing, video, documentaries, painting—and in almost all of this activity, in one way or other, moderate or radical, social and political criticism is central.

Third, despite experiencing a definite stagnation, the university student movement will revive. Almost all cultural and intellectual radicalism, as well as the activities of the myriad of other smaller political fragments, depend on student activists or former students recently graduated. High school students are also among those fragments to be found at protests outside government offices making themselves known. As they discover more of their past they will be at the forefront. It has been high school students at protests demanding more government spending on education in 2007, who carried pictures of Kartini and Soekarno, symbols of the national revolution and its struggle for free education.

Fourth, there are now a huge number of non-governmental organizations and sectoral organizations (trade unions, peasant groups, women's groups) whose policy concerns represent together a long list of criticisms of current development, cultural and political policies. They range from Indonesia's subordination to World Trade Organization regulations, the debt burden and debt trap, the need for agrarian reform, women's rights, protection for migrant workers, an end to impunity for generals who have committed crimes against humanity—the list is almost endless. Some are now dependent on foreign funding and their agendas sometimes reflect the latest concerns of international humanitarian discussions rather than what the local conditions demand of them. Many are wary of or even hostile to mass action strategies. But they house and sustain thousands of individuals—ex-student activists, as well as workers and peasants—whose outlook is opposed to the direction in which the country is going. These NGOs and sectoral organizations are also fragments, housing within them even more fragments at the individual level.

The forging of a new agency capable of taking the fragments beyond the conjuncture in which they are now treading water will not occur spontaneously by some automatic chemical process from within all these sectors. It will need conscious initiative, conscious intervention.

New Initiatives, New Polarizations

During the last months of 2007, an initiative to publish a new monthly journal supported by a large number of groups on the left or in the progressive camp was moving to a final stage prior to publication. Those involved in the initiative included Hilmar Farid, the dissident historian; Wilson, a member of the PRD in the 1990s and now an NGO activist; as well as members from a range of other activist groups, including the PRD, PRP and FMN. It is a first try and may falter or may not last—but it reflects the dynamic at work, the pressure for a new agency, to seek out a new basis of unity.

While by no means sufficient by itself to become the totality of a new agency that can present a post-conjunctural strategic outlook, the PRD will surely also play a role in the re-creation of agency. But here too a process of re-creation will be necessary. The PRD itself is a product of this history-less conjuncture. It was the vanguard of a movement that won a strategic victory in ending the Suharto dictatorship; but its leadership remained a tactical leadership. It consciously and systematically sought to reintroduce mass action as a method of struggle, and here it succeeded. Millions of people joined, initiated or otherwise supported mass actions in the 1990s. Tens of thousands still participate in the fragments of protest mobilizations that still occur every day. But even in the 1990s, when the PRD achieved a high profile, these millions did not move into action under the PRD's banner, nor were they won to its ideology, only its immediate demands, which quickly became everybody's demands.

This feature of the PRD's experience produces its own internal dynamics. What happens to a product of a history-less conjuncture when the conjuncture passes, as did this conjuncture when Suharto fell in 1998? First, tactical leadership loses its short-term strategic significance. Now everybody engages in street protest—even the right wing mobilizes on the streets. Some activists even start to fall into the thinking that mass action as a method of struggle has become degraded because everybody is doing it—left and right. Activists who previously scorned those who argued for the methods of lobbying the elite (rather than overthrowing them) start to counterpose the press release to street protests. While the PRD's consistency before and after 1998 has ensured it retains a strong respect among the masses, its leadership authority is weakened in these new circumstances. It faces the need to rebuild its authority on a new basis.

Second, the process of determining such a new basis starts from a heritage of the conjunctural experience, separated from any Pramoedya style longer term analysis of Indonesia's historical dynamics. In these circumstances, the specific experiences of different parts of the organization—those in trade unions, in the press, those doing united front work with other forces, those doing base organizing and so on—can loom larger in determining outlooks than if the experience had been located in a longer term historical framework. For ten years, since 1998, there has been constant debate, discussion and search for the next step forward. This is a long period for such a search to be the dominant issue and it is not surprising that many of the PRD leaders, both those active before 1998 and afterwards, have decided on other roads. Some have dropped out of politics altogether. Others have joined NGOs or other political groups, like the PRP. Some are trying to start a new political party.

Some have crossed to the other side of politics. In fact, every PRD chairperson between 1998 and 2005 has left the PRD to join one of the elite-controlled political parties.

As I write, this process seems to be coming to a head. Provoked by the reality that PAPERNAS is too small to break through the many bureaucratic obstacles put in the way of its electoral registration by the parliament (that is, by all the elite-controlled parties), a debate began over what PAPERNAS should be prepared to do in order to put up candidates in the 2009 parliamentary elections. The debate, which is raging as I write, has revealed a division reflecting different evaluations of the potential of continuing with mass action as the primary method of struggle. One section of the PRD has clearly developed a pessimistic assessment and is placing their hopes in achieving something through an electoral strategy. Another is reaffirming the mass action strategy. It is likely that this polarization will result in a new, recreated mass action-based party or political organization. The embryo of this formation emerged in late 2007 as the Political Committee of the Poor-PRD. Its leadership is drawn mainly from the younger generation, but includes Danial Indrakusuma.

But will re-creation of a vanguard organization on the basis of reaffirming the main lesson of the 1990s—the power of a mass action strategy— help in the re-creation of an agency of change?

Nothing is guaranteed, of course. However, in the aftermath of the fall of Suharto, a reaffirmation of a mass action strategy, of *aksi*, is also a reaffirmation of the centrality of the masses themselves as the agency for change that can bring solutions to their plight. The role of the PRD is as an agency of intervention and leadership. The huge, revolutionary changes required to win national liberation and then go on to ensure that the people are themselves in charge of their own solutions require the masses themselves to be the agency of change. Any reaffirmation of the mass action strategy as the basis for clarification and re-creation also reaffirms this fundamental outlook.

Now, as compared with the 1990s, the task that has already been identified is more than the dislodging of a dictator but rather the achievement of national liberation and the overturning of existing structures of oppression. The search for an understanding of how the masses in action can achieve that will itself inevitably lead back to the past, not only to the methods of struggle by the *pergerakan* between 1900 and 1965, but also to its ideas, not least of which will be socialism.

Notes

Introduction

1. W.S. Rendra, *The Struggle of the Naga Tribe: A Play*, trans. Max Lane, St. Lucia, Queensland: University of Queensland Press, 1979. There is no published version of the Indonesian text.
2. The most recent editions of these novels in English are by Penguin Books USA. The first Indonesian-language editions were by Hasta Mitra publishing house. The most recent have been published by Lentera Dipantara.
3. For materials on these campaigns explore the Southeast Asia section of the website. Available online at *http://www.asia-pacific-action.org/* (accessed 25 November 2007).
4. Daniel Dhakidae, *Cendikiawan dan Kekuasaan dalam negara Orde Baru*, Jakarta: Gramedia, 2003, p. 278.
5. Available online at *http://www.radix.net/~bardsley/prd-eng.html* (accessed 25 November 2007).
6. Pramoedya Ananta Toer, *Realisme Sosialis dan Sastra Indonesia*, Jakarta: Lentera Dipantara, 2003. No English-language version yet available.
7. Pramoedya Ananta Toer, *Sang Pemula*, Jakarta: Hasta Mitra, 1985. Also contains the journalistic and fictional writings of R.M. Tirto Adhisuryo. No English language version yet available.
8. Available online at *http://www.radix.net/~bardsley/prd-eng.html* (accessed 25 November 2007).
9. Available online at *http://www.radix.net/~bardsley/sambut.html* (accessed 25 November 2007).
10. Vedi Hadiz and Daniel Dhakidae (eds), *Social Sciences and Power in Indonesia*, trans. Max Lane, Jakarta: Ford Foundation and Equinox Press, 2005.

Chapter 1 Indonesia

1. Ruth McVey (ed.), *Indonesia*, Ithaca, NY: Cornell University Press, 1967, p. 24.
2. Anthony Reid, *Southeast Asia in the Age of Commerce 1450–1680, Volume Two Expansion and Crisis*, Ithaca, NY: Cornell University Press, 1993, p. 327.
3. Pramoedya did spell out the full name of Tirto Adhisuryo in the original manuscripts of *Footsteps* and *House of Glass*. They were removed from the published versions out of legal concerns.
4. In the 1990s Pramoedya Ananta Toer frequently argued that the naming of the country "Indonesia" was, in fact, a mistake. He pointed out that it was a term invented by a

British naturalist and is the Greek for "Indian islands." Pramoedya pointed out that the archipelago had no real connection with India, not sufficient for it to take such a name. He proposed terms that had been used in the past within the region itself to refer to the archipelago, namely Nusantara—meaning the islands in between—or Dipantara—the fortress in between.

5. Takashi Shiraishi, *An Age in Motion: Popular Radicalism in Java, 1912–1926*, Ithaca, NY: Cornell University Press, 1990, p. 341.

6. Herbert Feith in McVey, *Indonesia*, p. 317.

7. Everett D. Hawkins in McVey, *Indonesia*, pp. 260, 267.

8. Reid, *Southeast Asia*, p. 168.

9. In 2002 one of these initial self-critical assessments by PKI Central Committee member Sudisman was published by Teplok Press in Jakarta under the title, *Kritik Oto Kritik Seorang Politbiro CC PKI*,

Chapter 2 Counter-revolution

1. John Roosa, *Pretext for Mass Murder: The September 30th Movement and Suharto's Coup d'état in Indonesia*, Madison, WI: University of Wisconsin Press, 2006. In this new and convincing work, Roosa also argues that the chairperson of the Indonesian Communist Party, D.N. Aidit, was a leader of the group that planned the action but that he did not inform the rest of the party leadership. Later, argues Roosa, when the amateurish conspiracy went awry and Soekarno ordered it to stop, Aidit persisted in trying to bring it off and tried to replace Soekarno's cabinet.

2. Robert Cribb, *The Indonesian Killings of 1965–1966: Studies from Java and Bali*, Melbourne, Australia: Monash University, 1990.

3. David Bourchier and Vedi R. Hadiz, *Indonesian Politics and Society: A Reader*, London: Routledge, 2003, pp. 45–6 (emphasis added.)

4. *Panca Sila* was originally formulated and explained by Soekarno in a speech in 1945. Later, in 1958, he gave a series of public lectures explaining it again. These lectures stand as virtually the total negation of the New Order's interpretation of *Panca Sila*. While Soekarno connected democratic consultation, national unity, internationalism, social justice and monotheism to the major revolutionary upheavals in human history, the New Order ideologues distilled these principles to little more than the idea of obedience to authority.

5. For a new study of the militarization of Indonesian history, which includes a chapter on Nugroho, see Katherine E. McGregor, *History in Uniform: Military Ideology and the Construction of Indonesia's Past*, Singapore: Institute for Southeast Asian Studies, 2007.

6. The earliest English-language documentation of the new class was in Richard Robison, *Indonesia, the Rise of Capital*, Sydney: Allen and Unwin, 1986. For a more recent slightly different detailed mapping of these forces, see John T. Sidel, *Riots Pogroms Jihad Religious Violence in Indonesia*, Ithaca, NY and London: Cornell University Press, 2006, especially chapter 2. The most recent writing on corruption and business in Indonesia is George Aditjondro, *Korupsi kepresidenan: reproduksi oligarki berkaki tiga: istana, tangsi, dan partai penguasa*, Yogyakarta: LKiS, 2006. Aditjondro has published a series of such studies since 1998.

7. Two early English-language studies of rural conflict in Indonesia before 1965 are Rex Mortimer, *The Indonesian Communist Party and Land Reform, 1959–1965*, Melbourne Australia: Monash University, 1972, and Margo Lyon, *Bases of Conflict in Rural Java*, Berkeley, CA: Center for South and Southeast Asia Studies, University of California 1970. See also the essay by Benjamin White in Hadiz and Dhakidae, *Social Sciences*.

8. Jeffrey A. Winters, *Power in Motion: Capital Mobility and the Indonesian State*, Ithaca, NY: Cornell University Press, 1996, p. 69 for a table listing the Indonesian and foreign participants in the investment conference roundtable.

Chapter 3 Students

1. *Pedoman*, 16 January 1970.
2. *Pedoman* daily newspaper was sympathetic to the students and published reports on their actions and also reproduced some of their posters, such as in *Pedoman*, 16 January 1970.
3. For an account of these developments see P.J. Boole, "Corruption and Corruption Consciousness in Indonesia" (BA thesis), Melbourne University, 1973. See also J.A.C. Mackie, "The Commission of Four Report on Corruption," in *Bulletin of Indonesian Economic Studies*, vol. 6, no. 3, November 1980.
4. *Pedoman*, 11 February 1970.
5. Arief Budiman, "Portrait of a Young Indonesian Looking at His Surroundings," in *Internationales Asienforum*, vol. 4, 1973, p. 79.
6. Budiman describes the first meeting in ibid. He described the second meeting in *Kompas* newspaper on 8 August 1970.
7. See Roger Smith, *Southeast Asia: Documents of Political Development and Change*, Ithaca, NY: Cornell University Press, 1974, section on New Order.
8. The stream of student protests described below were reported daily in two newspapers considered to be connected to the anti-communist Socialist Party of Indonesia (PSI). These were *Pedoman* and *Indonesian Raya*. Many of these reports are available in English in the Indonesian Current Affairs Translation Service (ICATS), published in Jakarta until the late 1970s.
9. An almost complete set of the *Sendi* newspaper is held in the Australian National Library.
10. *Sendi*, Week I, January 1972, p. 2.
11. Translated into English and quoted in ICATS, January 1972, from *Pedoman*, 7 January 1972.
12. *Sendi* editorial, Week II, January 1972.
13. A comprehensive collection of newspaper reports on the events leading up to the major student protests and urban poor riots of January 1974 can be found in Marzuki Arifin, *Peristiwa 15 Januari, 1974*, Jakarta, 1974. Most of the incidents described here are reported in these clippings. Quotes, statements and so on have also been translated from the versions in this book. English language versions of newspaper reports, also composed as a chronology of events, can be found in the ICATS volumes for 1973–4.
14. See Arifin, *Peristiwa*, p. 104.
15. The speech was later reprinted in Hariman Siregar, *Hati Nurani Seorang Demonstran*, Jakarta: Mantika Media Utama, 1994, p. 6.
16. Ibid., p. 4.
17. Published in translation by Harry Aveling in W.S. Rendra, *State of Emergency*, Sydney: Wild and Woolley, 1980.
18. "Song of the Condors" in ibid.
19. Arifin, S.E., *Fakta, Analisa lengkap dan latar belakang Persitiwa 15 Januari 1974*, Jakarta, 1974, p. 164.
20. Brian May, *The Indonesian Tragedy*, London: Routledge, 1978.
21. P. Bambang Siswoyo, *Huru Hara Solo Semarang Solo Semarang—suatu reportase*, n.d.
22. David Bourchier, *Dynamics of Dissent in Indonesia: Sawito and the Phantom Coup*, Ithaca, NY: Cornell University Press, 1984, pp. 23–4.
23. INDOC, *Indonesian Workers and their Right to Organise*, Leiden, 1981
24. Wendy Stamp, "Internal Opposition to the Suharto Regime: The Student Movement 1977–1978 as a Case Study", BA thesis, Australian National University.
25. First circulated in photocopied form in 1977; see Bourchier and Hadiz, *Indonesian Politics*, p. 216 for English-language version.
26. See, for example, Ikranegara, "The struggle of the Naga Tribe: the irony of a propaganda piece," *Kompas* August 1975. Reprinted in English in Rendra, *Naga Tribe*, 1979.

Chapter 4 Memory

1. Anne Booth, *The Indonesian Economy in the Nineteenth and Twentieth Centuries*, New York: St. Martin's Press in association with the Australian National University, Canberra, 1998, p. 187.
2. "Wakil Presiden Adam Malik tentang 'Bumi Manusia'," in Adhy Asmara (ed.), *Analisa Ringan Kemelut Roman Karya Pulau Buru Bumi Manusia Pramoedya Ananta Toer*, Yogyakarta, 1981, p. 98.
3. Reprinted in ibid., p. 48.
4. Ibid., p. 38.
5. Goenawan Mohammed, "Dari 'Bumi Manusia' "; "From *This Earth of Mankind*', in Asmara, *Analisa*, pp. 76–7.
6. Ibid., p. 77.
7. Ibid., p. 78.
8. Mobilizations by workers, rural and urban, had occurred independently and separate from student mobilizations by the late 1970s.
9. Notosusanto was given the title Brigadier General so he could head the army History Center. He was earlier professor of history at the University of Indonesia, although already in close relations with the army officers.
10. *Garis-garis Besar Program Pengajaran Pendidikan Sejarah Perjuangan Bangsa untuk SMTA*, Departemen Pendidikan dan Kebudayaan, 1985.
11. *History for Senior High School Class 3*, Jakarta: Department of Education and Culture, 2001.
12. The title Bung was reintroduced into some activist circles around 1990 and has now become popular again.

Chapter 5 Plans

1. See PRD founding declaration in Appendix at the end of the chapter.
2. Typescript in author's possession, "Situasi Nasionaly", Jakarta, 1994, p. 2.
3. Ibid., p. 4.
4. Quoted in Bourchier and Hadiz, *Indonesian Politics*, p. 167.
5. Ibid., p. 168.
6. Ibid.
7. Ibid.
8. Ibid., p. 170.
9. Quoted in ibid., p. 167.
10. Translated from T. Mulya Lubis, Fauzi Abdullah and Mulyana W. Kusumah, *Laporan Keadaan Hak Asaasi Manusia di Indonesia 1981*, Jakarta: Yayasan Lembaiga Bantuan Hukum, 1983, pp. 13–14.
11. International Forum for Indonesia Development (INFID) Fact Sheet on Kedung Ombo.
12. Some issues of *Progres* are available in the library of the International Institute of Social History, the Netherlands and the Menzies Library, Australian National University.
13. Since the INDOC project closed down, its archives are housed at the International Institute of Social History in Amsterdam.
14. Samples of *kronologi* can be found by searching the internet archives available online at *http://www.library.ohiou.edu/indopubs/* (accessed 27 November 2007). One example is reproduced later in this chapter.
15. Translated from a report in *Suara Pembaruan* newspaper, 17 June 1992, entitled "Empat Barang Cetakan Dilarang Beredar."
16. *Progres*, vol. 3, no. 1, 1993, p. 21.

Chapter 6 *Aksi*

1. English-language accounts of these events can be found in D.K. Jana, "The 1994 Medan 'Unrest'," in ASIET, *The Fight for Workers Rights in Indonesia*, Sydney: Action in Solidarity with Indonesia and East Timor, 1996. Available online at *http://www.asia-pacific-action.org/southeastasia/indonesia/publications/doss1/contents.htm* (accessed 27 November 2007). Also Human Rights Watch, *The Medan Demonstrations and Beyond*, 1994, is available online at *http://www.library.ohiou.edu/indopubs/1994/05/16/0000.html* (accessed 27 November 2007).
2. *Kronologi Demonstrasi Mahasiswa 1989–1997*, Jakarta: Yayasan Insan Politika in cooperation with the Asia Foundation, 3 vols, 1999. The academic team comprised Muridan S. Widjojo, Arbi Sanit, Soewarsono, Abdul Mun'im DZ, Moch. Nurhasim, Irine H. Gayatri, Herman Sulistyo and Jamal Mashudi.
3. The YIP list appears to rely virtually completely on just one newspaper for the February–September 1995 period. This is the most likely explanation for its drop in the number of actions listed.
4. Solidaritas Mahasiswa untuk Demokrasi di Indonesia.
5. Student Solidarity For Democracy In Indonesia (SMID) and Center For Indonesian Working-Class Struggle (PPBI), "13,000 Workers March From Bogor Factories to Regional Parliament 10 Workers and Activists Arrested". Available online at *http://www.library.ohiou.edu/indopubs/1995/07/19/0000.html* (accessed 27 November 2007).
6. Action in Solidarity with Indonesia and East Timor, "Fighting Together: Indonesians and East Timorese Join in Struggle," Sydney, 1997 is a dossier containing documents and details of this action. Available online at *http://www.asia-pacific-action.org/south-eastasia/indonesia/publications/* (accessed 27 November 2007).
7. The presence of such activists is difficult to document given the fluid and temporary nature of these groups. However, throughout 1994, 1995 and 1996, I was in constant contact with the PRD leadership by telephone. They were able to pass on information on scores of actions, on almost the same day, sometimes even the day before, indicating their close proximity to all these activities.
8. These demonstrations and riots are also recorded in the YIP report.
9. From: "Indonesia: Tough international response needed to widening crackdown," Robert F. Kennedy Memorial Center for Human Rights: Human Rights Watch/Asia, August 1996, vol. 8, no. 8.
10. The most detailed description of the rise of the PDI as an opposition party, under the leadership of Megawati Soekarnoputri, is Ed Aspinall, *Opposing Suharto: Compromise, Resistance, and Regime Change in Indonesia*, Stanford, CA: University of Stanford Press, 2005, especially ch. 6.
11. Ibid., pp. 172–3.
12. Ibid., p. 175
13. Ibid.
14. Mikrolets are small station wagon-type vehicles that carry between ten and fifteen passengers. They travel back and forth along specific routes picking up and dropping off people where they wish on that route.
15. Peringatan Hari Ham, 10 Desember 1996, Mahasiswa, Pelajar, Sopir Mikrolet Lampung Bersatu Dalam Menuntut Ham dan Demokrasi, "Lampung Bergolak," 11 December 1996; statement and chronology issued by Komite Mahasiswa untuk Perjuangan Demokrasi (TesaPD) UBL, Perjuangan Mahasiswa untuk Keadilan (PERMAK) Unila, and Dewan Perjuangan Mahasiswa Pro Demokrasi (DPMPD) AAL/STIE Lampung.
16. H.A. Adiasyah, Boykee Soekapjo, Dana K. Anwari SB and Riyanto DW, *Pemilu 1997 Antara Fenomena lampanye Dialogis dan Mega-Bintang*, Jakarta: Penakencana, 1997, p. 49.
17. Commentary by People's Democratic Party: "Mega-Bintang-the People: A broad mass coalition against the Suharto dictatorship," typescript statement.

18. Hans Antlov and Sven Cederroth, *Elections in Indonesia: The New Order and Beyond*, London: Routledge Curzon, 2004, p. 29.

19. J. Kristiadi, T.A. Legowo, Nt Budi Harjanto, *Pemilihan umum 1997: perkiraan, harapan, dan evaluasi*, Jakarta, Centre for Stategic and International Studies, 1997, p. 98.

20. Ibid., pp. 99–100.

21. Kees van Dijk, *Country in Despair, Indonesia between 1997 and 2001*, Leiden: KTLV, 2002, pp. 32–3. Kees van Dijk's book provides the most detailed digest of political developments during the 1997–2000 period available in English.

22. Ibid., p. 33.

23. Adiasyah et al., *Pemilu 1997*, p. 77.

24. Kristiadi et al., *Pemilihan*, p. 93.

25. Adiasyah et al., *Pemilu 1997*, p. 209.

26. Discussions with PRD activists in 1997.

27. There are samples of these little leaflets in the *Reformasi* collection at the International Institute of Social History in Amsterdam, the Netherlands and in the Indonesian samizdat material—documents collection in the Menzies Library, Australian National University.

28. "Indonesia: Organising The Mass Struggle For Real Democracy: an Interview with Marlin," in *Links: International Journal of Socialist Renewal*, no. 5, 1998, pp. 8–9. Marlin is the pseudonym of a senior PRD leader who was involved in coordinating the intervention into the 1997 election campaign from underground.

29. Kristiadi et al., *Pemilihan*, p. 99.

30. This kind of revolt in the large towns of Pekalangan (Java), Sampang (Madura), Yogyakarta (Java) and Banjarmasin (Kalimatan) are well documented in Syamsuddin Haris, *Kecurangan dan Perlawanan Rakyat dalam Pemilu 1997*, Yayasan Obor, Indonesia, 1999. This book also contains an analysis of the relationship between the separatist movement in Aceh in the context of the 1997 elections.

31. Kristiadi et al., *Pemilihan, p. 29*.

32. Aspinall, *Opposing Suharto*, pp. 192–3.

33. For a chronology of events connected to the crisis in Indonesia see Hal Hill, *The Indonesian Economy in Crisis*, Singapore: Institute of Southeast Asian Studies (ISEAS), 1999, pp. 11–14. As to be expected from one of the economists from the Australian Department of Foreign Affairs-funded pro-New Order Indonesia Project at the Australian National University, the chronology does not mention any events relating to the impact on the mass of the population, such as from prices rises.

34. Budiman Sujatmiko, "Gerakan Mahasiswa Kini Bersama Rakyat Tuntaskan Reformasi Total," in *Kompas*, 20 December 2000.

35. *Aksi Mahasiswa Reformasi Total*, 1998, pp. 84, 117, 211 and 227. This book contains extensive data taken from newspapers on the day-to-day unfolding of *aksi* in scores of towns across Indonesia.

36. Translated from Sarlito W. Sarwono, "Aksi Mahasiswa bukan Aksi Massa," in Dedy Djamaludding Malik (ed.), *Gejolak Reformasi Menolak Anarki*, Jakarta: Zaman, 1998, p. 285.

37. See the booklet *Lengser Keprabon*, n.d., for coverage, including photos, of the actions in Yogyakarta. This publication also claims that 1 million people attended the Yogyakarta rally.

38. There are several such incidents recorded in the YIP list. An article in *Pembebasan* magazine mentions village heads from forty-one villages being chased out. This kind of incident continued to be reported for several months after the fall of Suharto.

39. The YIP listing also includes actions in various East Timorese and Papuan towns throughout the June–December 1998 period.

Chapter 7 Power

1. See data in next chapter.
2. *Deklarasi Dewan Rakyat Lampung*, 14 August 1998. Available online at *http://www.library.ohiou.edu/indopubs/1998/08/16/0006.html* (accessed 27 November 2007).
3. The exception to this trend was the demonstrations organized by the Islamic fundamentalist university student organization, KAMMI. KAMMI had only played a very small role before May 1998. It was part of a political current that had organized underground during the Suharto period and had avoided open politics. It was only after the fall of Suharto that actions by KAMMI became politically noticeable. It adopted some of the demands of the pre-army movement, such as repeal of the dual role of the armed forces and repeal of the repressive political laws. As regards the latter, it singled out the law imposing a single ideological outlook, the so-called *Panca Sila* ideology, on all political and social organizations. This law forbade any organization adopting Islam as its ideology. KAMMI also tended to accept the legitimacy of the Habibie government. Habibie had cultivated ties with Islamic intellectuals during the 1990s. This did not represent a split in the student or democratic movement that had developed during 1997 and 1998, but rather the emergence of a new player into post-dictator politics.
4. "Komunike Bersama," printed in full in *Suara Pembaruan* daily, 16 November 1998, reproduced in *Peta Politik di Indonesia*, CSIS, no. 22, November 1998, p. 24.
5. Van Dijk, *Country in Despair*, p. 345. Van Dijk presents the most detailed description of these events using mostly Indonesian sources.
6. The major routes included: Senen–Kramat–Alemba–Matraman–Proklamasi–Pramuka–Jatinegara–Kampung Melayu–Casablanca–Otista–Dewi Sartika–Cawang–Cilitan–Gatot Subroto–Kuningan–Warung Buncit–Mampang Prapatan–Sudirman–S. Parman–Bunderan Slipi–Pal Merah–Petambur–Tanah Abang–Kampung Bali–Grogol–Daan Mogot–Roxy. It was in the Cawang-Cilitan-Gatot Subroto neighborhoods where *kampung* populations turned against and killed members of the Pam Swakarsa.
7. *Belajar Dari Peristiwa Perlawanan November*, typescript document, 1998, p. 2.
8. By this time FORKOT was no longer the major cross-campus coalition in Jakarta. The debate inside FORKOT before May on the question of calling on non-students to join the May demonstrations had been just the first sign of political differences among the student leaders active at that time. Many students shifted into other groupings, such as the PRD-linked KOMRAD, or groups linked to Nahdatul Ulama students, such as FAMRED, or groups linked to PIJAR, such as FORBES, or to groups not attached to any organized ideological pole. FORKOT tended more and more to eschew alliances with other groups adopting a more radical language.
9. Translated from Reinhardt Sirait, "Pengalaman Pergolakan November 1998," in *Pembebasan*, August, 1999, p. 13.
10. Van Dijk, *Country in Despair*, p. 347.
11. Ibid., p. 348. Some elements of the marines had received good media publicity by refraining fron the use of force in confrontations with the masses. Marines accompanied crowds marching along some of the routes taken to the MPR.
12. *Belajar Dari Peristiwa Perlawanan November*, typescript document, p. 3.
13. Personal discussion, 1997.
14. "Sejumlah Kalangan Sesalkan Pernyataan Amien Rais Soal Nasakom," *Siar* magazine, 19 September 1998. Available online at *http://www.library.ohio.edu./indopubs/1998/09/15/0007.html* (accessed 27 November 2007).
15. For a critique of this interview see Lani Cahyani, *Mengapa Gus Dur, Amien Rais, Megawati, Dan Lain-Lain Lebih Takut Terhadap Radikalisme Dibanding Dengan Militerisme?*, Info Pembebasan, 17 December 1998. Available online at *http://www.library.ohio.edu/indopubs/1998/12/17/0006.html* (accessed 27 November 2007).
16. Dhakidae, *Cendikiawan dan Kekuasaan*.
17. Ibid., p. 56.

18. Ibid.
19. Aspinall, *Opposing Suharto*, p. 237.
20. Translated from Suharto, "Unjuk Rasa Ganggu Fungsi Kampus," in Dedy Djamalud-ding Malik (ed.), *Gejolak Reformasi Menolak Anarki*, Bandung: Zaman, 1998, p. 214.

Chapter 8 *Aksi* (and Politics After Suharto)

1. Translated from Munafrizal Manan, *Gerakan Rakyat Melawan Elit*, Yogyakarta: Resist Book, 2005, pp. 151–2.
2. Ibid., p. 152.
3. *Pembebasan*, 1–15 September 1998, p. 6.
4. Suraya Afif, Noer Fauzi, Gillian Hart, Lungisile Ntsebeza and Mancy Perluso, "Redefining Agrarian Power: Resurgent Agrarian Movements in West Java, Indonesia," 2005 p. 4. The paper is available online at *http://www.repositories.edlib.org/cseas* (accessed 28 November 2007), maintained by the Center for Southeast Asian Studies, University of California Berkeley.
5. Manan, *Gerakan*, pp. 154–5.
6. Keputusan Menteri Tenaga Kerja (Kepmennaker) Nomor 150/2000 tentang Penyelesaian Pemutusan Hubungan Kerja dan Penetapan Uang Pesangon, Uang Penghargaan Masa Kerja, dan Ganti Kerugian di Perusahaan.
7. See Manan, *Gerakan*, pp. 198–9.
8. Ibid., pp. 199–200.
9. Ibid.
10. I shall use the term *reformasi* mass movement and *reformasi* constituency to refer to the broad spectrum of radical political groups, as well as student, NGO, human rights, agrarian reform, women's rights, pro-reform intellectuals and journalists who adopted the term *reformasi* as the name for the democratic and social changes they were demanding.
11. *Awas PKI Bangkit Lagi!!! Dibalik gerakan radikalisme, anarkhisme dan barbarianisme PRD*, Jakarta: Masyarakat Anti Komunis Indonesia, March 2001, pp. 7–8.
12. The National Mandate Party (PAN) was headed by Amien Rais who was a part of the group of national elite figures considered to be opponents of Suharto, at least as of 1998. PAN had started off as a party led by intellectuals who prospered under the New Order but who had grown alienated from it in later years for a range of varying reasons. However, during this period PAN became more and more dominated by figures from a conservative, right-wing Islamic background. PAN joined PPP and other right-wing Moslem parties in a parliamentary caucus called the "Central Axis." This Central Axis joined GOLKAR as the core of the opposition to Wahid, with the PDIP and Megawati acting initially as quiet partners.
13. See chronology in *Indonesia Media Online Berita Tanah Air*, August 2001. Available online at *http://www.indonesia.com/2001/august/berta-0801-kronologus,htm* (accessed 27 November 2007).
14. *Indonesian Observer*, 7 January 2001.
15. *Indonesian Observer*, 24 January 2001.
16. Yudhoyono had been appointed by Wahid to replace General Wiranto. Yudhoyono had been depicted in the media as a more reforming general. Wahid dismissed him later on 1 June.
17. *Jakarta Post*, 10 January 2001.
18. *Pembebasan*, March 2001, p. 3.
19. There had been another example of how mass-scale *aksi* could quickly occur in late 1999, but in an arena that did not act directly on the processes being described here. In November 1999, an estimated 2 million people mobilized in the city of Banda Aceh demanding a referendum on self-determination in Aceh. In Aceh, the social and political discontent and the yearning for political liberalization and socio-

economic improvement found its expression in the demand for separation from Indonesia.
20. *Bernas,* 6 February, 2001.
21. *Kompas,* 9 February, 2001. Also see *Pembebasan,* March 2001, p. 3.
22. *Pembebasan,* March 2001.

Chapter 9 Political Economy of *Aksi*

1. See Rob Lambert, "Authoritarian State Unionism in New Order Indonesia," working paper no. 25, Asia Research Centre on Social, Political and Economic Change, Murdoch University, Western Australia, 1993, pp.1–25.
2. Interview with Domingus, President, FNPBI, Jakarta, July 2006.
3. A detailed and vivid picture of these trends in the peasant sector is contained in Afif et al., "Redefining Agrarian Power."
4. Royseptia Abimanyu, *Inside Indonesia,* October–December 2003, p. 76. Available online at *http://insideindonesia.org/content/view/274/29* (accessed 28 November 2007).
5. Bonnie Setiawan, *Inside Indonesia,* January–March 2004, p. 77. Available online at *http://insideindonesia.org/content/view/258/29* (accessed 28 November 2007).
6. Abimanyu, *Inside Indonesia,* p. 76.
7. AFP report, Jakarta, 3 September, 2006.
8. "Indonesia: Strategy for Manufacturing Competitiveness", Jakarta: United Nations Industrial Development Organization, 2000, p. 30 (emphasis added). Available online at *http://www.unido.org/doc/4859* (accessed 28 November 2007).
9. Ibid., p. 32.
10. Ibid., p. 33.
11. Ibid., p. 34.
12. Thanks to Doug Lorimer, journalist at *Green Left Weekly* newspaper, for these figures.
13. *Links,* no. 5, 1998, pp. 8–9.
14. Max Lane, "Winning Democracy in Indonesia: New Stage for the Progressive Movement," *Links—International Journal of Socialist Renewal,* no. 2, 1994; D. La Botz, *Made in Indonesia: Indonesian Workers since Suharto,* Cambridge, MA: South End Press, 2001.
15. M.S. Widjojo et al, *Penakluk Rezim Orde Baru: Gerakan Mahasiswa, 1998,* Jakarta: Pustaka Sinar Harapan, 1999.

Chapter 10 Back to the Future

1. For example, the chairperson of the PRD between 1996 and 2002, Budiman Sujatmiko, joined the PDIP in 2004.
2. James C. Scott, *The Moral Economy of the Peasant: Rebellion and Subsistence in Southeast Asia,* New Haven, CT: Yale University Press, 1976.
3. Soekarno also often discussed a theoretical and historical explanation of the phenomenon of this "Marhaen" or "little people" question in addition to the allegory of his meeting with the farmer named Marhaen. He compared Netherlands Indies society with, for example, India and the Philippines where an indigenous bourgeoisie had developed, pointing out that in Indonesia no such bourgeoisie was allowed to develop. Furthermore, even the working class and peasantry were prevented from developing their economic and cultural resources. In one lecture, after referring to the existence, even before independence, of the big Indian industrialist families, he stated: "There were no wealthy Indonesians, everybody was at a low level (small scale). Civil servants, small scale, there were no high civil servants. There may have been a few Bupati, but everybody else were clerks, messenger boys. In the colonial army, how many captains?

None. . . . Even among the ordinary people, everybody survived at the minimum level. There were workers getting only 8 cents a day. There were no big farmers, everything was small." Translated and abridged from *Bung Karno*, Menggali Pancasila: Kumpulan pidato, Jakarta: Gramedia Pustaka Utama, 2000, pp. 113–14.

4. This song is said to have been written by two students at Gajah Mada University, John Tobing and Dadang Juliantara. See Miftahuddin, *Radikalisa Pemuda PRD Melawan Tirani*, Jakarta: Desantara, 2004, p. 48. The Indonesian text can be found in this book.

5. Sidel, *Riots Pogroms*, p. 210.

6. Komite Perisapan Partai Rakyat Demokratik, *Demokrasi Multipartai*, Jakarta, 1998, p. 45.

7. In fact, in some respects the critique the PRD has developed adopts a starting point that includes a fundamental critique of the pre-1965 left. In particular, the PRD has raised criticisms of the left's and Soekarno's abandonment of parliamentary democracy in the late 1950s—although these have not been fully debated or articulated.

8. Pramoedya, "17 August 1945," in *Inside Indonesia*, October–December 2004, p. 76. Available online at *http://insideindonesia.org/content/view/281/29/* (accessed 28 November 2007).

9. Ibid., pp. 385–7.

Conclusion: *Aksi*, nation, revolution

1. See Greg Acciaioli, "Archipelagic culture as an exclusionary government discourse in Indonesia," in *The Asia Pacific Journal of Anthropology*, vol. 2 (1), April 2001.

2. The teaching of literature in schools that developed during the New Order period was confined to students learning by rote the names, dates, authors and synopses of major literary works.

3. After Pramoedya read a draft of this book, I received a SMS from him (sent by his daughter) emphasizing that I must make the point that the *Soempah Pemuda* was the start of the Indonesian nation.

4. Details are on the IMF website in the country information section on Indonesia, available online at *http://www.imf.org/external/country/IDN/index.htm* (accessed 28 November 2007).

5. Vedi Hadiz, *Decentralisation and Democracy in Indonesia: A Critique of Neo-Institutionalist Perspectives*, Southeast Asia Centre, City University of Hong Kong, working paper series, no. 37, May 2003, p. 20.

6. He was also a minister for a short period in the government of President Abdurrahman Wahid.

7. *Tempo*, 28 March–3 April 2006. There are several articles in this issue whose cover story theme was "Nationalism Rising!"

8. *Kompas*, 10 June 2006.

9. *Pokok-pokok Perjuangan, Program dan Struktur*, Jakarta: *KP-PAPERNAS*, 2006.

10. It can be noted, however, that the seeds of a struggle for literature can be identified. These still center on the figure and works of Pramoedya Ananta Toer. His pathbreaking historical novel, *This Earth of Mankind*, is currently under contract to be made into a movie, which has the potential to greatly boost the profile of literature. There is also another project to perform a dramatic adaptation of this novel, with a focus on the character Nyai Ontosoroh. Performances are scheduled to take place in ten cities across the country.

11. The most extreme and marginal form of this is the new phenomenon of suicide bomb attacks on symbols of the West.

12. The existence of secessionist sentiments in Aceh and Papua, two areas distinguished from the rest of Indonesia by the intensity of violent militarization of repression under Suharto, can also be partly explained by the suppression of the national revolution since 1965 and the consequent weakening of the ability to locate sources of problems outside the local region and in a national framework.

Index

Printed by Printforce, United Kingdom